THE EVOLUTION OF THE DOCTRINE AND PRACTICE
OF HUMANITARIAN INTERVENTION

THE EVOLUTION OF THE DOCTRINE AND PRACTICE OF HUMANITARIAN INTERVENTION

by

FRANCIS KOFI ABIEW
Lecturer, Department of Political Science,
University of Alberta, Canada

KLUWER LAW INTERNATIONAL
THE HAGUE / LONDON / BOSTON

A C.I.P. Catalogue record for this book is available from the Library of Congress.

981748

ISBN 90-411-1160-3

Published by Kluwer Law International,
P.O. Box 85889, 2508 CN The Hague, The Netherlands.

Sold and distributed in North, Central and South America
by Kluwer Law International,
675 Massachusetts Avenue, Cambridge, MA 02139, U.S.A.

In all other countries, sold and distributed
by Kluwer Law International, Distribution Centre,
P.O. Box 322, 3300 AH Dordrecht, The Netherlands.

Layout and camera-ready copy:
Anne-Marie Krens - Oegstgeest - The Netherlands

Printed on acid-free paper

Printed in the Netherlands.

PREFACE

The legitimacy of humanitarian intervention in international relations has long been a subject of controversy. In the wake of recent humanitarian crises and varying international responses to such situations, the debate surrounding humanitarian intervention has experienced a revival with important implications for the principle and its practice. On the one hand, there is the viewpoint that humanitarian intervention cannot be legal, justifiable, or permissible. On the other, there is a growing international concern for the protection of human rights and the right of intervention towards those ends, or for some, an obligation to intervene when violations reach a stage that incite the outrage of the international community.

This book attempts to demonstrate a legitimate basis for humanitarian intervention through an examination of the evolution of the principle and its practice. It argues that state sovereignty is not incompatible with humanitarian intervention. Sovereignty implies responsibility, and thus when egregious human rights violations occur either arising from governmental acts or in situations of internal conflict, intervention is justified to protect those rights.

The study outlines the historical development of humanitarian intervention before undertaking an investigation of the evolution and strength of the principle and its practice under the UN Charter during the Cold War period. It then proceeds to an examination of the scope of collective humanitarian intervention in the post-Cold War era by focusing on the cases of Iraq, the former Yugoslavia, Somalia, Rwanda, Liberia, and Haiti, and concludes by assessing contemporary developments in terms of sources of support for humanitarian intervention. It demonstrates

growing support for humanitarian intervention as a fundamental principle
of international relations.

Francis Kofi Abiew
Edmonton, September, 1998

ACKNOWLEDGEMENTS

This book is a revised and expanded version of my doctoral dissertation which was submitted to the Faculty of Graduate Studies and Research, University of Alberta, in October 1997. My thanks go primarily to my supervisor Professor Tom Keating for his invaluable comments and suggestions on earlier drafts of the manuscript. I would also like to express my thanks to various individuals who read and commented on earlier drafts of the manuscript, namely, Professors Fred Judson, Linda Reif, Wenran Jiang and Juris Leijneks. Professor Fernando Tesón's comments were a source of encouragement in the preparation of the manuscript for publication. My gratitude also goes to Dr. Leslie Green, University Professor Emeritus, who first introduced me to the complexities involved in the subject matter of humanitarian intervention. Parts of an earlier version of the manuscript were presented at the Academic Council on the United Nations System/American Society of International Law Summer Workshop on International Organization Studies at Brown University, Providence, Rhode Island, from July 28-August 9, 1996. I benefited from comments made by the directors and participants at the workshop.

The generosity of the staff of the Weir Memorial Law Library at the University of Alberta is beyond comparison. They provided a supportive environment in which to study and write over the years. For this, I am eternally grateful – especially to Mike Storozuk, Lillian MacPherson and Sandra Wilkins. Professor Shannon O'Byrne has been a friend and a source of advice throughout my years as a graduate student in Edmonton, and her assistance in printing the manuscript is very much appreciated. Thanks are also due to Lindy Melman and Peter Buschman at Kluwer for their cooperation.

Chapter 4 of the book entitled "Assessing Humanitarian Intervention in the Post-Cold War Period: Sources of Consensus" was previously published in *International Relations*, Vol. XIV, No.2, August 1998. My thanks to the editors for permission to reproduce the article here.

Finally, I would like to acknowledge the support of my family and friends too numerous to mention here. This book is dedicated to my mother and to the memory of my father. Any errors, omissions, or short-comings are, however, my sole responsibility.

Francis Kofi Abiew
Edmonton, September 1998

TABLE OF CONTENTS

INTRODUCTION

The doctrine of humanitarian intervention has long been a subject of controversy in international law and relations. The classical concept of the right of humanitarian intervention can be traced back to ancient times, but opinions of scholars, politicians, diplomats, and state practice still disagree whether the right exists, and, if it exists, what its precise normative scope is. On the one hand, there is the viewpoint that intervention for the sake of humanity cannot be legal, justifiable, or permissible. On the other, there is a growing international concern for protection of human rights and the right of intervention towards those ends, or for some, an obligation to intervene when violations reach a stage that incite the outrage of the international community. The debate continues. Thus, it is important to re-examine the evolution of the doctrine of humanitarian intervention in international law and relations, and also its place in the historical and contemporary practice of states. This is particularly pertinent since recent events relating to internal conflicts and the scale of human suffering resulting from these conflicts, have highlighted collective efforts to address the many humanitarian crises that have arisen. While state sovereignty is still important in international relations, humanitarian imperatives have led to more interventions in matters that are considered essentially within the domestic jurisdiction of states. It is in this context that the principle of humanitarian intervention has experienced a revival with ramifications for the extent to which it has been, or is, accepted in the international community.

Before embarking upon the extent to which the principle of humanitarian intervention has been accepted by the international community, some preliminiary considerations need to be addressed. In that regard, a brief general theoretically relevant discussion about how principles gain acceptance, or about indicators for acceptance of principles in international relations, and about how they come to be entrenched will be appropriate.

An important issue that often arises in international relations is that of whether there are any standards of behaviour applicable to states, and whether those standards can be regarded as universal, given the different cultural traditions represented in the international system. If there are any such standards, some would argue that they do not matter since the most obvious rule of state behaviour is grounded in self-interest. It is, however, argued that there are certain minimum standards that can be regarded as universal which states follow and that these standards matter in the assessment of state behaviour.

Jones argues "[t]he code that ... states have developed is not a rigid set of rules derived from static principles".[1] It is a set of guidelines that is designed towards the achievement of peace and security, although how that goal is attained is not specified. In that connection, "it is flexible, and it is, and has been, responsive to changing conditions and concepts".[2] These principles underlie relations between states, or as Jones puts it, "that ... states think ought to underlie" their relations. These standards have been derived from a whole range of interactions among states over the centuries, drawing on law, philosophy, religious and social concerns. These principles have come to be embodied in numerous treaties, conventions, declarations, diplomatic protocols, resolutions, and other international instruments that states (re) consider and reaffirm from time to time.

Specifically regarding the principle of humanitarian intervention, this study attempts to follow closely these international instruments and

---

1   The discussion that follows draws from Jones, *Code of Peace: Ethics and Security in the World of the Warlord States* (Chicago: The University of Chicago Press, 1991) at xi.

2   *Ibid.* There are nine fundamental principles in the international system on which this code relies. These are: 1. Sovereign equality of states 2. Territorial integrity and political independence of states 3. Equal rights and self-determination of peoples 4. Nonintervention in the internal affairs of states 5. Peaceful settlement of disputes between states 6. Abstention from the threat or use of force 7. Fulfilment in good faith of international obligations 8. Cooperation with other states, and, 9. Respect for human rights and fundamental freedoms.

what states have done and said in order to ascertain the extent of its acceptance in international relations. Even though the indicator or benchmark for acceptance of the principle is a grey area which lies along a continuum certain characteristics tend to be evident. Its use by states, scholarly writings on the subject, and its enshrinement in international institutions are but some of the characteristics that assist in knowing how the principle is or becomes accepted.

Another way of conceptualizing how principles get articulated and come to be entrenched in international relations is through the concept of epistemic communities.[3] The epistemic community approach focuses on the process through which consensus is reached within a given domain of expertise and through which consensual knowledge is diffused and carried forward by other actors. Its fundamental concern is the political influence that an epistemic community can have on collective policymaking. Haas argues that this approach may bring about "new patterns of reasoning to decision makers encourag[ing] them to pursue new paths of policymaking, which may in turn lead to unpredicted or unpredictable outcomes".[4]

An epistemic community is primarily a "network of professionals with recognized expertise and competence in a particular domain and an authoritative claim to policy-relevant knowledge within that domain or issue-area".[5] Epistemic communities have: a) a shared set of nor-

---

3   The epistemic community concept presents a research program with which students of world politics can empirically study the role of ideas in international relations. See Adler & Haas, "Conclusion: Epistemic Communities, World Order, and the Creation of a Reflective Research Program" (1992) 46 *International Organization* 367.

4   Haas, "Introduction: Epistemic Communities and International Policy Coordination" (1992) 46 *International Organization* 1 at 21.

5   Haas notes that the term "epistemic communities" has been defined or employed in diverse ways. It is used particularly in reference to scientific communities. However, epistemic communities need not be made up of natural scientists or of professionals applying the same methodology that natural scientists do. An epistemic community may consist of professionals from a variety of disciplines and backgrounds. According to Haas, members of an epistemic community may also "share intersubjective understandings;

mative and principled beliefs, providing value-based rationale for the social action of community members; b) shared causal beliefs deriving from their analysis of practices leading to a set of problems in their field which then serve as the basis for explaining the multiple linkages between possible policy actions and desired outcomes; c) shared notions of validity – that is, intersubjective, internally defined criteria for weighing and validating knowledge in the field of their expertise; and, d) a common policy enterprise – that is, a set of common practices relating to a set of problems to which their professional competence is directed, presumably out of the conviction that human welfare will be enhanced as a result.[6] Epistemic communities may either be national – where their activities are directed towards one country, or emerge as transnational[7] over time, as a result of the diffusion of community ideas through conferences, journals, research collaboration, and various informal communications and contacts.[8] A transnational community's ideas may have their source in an international organization or in various state agencies. These ideas are then diffused to other states through the decision makers who have been influenced by the ideas.[9]

Fundamentally, the epistemic community approach plays an important role in "articulating the cause-and-effect relationships of complex problems, helping states identify their interests, framing the issues for collective debate, proposing specific policies, and identifying salient points of negotiation".[10] Members of an epistemic community play both direct

---

have a shared way of knowing; have shared patterns of reasoning; have a policy project drawing on shared values, shared causal beliefs, and the use of discursive practices; and have a shared commitment to the application and production of knowledge". These are additional notions associated with epistemic communities which normally distinguish them from other groups involved in policy coordination. See, *ibid.*, at 3 and accompanying footnotes.

6   *Ibid.*

7   Collaboration in the absence of material interests binding together actors in different countries with common policy agendas suggest the existence of an epistemic community with transnational membership. *Ibid.*, at 17.

8   *Ibid.*

9   *Ibid.*

10   *Ibid.*, at 2.

and indirect roles in policy coordination. They spread ideas and influence the position adopted by a wide range of actors. These actors might include domestic and international bodies, government bureaucrats and decision makers, legislative and corporate bodies, as well as, the general public.[11] The community can directly make a contribution to informal convergence of policy preferences if it can simultaneously influence several governments through its transnational membership.[12] Epistemic communities with a transnational membership can influence national interests through identifying such interests for policymakers or by explaining and clarifying important issues and their implications from which policymakers may then deduce their interests.[13] Policymakers in one state may, in turn, influence the interests and behaviour of other states resulting in the likelihood of convergent state behaviour and international policy coordination, informed by the causal beliefs and policy preferences of the epistemic community. In the same vein, epistemic communities may contribute to the creation and maintenance of social institutions that guide international behaviour.[14] Haas notes that

> [b]y focusing on the various ways in which new ideas and information are diffused and taken into account by decision makers, the epistemic communities approach suggests a nonsystemic origin for state interests and identifies a dynamic for persistent cooperation independent of the distribution of international power.[15]

This approach thus supplements structural theories of international behaviour. In response to new knowledge expounded by epistemic communities, a state may choose to pursue entirely new objectives, in which case outcomes may be shaped by the distribution of information as well as by the distribution of power capabilities.[16]

---

11 *Supra*, note 3 at 379.
12 *Ibid.*
13 *Supra*, note 4 at 4.
14 *Ibid.*
15 *Ibid.*
16 *Ibid.*

The essential characteristic of epistemic communities is that members are respected within their own disciplines and have the ability to extend their direct and indirect influence eventually to major actors in the policy coordination process.[17] The timing of events is important in this regard. Crises and new developments in the international arena not only accelerate the diffusion process but also lend a sense of urgency to the task of re-evaluating current policies from which alternative results emerge.[18] In essence, some international relations scholars have argued that control over knowledge and information is a significant dimension of power. Thus, the diffusion of new ideas and information can result in new patterns of behaviour and prove to be an important determinant of international policy coordination.[19]

Thus, epistemic communities as an analytic approach to some particular issues in international relations, it would seem, can be usefully employed in an attempt to consolidate support or cooperation regarding intervention to protect human rights in the international system.[20]

The dilemma posed by intervention for human rights purposes rests on competing claims of state sovereignty and humanitarian assistance. However, recent events are leading to a re-evaluation or reassessment of normative assumptions concerning human rights, state sovereignty and nonintervention, particularly in situations of widespread violations of human rights occasioned by governmental acts or internal conflicts. Recent cases of humanitarian intervention seem to point to the emer-

---

17 *Supra*, note 3 at 380.

18 *Ibid.*

19 *Supra*, note 4 at 2-3.

20 The study of international relations as a discipline has come under criticism lately for lacking a credible theory and set of explanations for the sources of international institutions, state interests and state behaviour under conditions of uncertainty. In this regard, a prominent international relations theorist, Robert Keohane called for a "reflective" approach in the absence of "a research program that in particular studies that it can illuminate important issues in world politics". See, Keohane, *International Institutions and State Power: Essays in International Relations Theory* (Boulder: Westview Press, 1989) at 173. The epistemic communities approach thus amounts to a reflective response to the challenge posed by Keohane.

gence of a realignment regarding the basic notion of the inviolability of state sovereignty. The cases of intervention in Iraq, Bosnia, Somalia, Rwanda, Liberia, and Haiti have provided grounds for a reconsideration of the doctrine and practice of humanitarian intervention.

Most of the literature on humanitarian intervention argues for the primacy of state sovereignty over human rights or vice versa. Other scholars have called for a delicate balancing between state sovereignty and human rights. Whereas these approaches to the dilemma presented are commendable, this book argues that state sovereignty need not be interpreted as incompatible or inconsistent with concern for human rights protection. Sovereignty has always been limited by human rights concerns. This constraint is itself an attribute of sovereignty. In other words, the argument presented is that sovereignty cannot, and should not be a justification for preventing humanitarian intervention. The responsibilities that states have in relation to their citizens should be recognized as part of their sovereignty, and thus permitting intervention to redress those rights where violated. The effect of adopting such an interpretation is one of restoring state sovereignty as a cardinal principle of the international system, while at the same time, restoring notions of responsibility to state sovereignty.

The book attempts to establish a legitimate basis for humanitarian intervention. It asks three questions. First, are there minimum duties states have, in terms of protecting the rights of their citizens, that are attributes of their sovereignty? Second, can violation of these minimum duties constitute the justification for humanitarian intervention? Third, how should such intervention be effectively implemented? It presents answers to the questions by examining how the doctrine and practice of humanitarian intervention have evolved up to the present in order to throw light on future practice. It argues for intervention expressed in both legal and moral terms to alleviate the suffering of oppressed people and victims of internal armed conflict. Furthermore, in answering the third question, it employs the notion of epistemic communities as vehicles to build on the increasing support generated in the post-Cold War period in order to enhance the legitimacy and effectiveness of future interventions.

Humanitarian intervention, understood in the classical sense, involves forcible self-help by a state or group of states to protect human rights. Verwey, for instance, defines it as

> [t]he threat or use of force by a state or states abroad, for the sole purpose of preventing or putting a halt to a serious violation of fundamental human rights, in particular the right to life of persons, regardless of their nationality, such protection taking place neither upon authorization by relevant organs of the United Nations nor with the permission by the legitimate government of the target state.[21]

Ian Brownlie has defined it more broadly as "the threat or use of armed force by a state, a belligerent community, or an international organization with the object of protecting human rights".[22] Beyond these definitions, some writers have pointed to the concept of humanitarian access. They draw a distinction between forcible humanitarian intervention and humanitarian access. The latter takes account of situations where the United Nations or other humanitarian aid organizations negotiate with governments in order to gain access to affected civilian populations caught in the throes of internal armed conflict or other complex humanitarian emergencies. It also includes situations where humanitarian access is obtained without the consent of a government. In both situations the use of military force is absent. For purposes of this book, humanitarian intervention refers primarily to forcible means employed by a state, group of states, an international or regional organization, or humanitarian agencies with the aim (or at least one of its principal aims) of ending egregious human rights violations perpetrated by governments, or preventing or alleviating human suffering in situations of internal conflict.

In the chapters that follow, the traditional doctrine and practice of humanitarian intervention are examined, followed by a discussion of

---

21 Verwey, "Legality of Humanitarian Intervention after the Cold War" in Ferris ed., *The Challenge to Intervene: A New Role for the United Nations?* (Uppsala: Life and Peace Institute, 1992) 113 at 114.

22 Brownlie, "Humanitarian Intervention" in Moore ed., *Law and Civil War in the Modern World* (Baltimore: Johns Hopkins University Press, 1974) at 217.

humanitarian intervention in the United Nations Charter era (1945-1989). Analysis of post-Cold War practice is then undertaken, with the fourth chapter investigating the sources of support for the principle and practice of humanitarian intervention. Chapter five concludes the study.

In essence, this book attempts to show a legitimate basis for humanitarian intervention through an examination of the evolution of the doctrine and its practice. It argues that sovereignty is not incompatible with humanitarian intervention. Sovereignty connotes responsibility, and thus when human rights violations occur on a massive scale either arising from governmental acts or in situations of internal conflict, intervention is justified to protect those rights.

1

THE TRADITIONAL DOCTRINE AND PRACTICE OF HUMANITARIAN INTERVENTION

1   INTRODUCTION

The issue of intervention[1] by one state in the affairs of another has always been one that the international community has had to confront. External interference in the relationship between ruler and the ruled has been an enduring and pervasive characteristic of the Westphalian system since its inception. This has always been the case since issues pertaining to the relationship have an international dimension when the manner in which one state treats its subjects within its territory is challenged by other states. Intervention was common in the Greek city-state system, the Roman Empire, and in the religious wars of the 16th and 17th cen-

---

1   The term "intervention" as applied in the international system eludes any precise definition. It has been generally used to mean almost any act of interference by one state in the affairs of another. In a more specific sense, it denotes dictatorial interference in the domestic or foreign affairs of another state that impairs that state's independence. For various defenitions of intervention see for example, Falk, "The United States and the Doctrine of Nonintervention in the Internal Affairs of Independent States" (1959) *Howard Law Journal* 163 at 166; Stowell, *Intervention in International Law* (Washington D.C.: John Byrne & Co., 1921) at 318, note 48; Thomas & Thomas, *Non Intervention – The Law and its Import in the Americas* (Dallas: Southern Methodist University Press, 1956) at Chap.IV; Winfield, "The History of Intervention in International Law"(1922-1923) 3 *British Yearbook of International Law* 130 (commenting that "intervention may be anything from a speech of Lord Palmerston's in the House of Commons to the partition of Poland".); Kelsen, *Principles of International Law* (1956) at 64; Leurdijk, *Intervention in International Politics* (Leeuwarden: Eisma BV Publishers, 1986) at Chap.5.

turies.[2] Two main motivations have been responsible for interventions in the relationship between rulers and the ruled. Firstly, states have intervened in the internal affairs of other states due to the fact that domestic developments elsewhere could undermine their own security, either by increasing the chance of conflict between states, or by undermining the legitimacy of their own regimes. Secondly, interventions have occurred because values related only loosely to material or security interests, or in the interests of humanity, have prompted states to bring pressure to bear on others to alter the way in which they treat their own citizens or subjects.[3] The latter motivation for intervention, especially that in the interests of humanity, is the primary concern of this chapter. The chapter outlines the historical development of the doctrine and practice of humanitarian intervention in the pre-United Nations Charter period. It attempts to show the doctrine coexisted with state sovereignty. Its underpinnings can be found in international law, morality, scholarly opinions, treaties and state practice. Thus, the approach used here is to progress from an examination of the origin and development of the doctrine of humanitarian intervention to a study of contemporary attitudes and practices.

Before embarking on an enquiry into the doctrinal evolution and practice of humanitarian intervention however, it would be appropriate to make some brief comments or observations on the concept of state sovereignty. This is pertinent because debates over the current status and future role of humanitarian intervention are embedded in the changing character of state sovereignty. The juxtaposition of state sovereignty with intervention reveals the examination of a wide range of issues and

---

2   Morgenthau, for example, observes that "[f]rom the time of the ancient Greeks to this day, some states have found it advantageous to intervene in the affairs of other states on behalf of their own interests and against the latter's will". Morgenthau, "To Intervene or not to Intervene" (1967) 45 *Foreign Affairs* at 425. See also, Phillipson, *The International Law and Custom of Ancient Greece and Rome*, Vol. 1 (London: MacMillan & Co. Ltd, 1911) at 100-101, Vol 2 at 90.

3   See for example, Krasner, "Sovereignty and Intervention" in Lyons & Mastanduno eds., *Beyond Westphalia? State Sovereignty and International Intervention* (Baltimore: Johns Hopkins University Press, 1995) 228 at 233.

raises a series of questions. However, a paramount concern here is: under what circumstances can a state or group of states, or the United Nations intervene in the domestic affairs of states to bring governments to account for failing to fulfil an international obligation viz., to provide their citizens with basic human rights? The question is one that does not yield an easy answer. It is one that the international community is continuing to grapple with and prompts a reexamination. Sovereignty features in the question of whether or not to intervene on humanitarian grounds. Definitions or conceptions that tend to emphasise the absolute nature of state sovereignty provide a bulwark against developing a robust practice of humanitarian intervention in international relations. It is contended that the meanings or interpretations of sovereignty are not, and have not been incompatible or inconsistent with intervention to protect human rights. In other words, the responsibilities of states toward their citizens mean that human rights protection must be seen as part of the definition of sovereignty.

2   HISTORICAL EVOLUTION OF STATE SOVEREIGNTY AND THE DOCTRINE AND PRACTICE OF HUMANITARIAN INTERVENTION

a.   State Sovereignty

A defining feature of the modern international system is the division of the world into sovereign states. Most of the basic norms, rules, and practices of international relations have thus rested on the premise of state sovereignty. In other words, over the centuries, this sovereignty of nation-states – the idea of final and absolute authority in the state – has been a principal, constitutive, feature of the modern world.[4] Yet

---

4   See Jackson, "Quasi-States, Dual Regimes, and Neoclassical Theory: International Jurisdiction and the Third World" (1987) 41 *International Organization* 519; Walker, "Sovereignty, Identity, Community: Reflections on the Horizons of Contemporary Political Practice" in Walker & Mendlovitz eds., *Contending Sovereignties: Redefining Political Community* (Boulder: Rienner, 1990) at 159; Verhoeven, "Sovereign States: A Collectivity or Com-

its role in the relations between states has been "so thoroughly deline-ated, demarcated, explicated, qualified and categorized [so much so that] the term's continued useful precision is open to question".[5] Some writers have even called for the introduction of other concepts that may provide more insights for analyzing the authority of nation-states in contemporary international relations, or for its abandonment altogether.[6] It is, however, unlikely that sovereignty will be eliminated in the relations between states since the view persists that it is the best mechanism for organizing human society at the international level. Although the formal principle of sovereignty remains the basic norm of international relations, its con-tent has shifted as will be argued later regarding the concept of human rights.

Definitions of sovereignty tend to focus on its legal content which is often perceived to change little and thus the concept is viewed as a static, fixed one. Internally, sovereignty connotes the exercise of supreme authority by states within their individual territorial boundaries. External-

---

munity" (1994) *Hitotsubashi Journal of Law and Politics* 149. Although various definitions of sovereignty have been proffered and distinctions drawn between internal, external, legal and political, shared or exclusive sovereignty, in an attempt at clarification, its exact meaning has not been authoritatively defined. The brief discussion here is to show the evolution of the concept in an attempt to determine in subsequent chapters, the current understandings and meanings of the term.

5 Philpott, "Sovereignty: An Introduction and Brief History" (1995) 48 *Jour-nal of International Affairs* 353 at 354. The term 'sovereignty' has a long and troubled history, and a variety of meanings. See Crawford, *The Creation of States in International Law* (Oxford: Clarendon Press, 1979) at 26. Ac-cording to Oppenheim it is "doubtful whether any single word has caused so much intellectual confusion". See, Oppenheim, *International Law*, Vol. 1 (London: Longman, 1905) at 103; Fall, "Sovereignty" in *Oxford Compan-ion to Politics of the World* (Oxford: Oxford University Press, 1993) at 854.

6 Goodman, "Democracy, Sovereignty, and Intervention" (1993) 9 *American University Journal of International Law and Policy* 27 at 30. Laski for example suggests that "it would be of lasting benefit to political science if the whole concept of sovereignty were surrendered". Laski, *A Grammar of Politics* 4th ed. (London: Allen & Unwin, 1938) at 44-45.

ly, it connotes equality of status between states comprising the society of states. Thus, the formal position of the concept in legal and diplomatic convention has implied both supremacy within and equality of status without.

The original meaning of sovereignty, according to Paasivirta, employing both etymology and the usage of the concept in legal and political theory, is related to the idea of superiority.[7] It stems from the Latin word 'supra'. In mainstream legal and political theory, therefore, the sovereign is the holder of ultimate power.[8] In the Westphalian international system the ultimate power holder is the state. This particular view of sovereignty maintains that because the state is under the legal influence of no superior power, sovereignty resides in the state. In other words, to be sovereign is to be subject to no higher power. The upshot of this theory of state sovereignty, therefore, is that human rights are considered a matter of domestic, and not international concern.

This absolute notion of state sovereignty discussed above has its origins in Aristotle's *Politics*, and the classic body of Roman Law.[9] In the *Politics*, Aristotle recognizes the fact that there must be a supreme power existing in the state, and that this power may be in the hands of

---

7   Paasivirta, "Internationalization and Stabilization of Contracts Versus State Sovereignty" (1990) *British Yearbook of International Law* 315 at 331.

8   In international law the meaning of sovereignty relates to the idea of independence. The right to be independent assumes the right of state autonomy in issues pertaining to its internal affairs and the carrying out of its external relations. The classic definition given by Judge Max Huber in the *Island of Palmas case* in 1928, states that: "sovereignty in the relations between states signifies independence. Independence in regard to a portion of the globe is the right to exercise therein, to the exclusion of any other state , the functions of a state". Permanent Court of Arbitration, April 4, 1928. *UN Reports of International Arbitral Awards*, Vol.2, 829 at 838. Again, in the *Wimbledon Case*, the Permanent Court of International Justice held that the sovereign state "is subject to no other state and has full and exclusive powers within its jurisdiction without prejudice to the limits set by applicable law". PCIJ, Series A, no.1, 1923 at 25.

9   Merriam, *History of the Theory of Sovereignty since Rousseau* (New York: Ams Press, 1968) at 11.

one, or a few, or of many.[10] The idea of sovereignty as formulated in ancient Rome sought to establish the theoretical absolutism of the powers of the Emperor and to consolidate the despotism of his rule.[11] Among the Romans the idea of sovereignty found expression in the fact that "[t]he will of the Prince has the force of law, since the people have transferred to him all their right and power".[12]

In the Middle Ages, government based on the consent of the governed was the ruling theory. The idea of original popular sovereignty was universally prevalent. It was an axiom of political theory from the end of the 13th century that the justification of all government lay in the voluntary submission of the community ruled.[13] At this time, however, a strong doctrine on the nature of sovereignty was inhibited; firstly, by the prevalent idea of the dominance of divine and natural law over positive law; secondly, by the idea of the so-called mixed form of state – politically by the conflict between Church and State, and by the feudal conditions prevalent within the State itself.[14] In this era, the conception of sovereignty as representing some absolute and even arbitrary authority in the State or Church was unknown.[15] One writer notes that

[t]here is nothing more characteristic of the Middle Ages than the absence of any theory of sovereignty as this conception has been sometimes current during the last three centuries. The King or ruler of the Middle Ages was conceived of not as the master, but as the servant of the law; the notion of an absolute king was not medieval, but grew

---

10 Book III, chp.7. *Jowett's translation.* Cited in *ibid.*
11 See Hinsley, *Sovereignty* (London: Watts & Co. Ltd., 1966) at 126.
12 *Supra,* note 9. Cicero for example wrote with reference to sovereignty that "there exists a supreme and permanent law, to which all human order, if it is to have any truth or validity, must conform" and that there is "no other foundation of political authority than the consent of the whole people". Quoted in Carlyle, *A History of Medieval Political Theory in the West* (1950) at 16-17.
13 See, Merriam, *ibid.* at 12.
14 *Ibid.,* at 13.
15 Larson, Jenks et al., *Sovereignty Within the Law* (New York: Dobbs Ferry, 1965) at 23.

up during the period of the decline of the political civilisation of the Middle Ages.[16]

Further development of the concept was to come with the formation of the national state. As the Roman Empire declined the idea of sovereignty was reinvigorated to reinforce and legitimize secular authority.

The concept received its first systematic articulation in the works of scholars such as Jean Bodin, Hugo Grotius and Thomas Hobbes in the 16th and 17th centuries. Bodin defined sovereignty as "the most high, absolute and perpetual power over the citizens and subjects in a Commonweale ... the greatest power to command".[17] For him, the nature of the supreme power is absolute, wholly free from the restraint of law, and held subject to no conditions or limitations. Even though he stated in very strong terms the nature of sovereignty, he was prepared to place limitations on the sovereign power. The sovereign was constrained by natural law, divine law and the law of nations.[18]

To Grotius, sovereignty was "that power whose acts are not subject to the control of another, so that they may be made void by the act of any other human will".[19] The supreme power is, however, limited by divine law, natural law, the law of nations, and by such agreements as are made between ruler and the ruled.[20] He aptly points out that

...an indefinite number of rights may be subtracted from the authority of the ruler; his acts may be rendered subject to ratification by a senate or other body; it may even be provided that in certain cases a right of

---

16 Carlyle, *supra*, note 12 at 457.
17 Bodin, *Six Bookes of a Commonweale* (London, 1606) trans. Knolles, Mac-Rae ed., (Cambridge, Mass: Harvard University Press, 1962) bk.1, chp.8 at 84. Quoted in Beitz, *"Sovereignty and Morality in International Affairs"* in Held ed., Political Theory Today (Stanford University Press, 1991).
18 *Supra*, note 9 at 15-16. See also, Skinner, *The Foundations of Modern Political Thought*, 2 Vols.(Cambridge: Cambridge University Press, 1978) 2: at 244-254.
19 Cited in Merriam, *ibid.*, at 21.
20 *Ibid.*, at 23.

insurrection falls to the people *yet the sovereignty still retains its essential quality unimpaired* [Emphasis added].[21]

Sovereignty for Hobbes was far more absolute than the theory of Bodin or Grotius. He regarded sovereignty as absolute, unified, inalienable, based upon a voluntary but irrevocable contract.[22] The idea of absoluteness regarding this classical notion of sovereignty has been interpreted as complete or unlimited freedom of action with no political or institutional constraints regarding the capacity to act.[23] On another interpretation, an absolute sovereign is not limited by moral considerations, so that for a sovereign power nothing can be unjust.[24] In this formulation, thus, sovereignty is regarded as final political authority.[25]

It is pertinent to note that both Bodin and Hobbes wrote long after territorial states or city-states had formed in Europe. They were driven to a more extreme defence of sovereign control by the disorders that were engendered by the religious wars of the sixteenth and seventeenth centuries. The importance of these theorists to the development of state sovereignty is that they "provided European rulers with a variegated menu of intellectual ideas from which they could draw to justify their policies".[26]

Although the concept of state sovereignty has been influential from the sixteenth century onwards, it has nevertheless been contested or qualified by the continuing influence of developments within the international system over the past four centuries. The European pattern of territorial entities ruled by sovereigns equal as between themselves received its confirmation at Westphalia following the end of the Thirty Years War that had raged over Europe in the early 17th century. The Peace of West-

---

21 *Ibid.*

22 *Ibid.*, at 27.

23 See, Beitz, "Sovereignty and Morality in International Affairs" in Held ed., *Political Theory Today* (Stanford University Press, 1991) at 238.

24 *Ibid.*

25 *Ibid.*

26 Krasner, "Westphalia and All That" in Goldstein & Keohane eds., *Ideas and Foreign Policy: Beliefs, Institutions and Political Change* (Ithaca, NY: Cornell University Press, 1993) at 263.

phalia (1648) marked the acceptance of the idea of the sovereign authority of the state.[27] The international system that evolved, initially centred in Europe, was based on the idea that states were the major actors. Their sovereignty was to be regarded as absolute. The supposition was that states would maintain domestic order within their borders and command the resources necessary to carry on effective relations with other states outside their own jurisdiction.[28] Institutions eventually evolved to maintain order and stability in a system of international relations. These institutions were: a balance of power to prevent the rise of a powerful state and to contain aggression; the codification of rules of behaviour through international law; the convening of international conferences to settle major differences; and diplomatic practices through which states would be encouraged to negotiate differences among themselves.[29]

Within the institutions noted above, however, it is significant to note that the Peace of Westphalia did not sanction the right of rulers to do whatever they pleased within their own territories. There were important limitations contained in its provisions on the authority of the sovereign, especially regarding the practice of religion, which was the dominant political question of the seventeenth century.[30] It provided for a set of internal practices by recognizing rights for both Protestants and Catholics, thus rejecting the right of rulers to change the religious practices within their territories arbitrarily. A sovereign, for example, who changed

---

27 There is some disagreement as to whether the Peace of Westphalia marked a decisive break between the medieval and modern worlds by creating a system of sovereign states or consolidated 300 years of evolution towards such a system. See for example, *ibid.*, at 235-264; Tilly, *Coercion, Capital, and European States, AD 990-1992* (Oxford: Basil Blackwell, 1990) at 167.
28 Lyons & Mastanduno, "Introduction: International Intervention, State Sovereignty, and the Future of International Society" in Lyons & Mastanduno, *supra*, note 3 at 5-6.
29 Watson, "European International Society and its Expansion" in Bull & Watson eds., *The Expansion of International Society* (New York: Clarendon Press, 1894) at 23-25.
30 *Supra*, note 26 at 244.

his religion could not compel his subjects to change theirs.[31] The tension between the scope of sovereign authority and international pressures indicated in the treaties of Westphalia is analogous to the ongoing debates regarding a universal human rights regime.

It would seem to be the case that the actual content of sovereign authority – its content both internally and externally – has never been generally agreed upon and recognised in absolute terms.[32] A discussion of sovereignty in its broad historical context and as an abstract theoretical construct suggests its meanings and practices are historically variable.

b.   Humanitarian Intervention

Humanitarian intervention has long been a routine feature of the international system and has coexisted with the development of state sovereignty. The theory of humanitarian intervention is based on the assumption that States in their relation with their own nationals have the international obligation to guarantee to them certain basic or fundamental rights which are considered necessary for their existence, and for the maintenance of friendly relations among nations. It holds further that these rights are so essential, universal, and of such high value to the human person that violations by any state cannot be ignored by other states. This assumption would authorize intervention by other States, in case of flagrant denial of these rights by any State to her own citizens.[33]

---

31 *Ibid.*

32 *Ibid.*, at 261. Also see generally, Biersteker and Weber, eds., *State Sovereignty as Social Construct* (Cambridge: Cambridge University Press, 1996) at 1-21, 278-286 (arguing "throughout the course of history, the meaning of sovereignty has undergone important change and transformation – from the location of its legitimacy (in God, in the monarch, or in a people) – to the scope of activities claimed under its protection").

33 See Ganji, *International Protection of Human Rights* (Geneve: Librairie E. Droz, 1962) at 9.

Although a "usable general definition" of humanitarian intervention is "extremely difficult and virtually impossible to apply rigorously" according to some commentators, [34]the concept may be defined as "the reliance upon force for the justifiable purpose of protecting the inhabitants of another state from treatment which is so arbitrary and persistently abusive as to exceed the limits of that authority within which the sovereign is presumed to act with reason and justice".[35] In a frequently used definition, "the theory of intervention on the ground of humanity ... recognizes the right of one state to exercise international control over the acts of another in regard to its internal sovereignty when contrary to the laws of humanity".[36] Tesón defines it as the "proportionate transboundary help, including forcible help, provided by governments to individuals in another state who are being denied basic human rights and who themselves would be rationally willing to revolt against their oppressive government".[37] These definitions do overlap in important aspects and provide a fundamental understanding of the employment of the term by scholars. It is generally an act performed for the purpose of compelling a sovereign to respect fundamental human rights in the exercise of its sovereign prerogatives.[38] The classical concept covered any use of armed force by a state against another state for the purpose

---

34 Franck & Rodley, "After Bangladesh: The Law of Humanitarian Intervention by Military Force" (1973) 67 *American Journal of International Law* 275 at 305.

35 Stowell, *supra*, note 1 at 53. Arntz, for example, maintains that "[w]hen a government, although acting within its rights of sovereignty, violates the rights of humanity, either by measures contrary to the interests of other States or by an excess of cruelty and injustice, which is a blot on our civilization, the right of intervention may lawfully be exercised, for, however worthy of respect are the rights of state sovereignty and independence, there is something yet more worthy of respect, and that is the right of humanity or of human society, which must not be outraged". Payne trans., *Cromwell on Foreign Affairs* at 72, quoted in *ibid*.

36 Quoted in *ibid*.

37 Tesón, *Humanitarian Intervention: An Inquiry into Law and Morality* (Ardsley-on-Hudson, New York: Transnational Publishers, 1988) at 5.

38 *Supra*, note 33.

of protecting the life and liberty of the nationals of the latter state unable
or unwilling to do so itself.[39]

---

39 Beyerlin, "Humanitarian Intervention" in Bernhardt ed., *Encyclopedia of
    Public International Law* 3 (Amsterdam: North Holland Publishing Co.,
    1981) at 211. In International Law, some commentators tend to draw a
    distinction between intervention for the purpose of protecting a state's
    nationals abroad from other types of humanitarian intervention. The claim
    is made that although the former is a humanitarian act, the legal ground
    for protection of nationals is traceable to the independence of States, and
    thus it is not proper to consider both under the umbrella of humanitarian
    intervention. Asrat, *Prohibition of Force Under the UN Charter: A Study
    of Art. 2(4)* (Uppsala: Juridiska Foreningen i, 1991) at 184-185. Bowett
    claims the legality of humanitarian intervention is far more controversial
    than the right of protection of nationals abroad thus the two principles
    should not be lumped together;the reason being that if they are grouped
    together it might undermine the latter principle. Bowett, "The Use of Force
    for the Protection of Nationals Abroad" in Cassese ed., *The Current Regu-
    lation of the Use of Force* (Dordrecht: Martinus Nijhoff Publishers, 1986)
    at 49. See also, Ronzitti, *Rescuing Natioanls Abroad Through Military Co-
    ercion and Intervention on Grounds of Humanity* (Dordrecht: Martinus Nij-
    hoff Publishers, 1985). Fairley contends that this distinction exists in theory
    but should be abolished in practice. He states that "with respect to the use
    of force by states for humanitarian ends ... the utility of the two-fold clas-
    sification of customary international law collapses for the purpose of asses-
    sing the legal propriety of humanitarian intervention in the post-1945 era...".
    Fairley, "State Actors, Humanitarian Intervention and International Law:
    Reopening Pandora's Box" (1980) 10 *Georgia Journal of International and
    Comparative Law* 29 at 35; Gordon, however, indicates that humanitarian
    Intervention "is employed to describe three very different situations: first,
    where a state uses force to protect the lives or property of its own nationals
    abroad ... second, where the use of force serves to prevent a foreign govern-
    ment from initiating or perpetuating a massive and gross violation of the
    human rights of its own or a third state's nationals; third, where a state
    intervenes in a foreign state's civil war or so-called war of national liber-
    ation". Gordon, "Article 2(4) in Historical Context" (1985) 10 *Yale Journal
    of International Law* at 277. It is suggested that the nature of interventions
    today does not warrant such a distinction. Whether the right of protection
    of nationals flows from self-defence or not, the ultimate objective involved
    here is the protection of human rights. For purposes of this book humanit-
    arian intervention will be taken to encompass intervention for protection

The genesis of the doctrine is traceable to ancient times and the religious wars of the 16th and 17th centuries. Its institution, however, seems to be largely a creation of the 19th century.[40] Prior to the 19th century humanitarian intervention was based on Christian Beliefs and the religious concept of the dignity of man.[41] St. Thomas Aquinas made references on the basis of religious solidarity to the effect that a sovereign has the right to intervene in the internal affairs of another when the latter greatly mistreats its subjects.[42] Similarly, the Spanish scholar Vitoria argued that

> if any of the native converts to Christianity be subjected to force or fear by their princes in order to make them return to idolatry, this would justify the Spaniards ... in making war and in compelling the barbarians by force to stop such misconduct, ... and in deposing rulers as in other just wars ... Suppose a large part of the Indians were converted to Christianity, and this whether it were done lawfully or unlawfully, ...so long as they really were Christians, the Pope might for a reasonable cause, either with or without a request from them, give them a Christian Sovereign and depose their other unbelieving rulers.[43]

Vitoria thus contended that resistance by the heathen princes to the Christian missionaries and measures to force converted Indians to return

---

of nationals.

40   Fonteyne, "The Customary International Law Doctrine of Humanitarian Intervention: Its Current Validity Under the UN Charter" (1974) 4 *California Western International Law Journal* 203 at 205-206.

41   Green, *Law and Society* (Leyden: A.W. Sijthoff, 1975) at 294. Fonteyne comments that earlier examples of humanitarian intervention are too closely associated with the feeling of religious solidarity to consider them as genuinely humanitarian. *Ibid.*, at 206.

42   *Supra*, note 40 at 214.

43   Scott, *The Spanish Origins of International Law, Francisco de Vitoria and His Law of Nations* (Carnegie Endowment for International Peace, 1934) at Para.401 (XLIII). Quoted in Green, *supra*, note 41 at 289. Vitoria's argument in justifying the conversion of heathens to Christianity whether it was done lawfully or unlawfully, does not suggest any criteria but instead opens the door for all kinds of pretextual intervention.

to paganism would entitle the Pope to remove the Indian Princes and justified war.[44] These statements provided the ideological grounds for most interventions undertaken by "civilized nations" in the affairs of "non-civilized nations".[45] When Christian populations in "non-civilized" nations were subjected to persecutions or atrocities it was lawful to intervene. It was also lawful to intervene to end such practices as human sacrifice, although it is noteworthy that these statements also provided the basis for European Powers who invoked such principles to justify their imperialistic behaviour.

Moving from the ecclesiastical underpinnings of the doctrine, the question of when humanitarian intervention is permissible became secularised in the principle of lending lawful assistance to peoples struggling against tyranny. Support was found for the doctrine among many international scholars.[46] For Grotius writing in 1625, it was important that the law governing every human society be limited by a widely recog-

---

44 Suarez, writing around the same period unlike Vitoria, narrowed the right to wage war on behalf of nationals by maintaining "only on condition that the friend himself would be justified in avenging himself and actually proposes to do so... but if the injured party does not entertain such a wish, no one else may intervene, since he who committed the wrong has made himself subject not to everyone indiscriminately, but only to the person who has been wronged". He, however, went further to state that a punitive war might be waged to preserve a people's right to worship "on the ground of the defence of the innocent ... (and) if the prince forcibly compelled his subjects to practise idolatry; but under other circumstances, (such a ground) would not be a sufficient cause for war, unless the whole state should demand assistance against its sovereign ... [A] Christian prince may not declare war save either by reason of some injury inflicted or for the defence of the innocent ...[which latter] is permissible in a special sense to Christian princes...". Suarez, *De Triplici Virtute Theologica* (1621), "De Charitate, Disputatio XIII", s.4, para.3, Carnegie Translation, *Selections From Three Works* (1944) at 817;s.5, paras.3, 6-8, at 824, 826-827. Quoted in Green, "International Criminal Law and the Protection of Human Rights" in Chen & Brown eds., *Contemporary Problems of International Law: Essays in Honour of Georg Schwarzenberger* (London: Stevens & Sons Ltd., 1988) 116 at 122-123.

45 Green, *supra*, note 41.

46 See Stowell, *supra*, note 1 at 55.

nized principle of humanity. If a sovereign, although exercising his rights, acts contrary to the rights of humanity by grievously ill-treating his own subjects, the right of intervention may be lawfully exercised.[47] In his oft-quoted words, he asserts:

> [t]here is also another question, whether a war for the subjects of another be just, for the purpose of defending them from injuries by their ruler. Certainly it is undoubted that ever since civil societies were formed, the rulers of each claimed some especial rights over his own subjects ... [But] ... [i]f a tyrant ... practices atrocities towards his subjects, which no just man can approve, the right of human social connexion is not cut off in such a case ... [I]t would not follow that others may not take up arms for them.[48]

---

47 He writes: "The fact must be recognized that kings, and those who possess rights equal to kings, have the right of demanding punishments not only on account of injuries committed against themselves or their subjects, but also on account of injuries which do not affect them but excessively violate the law of nature or of nations in regard to any persons whatsoever... Truly it is more honourable to avenge the wrongs of others rather than one's own, in the degree that in the case of one's own wrongs it is more to be feared that through a sense of personal suffering one may exceed the proper limit or at least prejudice his mind ... Kings in addition to the particular care of their own state, are also burdened with a general responsibility for human society ... The ... most wide-reaching cause for undertaking wars on behalf of others is the mutual tie of kinship among men, which of itself affords sufficient ground for rendering assistance". Grotius, *De Jure Belli ac Pacis Libri Tre*(1625), Kelsey trans. (New York: Bobbs-Merrill Co., 1925) at 504-505, 508, 582. Another writer of the period, Pufendorf, also maintained that "common descent alone may be a sufficient ground for our going to the defense of one who is unjustly oppressed, and implores our aid, if we can conveniently do so". See *De Officio Humanis et Civis* (1682), Moore trans. (1927) at Lib.II, cap. XVI, s.11.

48 Grotius, 2 *De Jure Belli est Pacis* (Whewell trans.1853) at 288. Grotius also recognized the abuses inherent in exercising the right of humanitarian intervention but nevertheless supported it by drawing interesting analogies, for he states, "the desire to appropriate another's possessions often uses such a pretext as this: but that which is used by bad men does not necessarily therefore cease to be right. Pirates use navigation, but navigation is

Consequently, the sovereignty or independence of states stopped where
it was violated beyond the point of tolerance. Another writer of the
period, Vattel, [49]in his thoughts on the subject, stated:

> [I]f the prince, attacking the fundamental laws, gives his people a
> legitimate reason to resist him, if tyranny becomes so unbearable as
> to cause the Nation to rise, any foreign power is entitled to help an
> oppressed people that has requested assistance.[50]

Thus, authorities on international law considered humanitarian intervention to be in conformity with natural law. Their writings pointed to
the permissibility of the use of force against tyrants who mistreated their
subjects. Whereas publicists around the period in which Grotius and
Vattel were writing formulated the rules of international law in terms
of the recognition of natural rights, the nineteenth century saw the
ascendancy of legal positivism as the basis of international jurisprudence.[51] Arntz, for example, developed the theory of humanitarian intervention by recognizing it in an absolute way against all states. He maintains that

---

not therefore unlawful. Robbers use weapons, but weapons are not therefore
unlawful". *Ibid.*

49 Vattel had earlier observed that "[t]he Sovereign is the one to whom the
    Nation has entrusted the empire and the care of government; it has endowed
    him with his rights; it alone is directly interested in the manner in which
    the leader it has chosen for itself uses his power. No foreign power, accor-
    dingly, is entitled to take notice of the administration by that sovereign,
    to stand up in judgment of his conduct and to force him to alter it in any
    way. If he buries his subjects under taxes, if he treats them harshly, it is
    the Nation's business; no one else is called upon to admonish him, to force
    him to apply wiser and more equitable principles". De Vattel, 2 *Le Droit
    Des Gens*, Pradier-Fodere ed. (1863) Ch. IV, para. 55. Quoted in *supra*,
    note 40 at 214.

50 Quoted in *ibid.*, at 215

51 For an exposition on the distinctions between "natural" and "positive" law
    as applied to humanitarian intervention see generally, Harff, *Genocide and
    Human Rights: International Legal and Political Issues* (Denver: Graduate
    School of International Studies Univ. of Denver, 1984).

When a government, even acting within the limits of its rights of sovereignty, violates the rights of humanity, either by measures contrary to the interests of other States, or by excessive injustice or brutality which seriously injure our morals and civilization, the right of intervention is legitimate. For, however worthy of respect the rights of sovereignty and independence of States may be, there is something even more worthy of respect, namely the law of humanity, or of human society, that must not be violated. In the same way as within the State freedom of the individual is and must be restricted by the law and the morals of society, the individual freedom of the States must be limited by the law of human society.[52]

Some writers, however, recognizing the independence of sovereign states denied the right of another state to intervene even though a neighbouring state treats its nationals in an atrocious manner. To intervene was to usurp the sovereign characteristics of the state against which it was invoked. Mamiani[53] and Carnazza-Amari, both Italian scholars, for example, did not recognize the legality of intervention for humanitarian purposes. The latter states that "...[n]either can one justify intervention in the case where the local government does not respect the elementary laws of justice and humanity".[54] The French scholar Pradier-Fodere in essence observed that the doctrine is illegal since it constitutes a

---

52 Quoted in *supra*, note 40 at 220.
53 Carnazza-Amari, quoting Mamiani, considered " the actions and the crimes of a people within the limits of its territory do not infringe upon anyone else's rights and do not give a basis for a legitimate intervention...". Carnazza- Amari, 1 *Traite De Droit International En Temps De Paix* (Montanari- Revest Transl. 1880). Quoted in *supra*, note 40 at 215.
54 *Ibid.* at 555.
55 He writes that "[t]his [humanitarian] intervention is illegal because it constitutes an infringement upon the independence of States because the powers that are not directly, immediately affected by these inhuman acts are not entitled to intervene. If the inhuman acts are committed against the nationals of the country where they are committed, the powers are totally disinterested. The acts of inhumanity, however condemnable they may be, as long as they do not affect or threaten the rights of other States, do not

violation of the independence of states.[55] Other writers such as Halleck, Bonfils, and Despagnet expressed similar views.[56]

Nevertheless, the doctrine still had its advocates among scholars.[57] Some writers, however, partially accepted the doctrine. They seemed concerned about whether the doctrine could be incorporated into the principles of traditional international law. Their worries apparently were heightened by their fundamental ideological or political beliefs regarding sovereignty and non-intervention versus feelings of humanitarianism. Bernard stated that "the [positive] law ... prohibits intervention ... [However,] there may even be cases in which it becomes a positive duty to transgress [positive law]".[58] Referring to humanitarian considerations, Harcourt argues: "Intervention is a question rather of policy than of law. It is above and beyond the domain of law, and when wisely and equit-

---

provide the latter with a basis for lawful intervention, as no State can stand in judgement of the conduct of others. As long as they do not infringe upon the rights of the other powers or of their subjects, they remain the sole business of the nationals of the countries where they are committed". Pradier-Fodere, *Traite De Droit International European et Americain* (1885) 655. Quoted in Hassan, *"Realpolitik in International Law: After Tanzanian-Ugandan Conflict 'Humanitarian Intervention' Reexamined"* (1980-1981) 17 Willamette Law Review 859 at 863.

56 See Halleck, *International Law;or Rules Regulating the Intercourse of States in Peace and War* (1861) at 340; Bonfils, *Manuel le Droit International Public* 4th ed.(Droits des Gens) (1905) at 168 et seq.;Despagnet, *Cours de Droit International Public* 4th ed.(1910) at 258 et seq. Cited in Ronzitti, *supra*, note 37 at 89 and accompanying footnotes. Stowell also provides authorities denying the existence of humanitarian intervention. Stowell, *supra*, note 1 at 58-60 and accompanying footnotes. Some South American jurists also rejected the doctrine. Writing at the beginning of the 20th century, Pereira, for instance, states: "[i]nternal oppression, however odious and violent it may be, does not affect, either directly or indirectly, external relations and does not endanger the existence of other States. Accordingly, it cannot be used as a legal basis for use of force and violent means". Pereira, *Principios De Direito Internacional* (1902), quoted in Hassan, *ibid.* at 864, footnote 11.

57 See, Hassan, *supra*, note 55 at 860.

58 Bernard, *On the Principle of Non-Intervention*(1860) at 33-34, quoted in *supra*, note 40 at 218.

ably handled ... may be the highest policy of justice and humanity".[59]
Similarly, Lawrence considered "intervention to put a stop to barbarous
and abominable cruelty a high act of policy above and beyond the domain of law". He furthermore stated that it "is destitute of technical
legality, but it may be morally right and even praiseworthy to a high
degree... [international law, therefore,] will not condemn interventions
for such a cause".[60] Phillimore maintained that in the absence of specific
treaty provision, the right of intervention could be exercised only

> in the event of *persecution* of large bodies of men, on account of their
> religious belief, [in which case] an armed intervention on their behalf
> might be as warrantable in international law, as an armed intervention

---

59 Harcourt, *Historicus: Letters on Some Questions of International Law*
(1863) 14, quoted in Stowell, *supra*, note 1 at 60.

60 Furthermore, Lawrence forcefully argues for maintaining a right of intervention by stating" [s]o prone are powerful states to interfere in the affairs
of others, and so great are the evils of interference, that a doctrine of absolute non-intervention has been put forth as a protest against incessant meddl-
ing. If this doctrine means that a state should do nothing but mind its own
concerns and never take an interest in the affairs of other states, it is fatal
to the idea of a family of nations. If, on the other hand, it means that a
state should take an interest in international affairs, and express approval
or disapproval of the conduct of its neighbors, but never go beyond moral
suasion in its interference, it is foolish. To scatter abroad protests and
reproaches, and yet to let it be understood that they will never be backed
by force of arms, is the surest way to get them treated with angry contempt.
Neither selfish isolation nor undignified remonstrance is the proper attitude
for honorable and self-respecting states. They should intervene very sparingly, and only on the clearest grounds of justice and necessity; but when they
do intervene, they should make it clear to all concerned that their voices
must be attended to and their wishes carried out". See Lawrence, *The Principles of International Law* 4th ed.(London: Macmillan & Co., 1910) at
129, 137-138. Hall also observes that "[w]hile however it is settled that
as a general rule a state must be allowed to work out its internal changes
in its own fashion ... intervention for the purpose of checking gross tyranny
or of helping the efforts of a people to free itself is very commonly regarded without disfavour". Hall, *A Treatise on International Law* 2nd. ed.
(1884) at 265.

to prevent the shedding of blood and protracted internal hostilities ...
[N]o writer of authority upon International Law sanctions such an Intervention, except in the case of a positive *persecution* inflicted avowedly
upon the ground of religious belief.[61]

Westlake, one of the prominent English writers of the period, on the
other hand, recognized a right to intervene in the interest of humanity,
especially in response to popular feeling. He was of the view that even
a single state could exercise this right.[62]

By the early 20th century, the right of humanitarian intervention had
gained wide acceptance in the doctrine of non-intervention.[63] Many

---

61 Phillimore, *International Law*, vol.1, (1879) at 622-623.
62 He asserts that "[i]ntervention in the internal affairs of another state is jus-
    tifiable ... when a country has fallen into such a condition of anarchy or
    misrule as unavoidably to disturb the peace, external or internal of its
    neighbours, whatever the conduct of its government may be in that respect
    ... In considering anarchy and misrule as a ground for intervention ... [t]he
    moral effect on the neighbouring population is to be taken into account.
    Where this include considerable numbers allied by religion, language or
    race to the population suffering from misrule, to restrain the former from
    giving support to the latter in violation of the legal rights of the misruled
    state, may be a task beyond the power of their government, or requiring
    it to resort to modes of constraint irksome to its subjects, and not necessary
    for their good order if they were not excited by the spectacle of miseries
    which they must feel acutely. It is idle to argue in such a case that the duty
    of the neighbouring peoples is to look on quietly. Laws are made for men
    and not for creatures of the imagination, and they must not create or tolerate
    for them situations which are beyond the endurance ... of the best human
    nature that at the time and place they can hope to meet with".
    Westlake, *International Law*, Part I, Peace, (Cambridge: Cambridge Univer-
    sity Press, 1904) at 305-307.
63 See Mandelstam, The Protection of Minorities I (1923) *Recueil Des Cours*
    367 at 391. Brownlie writes that: "by the end of the nineteenth century the
    majority of publicists admitted that a right of humanitarian intervention
    ... existed". Brownlie, *International Law and the Use of Force by States*
    (Oxford: Clarendon Press, 1963) at 338, although he notes elsewhere that
    "unilateral action by a State in the territory of another State on the ground
    that human rights require protection, or a threat of force against a State
    for this reason, is unlawful" *Ibid.* at 226.

writers refused to recognize state sovereignty as absolute. It was a principle that was susceptible to restrictions or exceptions. Consequently, absolute sovereignty and non-intervention were relegated to the background in favour of protecting higher humane values in some situations.[64] According to Borchard:

> ...where a state under exceptional circumstances disregards certain rights of its own citizens over whom presumably it has absolute sovereignty, the other states of the family of nations are authorized by international law to intervene on grounds of humanity. When these "human" rights are habitually violated, one or more states may intervene in the name of the society of nations and may take such measures as to substitute at least temporarily, if not permanently, its own sovereignty for that of the state thus controlled. Whatever the origin, therefore, of the rights of the individual, it seems assured that these essential rights rest upon the ultimate sanction of international law, and will be protected, in the last resort, by the most appropriate organ of the international community.[65]

Similarly, Oppenheim pointed out:

> [T]here is no doubt that, should a State venture to treat its own subjects or a part thereof with such cruelty as would stagger humanity, public opinion of the rest of the world would call upon the Powers to exercise intervention for the purpose of compelling such State to establish a legal order of things within its boundaries sufficient to guarantee to its citizens an existence more adequate to the ideas of modern civilisation.[66]

---

64 See *supra*, note 40 at 222-223.

65 Borchard, *The Diplomatic Protection of Citizens Abroad* (New York: The Banks Law Publishing Co., 1922) at 14.

66 Oppenheim, *International Law* (London: Longmans & Co., 1905) Vol.I at 347. The editor of Oppenheim's treatise (Sir Hersch Lauterpacht) in 1955 observed that "[t]here is general agreement that, by virtue of its personal and territorial supremacy, a State can treat its own nationals according to discretion. But there is a substantial body of opinion and of practice in support of the view that there are limits to that discretion and that when

The doctrine of humanitarian intervention had come to be justified as "an instance of intervention for the purpose of vindicating the law of nations against outrage. For it is a basic principle of every human society and the law which governs it that no member may persist in conduct which is considered to violate the universally recognized principles of decency and humanity".[67] It was grounded upon a minimum standard for the treatment of individuals within a state, or to put it otherwise, minimum conditions for the survival of humanity. In situations where these standards were encroached upon, the offending state was to be held responsible for such actions.

It is worth noting from an examination of doctrinal writings on the subject that while they concentrated on the philosophical, religious and ideological foundations of the doctrine they failed to provide definite criteria for exercise of the right of humanitarian intervention. However, gleaning through the various writings it is possible to discern some yardstick for exercise of the right.[68] This included firstly, lack of other interests or motives than for purely humanitarian reasons on the part of the intervenor.[69] Secondly, there must be a preference for collective

---

a State renders itself guilty of cruelties against and persecution of its nationals in such a way as to deny their fundamental rights and to shock the conscience of mankind, intervention in the interest of humanity is legally permissible". Lauterpacht, ed. 8th ed., (1955) at 312-313.

67 Stowell, *supra*, note 1 at 51-52. Regarding the doctrine's future status in international law, one writer concluded at the beginning of the twentieth century that "as the feeling of general interest in humanity increases, and with it a world-wide desire for something approaching justice and international solidarity, interventions undertaken in the interest of humanity will also doubtless increase ... We may therefore conclude that future public opinion and finally international law will sanction an ever increasing number of causes for intervention for the sake of humanity". Hodges, *The Doctrine of Intervention* (1915) at 87, quoted in *supra*, note 40 at 223, footnote 70.

68 See generally, *supra*, note 40 at 226-267.

69 Amos indicated that "so far as [humanitarian] intervention is concerned, it is above all, desirable that the purity of the motives should be conspicuous...". Amos, *Political and Legal Remedies for War* (New York: Harper, 1880) at 159. Quoted in *ibid.* at 227.

action.[70] Thirdly, intervention must be in response to situations such as tyranny,[71] extreme atrocities,[72] and violations of specific fundamental human rights.[73] Lastly, intervention was to be restricted to certain situations such as "civilized" against "non-civilized nations".[74] Interestingly, an attempt at setting out some normative criteria as to when it is permissible to exercise the right was provided by Rougier in his "Theory of Humanitarian Intervention" in 1910. Starting from a critique of the concepts of absolute sovereignty and non-intervention he rejected the legality of individual intervention but accepted collective action instead, basing his reasons on various policy and legal grounds.[75]

In essence, whilst there was no unanimity regarding the incorporation of the doctrine into customary international law, a great number of authorities held consistent views on the subject matter, acknowledged its existence, and not only sanctioned permissible intervention, but also

---

70 Fonteyne, *ibid.*

71 Creasy, *First Platform of International Law* (1876) at 303-305.

72 Higgins ed., *Hall's Treatise on International Law* 8th ed., (1924) at 344.

73 See *supra*, note 40 at 227.

74 According to Stowell, however, "...when by exception a civilized state transgresses the dictates of humanity, it also may be constrained to reform its conduct". Stowell, *supra*, note 1 at 65.

75 He established three requirements for legality. Firstly, "that the event which ... motivates intervention be an action of the public authorities and not merely of private individuals". These included actions authorized by states as well as those by persons in a private capacity but condoned by the State. Secondly, "that the action constitutes a violation of the law of humanity and not merely a violation of national positive law". The only rights which justified intervention were the rights to life, freedom and justice. Thirdly, "that the intervention fulfils certain [circumstantial] requirements". Factors relevant to this requirement included, "the extent of the scandal, a pressing appeal from the victims, the very constitution of the guilty state, and certain favourable conditions relating to the political balance, economic rivalries, and the financial interests of the intervenors". Rougier, "The Theory of Humanitarian Intervention" (1910) 17 *Revue Generale De Droit Internatio-nal Publique* at 497-525.

argued that it was necessary.[76] The doctrine also sought a balance between the sovereignty of states and certain basic or 'natural' laws aimed
at the protection of human dignity. For, when a state's conduct toward
its subjects is such that it leads to massacres, brutality, religious or racial
persecution, and when these acts are of such nature that they shock the
conscience of mankind, the international community has the right to
intervene to restore some semblance of civilized conduct. In some situations, such action may even lead to the removal of a tyrannical sovereign.

The extent to which precedents in state practice tended to support
such a right is the subject of the next section.

c.   *State Practice in the Nineteenth and Early Twentieth Century*

State practice regarding interventions on humanitarian grounds date back
to earlier times. One of the earliest known instances occurred in 480
B.C.. The Prince of Syracuse, in defeating the Carthaginians, laid down
as one of the conditions of peace that they refrain from the barbarous
custom of sacrificing their children to Saturn.[77] The history of international relations shows many instances of humanitarian protest and
representation by one or more states on behalf of the citizens of other

---

76 Corbett writes that "since the very beginnings of the literature of inter-
    national law, many jurists have asserted that a just cause of war or other
    form of intervention existed against a State persecuting residents for racial,
    religious or political reasons. [And adds that] [f]rom time to time, also,
    governments have justified interventions in foreign territory on such
    grounds". Corbett, *Law and Society in the Relations of States*(New York:
    Harcout, Brace & Co.1951)

77 It is claimed, however, that a century later the Carthaginians suffered
    another defeat at the hands of a Sicilian Prince. This defeat was considered
    by the Prince a punishment for stopping human sacrifices, thus restoring
    it. See Sohn & Buergenthal, *International Protection of Human Rights* (New
    York: Bobb-Merrill Co., 1973) at 178.

states.[78] For the most part, and especially from the latter half of the seventeenth century, humanitarian action was undertaken mostly on behalf of persecuted religious minorities or coreligionists. Intervention was also undertaken on behalf of other recognizable groups, often constituting minorities.

Perhaps an initial step in the protection of minorities was to be found in the 1555 Treaty of Augsburg. This affirmed the principle *cujus regio, ejus religio*, ("whose the region, his the religion") but provided that in the Free Cities of the Holy Roman Empire Protestants and Catholics, often only constituting small minorities, were to live "quietly and peacefully".[79] A more significant treaty was the Peace of Westphalia, providing that

> for Catholics and Protestants living under the opposite faith, the conditions of public and private religious worship which had obtained at the most favourable date in the year 1624 were to be accepted as decisive, and to be maintained *semper et ubique* ... Subjects who in 1627 had been debarred from the free exercise of a religion other than that

---

78   Lord Phillimore in 1789 writes that "[t]he practice (if it can be called such) of intervention of one Christian State on behalf of the subjects of another Christian State upon the ground of religion, dates from the period of the Reformation... The great Treaty of Westphalia, in its general language respecting Germany, established, as a maxim of public law, that there should be an equality of rights between the Roman Catholic and Protestant religions; a maxim renewed and fortified by the Germanic Confederation of 1815. In these instances, it is true, that several States to which the stipulation related were all members of one confederation, though individually independent of each other. But the precedent does not stop here; for passing by the interventions of Elizabeth, Cromwell and even Charles II, on behalf of foreign Protestants, and going back no later than 1690, we find in that year Great Britain and Holland intervening in the affairs of Savoy, and obtaining from that kingdom a permission that a portion of the Sardinian subjects might freely exercise their religion." Lord Phillimore, *Commentaries Upon International Law*, Vol.1, 3rd.ed.(London: Butterworth, 1879), quoted in *supra*, note 33 at 3.

79   See Schwarzenberger, *Power Politics – A Study of World Society* (London: Stevens & Sons, 1964) at 450.

of their ruler were by the Peace granted the right of private worship and of educating their children at home or abroad, in conformity with their own faith; they were not to suffer in any civil capacity nor to be denied religious burial, but were at liberty to emigrate, selling their estates or leaving them to be managed by others.[80]

As noted earlier, Westphalia recognized some rights for both Protestants and Catholics, rejecting the right of rulers to change religious practices within their territories arbitrarily. While there was no provision for international enforcement, the relevant provisions were described as

a perpetual Law and establish'd Sanction of the Empire, to be inserted like other fundamental Laws and Constitutions of the Empire, and the Empire was obligated not to pass any legislation which would discriminate as between Catholics and Protestants.[81]

Other Treaties of Peace signed during this period included, for example, that between Brandenburg and Poland, 1657 (Treaty of Velau); between Sweden, Poland, Austria and Brandenburg, 1660 (Treaty of Oliva); and between the Holy Roman Empire and France, 1679 (Treaty of Nimeguen).[82] All these treaties constituted examples of Roman Catholic intervention on behalf of their subjects in countries ceded to Protestant sovereigns. One writer notes that almost without exception, major peace treaties concerning changes of sovereignty contained clauses protecting the rights and properties of populations transferred to new sovereignties.[83]

---

80 See Ward, "The Peace of Westphalia" (1934) 4 *Cambridge Modern History* at 412.

81 Art. CXX, quoted in Green, "Group Rights, War Crimes and Crimes against Humanity" (1993) *International Journal on Group Rights* 27 at 31.

82 For the full text of the Treaty of Velau, see Parry ed., *The Consolidated Treaty Series (1655-1658)* Vol.4 (Dobbs Ferry: Oceana Publications, 1969) at 435-436;Treaty of Oliva, *ibid.*(1658-1660) Vol.6, at 60-87;Treaty of Nimeguen, *ibid.*(1679-1680) Vol.15, at 55-66.

83 See for example, Article 16 of the Treaty of Velau which provided for "the free exercise ... of the Catholic religion...". *Ibid.* Vol.4, at 435-436. Similarly, Section 3 of the Treaty of Oliva stated: "[t]he towns of Royal Prussia

The doctrine as practised in the 18th and 19th centuries was mainly concerned with the rights of Christians, although secularization of religious belief led to basing such intervention on behalf of the dignity of man, [84]as well as Jews, and other minority groups in various countries, and in parts of the Ottoman Empire.[85] It was mainly done through dip-

---

which have been during this War in the possession of his Royal Swedish Majesty, and of the Kingdom of Sweden, shall likewise be continued in the Enjoyment of all Rights, Liberties and Privileges, in matters Ecclesiastical and Civil, which they enjoy'd before this War, (saving the free Exercise of the Catholic and Protestant Religion) as it prevail'd in the Citys before the War...". *Ibid.* Vol.6, at 60-87. See also, Feinberg, "International Protection of Human Rights and the Jewish Question (An Historical Survey)" (1968) 3 *Israel Law Review* 487 at 490;Israel, *Major Peace Treaties of Modern History: 1648-1967* Vol.1 (New York: Chelsea House, 1967) at 7-49.

84   See Green, "General Principles of Law and Human Rights" (1955-56) 8 *Current Legal Problems* 162.

85   The principle of international protection of Jews, for example, was stated succinctly in a speech in the English Parliament by Burke as follows: "[h]aving no fixed settlement in any part of the world, no kingdom nor country in which they have a government, a community nor a system of laws, they are thrown upon the benevolence of nations ... If Dutchmen are injured and attacked, the Dutch have a nation, a government and armies to redress or revenge their cause. If Britons are injured, Britons have armies and laws, the law of nations ... to fly for protection and justice. But the Jews have no such power and no friend to depend on. Humanity, then must be their protection and ally". To further illustrate the principle, the British representative in a dispatch to the Rumanian Government in 1867 stated: "[t]he peculiar position of the Jews place them under the protection of the civilized world". Burke, 13 Parliamentary History of England From the Earliest Period to the Year 1803 (1814). Quoted in Feinberg, *supra*, note 83 at 490. See also Kutner, "World Habeas Corpus and Humanitarian Intervention" (1985) 19 *Valparaiso University Law Review* 593. Generally the doctrine of humanitarian intervention embodied in these principles during this period protecting Jews and other minorities became part of diplomatic practice. The question of the situation of Jews in various countries was discussed either directly or indirectly at various Congresses. At the Congress of Vienna (1814-1815) for example, the question of the situation of Jews in the German Confederated States was addressed. Further-

lomatic intercession, although there were instances of military intervention. It was not until the nineteenth and early twentieth centuries that the institution of humanitarian intervention reflected in state practice gained ground, as the great powers occasionally sought to protect individuals and groups of individuals against their own states, though power politics was also involved. Although individual states invoked the doctrine, in most cases, several of the major powers acted collectively under the aegis of the concert of Europe, typically against the Turkish/Ottoman Empire.[86]

During the period 1827-1830, France, Britain and Russia intervened in Greece to protect the Greek right of self-determination and Greek Christians from the oppressive rule of the Turks following a number of massacres.[87] This action resulted in acceptance by the Porte of the

---

more, at that same Congress an obligation was imposed on Holland not to discriminate between the members of all religious faiths (which included members of the Jewish faith). Also, another example of intervention by one or more of the Great Powers through diplomacy occurred in 1840 on behalf of the Jews in Rumania, when the Government, in breach of the Treaty of Berlin refused them recognition as citizens and denied them fundamental rights. See generally, Feinberg, *ibid.*

86 The interventions under the Concert of Europe (which functioned successively for some years) had some religious impetus as well, since most were carried out to protect Christian minorities in non-Christian states. *Supra*, note 40 at 232. Rougier, however, notes other than the intervention in Syria in 1860 which was humanitarian, other interventions in the Ottoman Empire were exercised "less in the interests of the Ottoman subjects than in order to resolve the conflicting interests of England, Austria, France and Russsia in the Black Sea area". *Supra*, note 73 at 525. Quoted in Feinberg, *ibid.* at 492.

87 On the question of motives for that intervention, Stowell notes that the "motive of the intervention would seem to have been to protect the rights of [Greek] self determination". Stowell, *supra*, note 1 at 126-127. Other writers, like Oppenheim, point out the interest mainly to be the European Powers' concern for the Christian population being subjected to great cruelty in an attempt to forcibly absorb them into the Muslim empire. *Supra*, note 66, 2nd.ed., at 194; The contention that this intervention was humanitarian in character is borne out by the terms of the London Treaty of 1827 (for the "Pacification of Greece") to which Britain, France and Russia were

1827 London Treaty,[88] and ultimately in the independence of Greece in 1830. As noted, the major powers indicated in the London Treaty that their action was mandated "no less by sentiments of humanity, than by interests for the tranquillity of Europe".[89] On the question of whether considerations other than humanitarianism were involved, Brownlie points out the fact that a realist might see this action from the perspective of the other Powers being afraid of a unilateral Russian intervention.[90] This comment, perhaps, recalls the presence of power politics in the theatre of international relations. The tendency of powerful states in the system to invade weaker ones for a variety of reasons[91] cannot be totally discounted. Nevertheless, it should be borne in mind that a number of scholars have accepted this intervention as based on humanitarian considerations.[92]

---

parties. The preamble to that treaty stated that the contracting powers "... having moreover received from the Greeks an earnest invitation to interpose their mediation with the Ottoman Porte ... being animated with the desire of putting a stop to the effusion of blood ... have resolved to combine their efforts, and to regulate the operation thereof, by a formal Treaty, for the object of re-establishing peace between the Contending Parties, by means of an arrangement called for, no less by *sentiments of humanity*, than by interests for the tranquility of Europe". British and Foreign State Papers, Vol.14, (1826-1827), 633, quoted in *supra*, note 33 at 22. For a detailed discussion see *supra*, note 34 at 280-283.

88   The treaty also proposed a limited local autonomy for the region within the Ottoman Empire. The Turkish government rejected this proposal which consequently, resulted in an armed intervention by the Major Powers on 14th September 1829 and acceptance of the treaty. See Ganji, *ibid*.

89   *Ibid.*

90   Brownlie, *supra*, note 63 at 339.

91   Verwey suggests that this particular intervention was also justified as a protection of commercial interests. Verwey, "Humanitarian Intervention Under International Law" (1985) 32 *Netherlands International Law Review* 357 at 399.

92   See Stowell, *supra*, note 1 at 126, 489. Moskowitz notes the 1827 intervention as an "... occasion ... on which the doctrine of 'humanitarian intervention' has been invoked on behalf of nationals or inhabitants of foreign countries felt to have been subjected to practices which 'shock the conscience of mankind'". He goes on to cite other examples like the

Another important instance of invocation of the doctrine to prevent religious persecution occurred in Syria between 1860 and 1861.[93] From the sixteenth century until World War I, geographical Syria, an area encompassing present-day Lebanon, Jordan, Israel, Syria, the West Bank and Gaza, constituted an integral part of the Ottoman Empire. For centuries before the Ottoman conquest of Syria, the mountains of Lebanon offered a refuge for persecuted religious communities, particularly for Maronite Christians immersed in a generally hostile Islamic region. Turkish rule led to the suppression and massacre of thousands of Maronite Christians by the Muslim population. Consequently, France was authorized by Austria, Great Britain, Prussia, Russia and Turkey, meeting at the Conference of Paris of 1860, to intervene in Syria to restore order. As a result 6, 000 French troops were deployed. A Constitution for the Lebanese region was adopted requiring a Christian governor who was responsible to the Porte. The French forces withdrew in 1861 after accomplishing their tasks.[94]

Although the Sultan was a formal party to this intervention as a result of the Protocol of Paris, Turkey assented "only through constraint and

---

numerous interventions protesting Turkish treatment of Armenians and other Christians, and the protests by the United States in 1891 and 1905 against anti-Semitic outrages in Russia". Moskowitz, *Human Rights and World Order* (New York: Oceana Publications, 1958) at 16; Ganji also suggests "[t]his intervention ... can be identified as humanitarian intervention mainly because its primary motive was to bring an end to the effusion of blood and the human sufferings which had accompanied the six years of war between Greece (then part of the Ottoman Empire) and the Sublime Porte". *Supra*, note 33 at 22; See also, Lillich, "Forcible Self-Help by States to Protect Human Rights" (1967-1968) 53 *Iowa Law Review* 325 at 332; Reisman & McDougal, "Humanitarian Intervention to Protect the Ibos" in Lillich ed., *Humanitarian Intervention and the United Nations* (1973) at 180. But see Brownlie, *supra*, note 63 at 339.

93   Stowell, *supra*, note 1 at 63.
94   For details of this intervention see *ibid.* at 63-66.

desire to avoid worse".[95] This constraint was however deemed lawful by virtue of the humanitarian considerations involved.[96]

Again in 1866, when Crete revolted alleging Turkish oppression and persecution of Christians among other complaints, the European Powers called for establishment of an International Commission of Enquiry to investigate the allegations. Turkey refused on grounds that the issue was one that fell within its domestic jurisdiction. Great Britain stepped in as a neutral mediator offering friendly advice to Turkey, thus preventing armed intervention. Consequently, the Turkish government adopted a constitution deemed acceptable to the Christian population as well as making commitments for the protection of human rights.[97]

Similarly, Russian intervention in Bosnia, Herzegovina, and Bulgaria in 1877 offers an illustration of state practice. Following Turkish misrule and harsh treatment of the Christian populations of Bosnia, Herzegovina and Bulgaria within the Ottoman Empire, the Concert of European Powers became concerned about the possibility of the creation of effective and equal guarantees for the rights of the Christian population of these areas in comparison with the rights enjoyed by the Moslem inhabitants of the empire.[98] The European Powers thus requested that an International Commission operate in the areas to observe and protect the

---

95 *Ibid.* at 66.

96 Some writers have questioned the humanitarian objectives involved here, contending the French expeditionary force stayed on after the rescue operations were completed and actually behaved like an occupational force. See for example, *supra*, note 89. For further discussions on the French intervention in Syria see, Pogany, "Humanitarian Intervention in International Law: The French Intervention in Syria Re-examined" (1986) 35 *International and Comparative Law Quarterly* 182; Kloepfer, "The Syrian Crisis, 1860-61: A Case Study in Classic Humanitarian Intervention" (1985) 23 *Canadian Yearbook of International Law* 246.

97 *Supra*, note 33 at 26-29.

98 In describing the situation at the time, Stowell quotes Morley as saying: "[f]ierce revolt against intolerable misrule slowly blazed up in Bosnia and Herzegovina, and a rising in Bulgaria, not dangerous in itself, was put down by Turkish troops ... with deeds described by the British agent who investigated them on the spot, as the most heinous crimes that had stained the history of the century". See Stowell, *supra*, note 1 at 127.

Christians. Turkey rejected the proposal, but the Powers signed a Protocol, stating that they reserved to themselves a right of action should
Turkey fail to maintain the minimum conditions demanded in these
areas. Russia declared war on Turkey with the consent of Austria, Prussia, France, and Italy.

The war between Turkey and Russia ended with the preliminary treaty concluded between them at San-Stefano. This treaty provided the basis
for deliberations and adoption of the Berlin Treaty of 1878. By this treaty, a system of Christian autonomy was set up for Bulgaria and Montenegro, the independence of Serbia and Rumania were recognized, and
Bosnia and Herzegovina were occupied and annexed by Austria-Hungary.[99] It further provided for freedom of worship and for the principle
of non-discrimination on the grounds of religion where it concerned the
enjoyment of civil and political rights, admission to public employment,
and the right to the exercise of any profession in any locality in all these
States or territories.[100]

Although this particular example appears to have been justified by
the overriding humanitarian concerns of the major powers, it also por-
trays the inherent risks in exercising the right of humanitarian intervention. The British government insisted at the time that whatever the
repressive nature of Turkish rule over the Bulgarians, Herzegovinians,
and Bosnians, the Russian intervention, sanctioned by the other powers,
"based in theory upon religious sympathy and upon humanity ... was
a move, in fact, upon the Straits and Constantinople, in pursuance of
Russia's century long program".[101] One writer suggests and as a fact
pertaining to this example, the "alleged humanitarian motives were ...

---

99 *Supra*, note 33 at 29-33. For an exposition on the question of treaty obli-
    gations on the successor states see, Green, "Protection of Minorities in the
    League of Nations and the United Nations" in Gotlieb ed., *Human Rights,
    Federalism amd Minorities* (Toronto: Canadian Institute of International
    Affairs, 1970) 180.
100 *Ibid.* at 33.
101 Woolsey, *America's Foreign Policy* (New York, 1898), quoted in *supra*,
    note 32 at 283.

influenced or affected by the political interests of the intervening state...".[102] It appears that there was lack of inclusive supervision in implementation which facilitated abuse by Russia, ultimately resulting in only partial relief for the victims of oppression and misrule.[103]

Another instance of intervention in the Ottoman Empire occurred in 1903. In the course of a rebellion, fuelled partly by attempts to convert the Christian population in Macedonia, Turkish troops committed atrocities by attacking the civilian population and destroying many villages with a considerable loss of life. Austria-Hungary and Russia, acting under the aegis of the European powers, demanded the Sultan put into effect a programme to provide for among other things, future protection of the population including a year's remission of taxes as reparation for the loss and destruction suffered by the local population.[104] Although Turkey accepted the demands, there was a subsequent revolution which led to perpetration of new atrocities in Macedonia. This led to a declaration of war by Greece, Bulgaria and Serbia on Turkey. The war ended with the signing of the 1913 Treaty of London, wherein Turkey ceded the greater part of Macedonia for partition among the Balkan allies.

Although the Balkan allies were not able to invoke treaty commitments of the 1878 Berlin Treaty (since they were not parties to it), it is important that they did not hesitate to resort to armed force. They justified their action on grounds of humanitarian concern for the continuing atrocities that were being perpetrated upon the Macedonian population.[105]

Also, the American action against Cuba in 1898 could possibly be characterized as a case of humanitarian intervention.[106] Following the

---

102 Fenwick, "Intervention: Individual and Collective" (1945) 39 *American Journal of International Law* 645 at 650.
103 See *ibid.*
104 *Supra*, note 33 at 33-38.
105 *Ibid.* at 37.
106 Various interpretations have been placed on the American action; while some commentators perceive it as an example of humanitarian intervention, others have seen it as "the powerful influence of endangered investments and trade". See Fitzgibbon, *Cuba and the United States*, 1900-1935 (1964)

rebellion of Cubans against Spanish rule, the President of the United States of America reserved to the United States the right of intervention. In President McKinley's war message to Congress, he declared the purpose of the United States intervention, among other things, as being

> ...[i]n the cause of humanity and to put an end to the barbarities, bloodshed, starvation, and horrible miseries now existing there, and which the parties to the conflict are either unable or unwilling to stop or mitigate. It is no answer to say this is all in another country, belonging to another nation, and therefore none of our business...[107]

A joint resolution of Congress[108] authorized an armed intervention by the United States in Cuba leading to the defeat of Spanish forces. A general election was held on the island under the authority of the United States, a constitutional convention was convened and, within two years, the Republic of Cuba was established.

While other motives may have prompted the United States action, the evidence points to the presence of humanitarian ideals as well, and thus may well be considered to fall within the ambit of intervention for the cause of humanity.

Perhaps a general observation to be made is that international scholars examining these various instances of intervention have recog-

---

at 22, quoted in *supra*, note 34 at 285. Woolsey after studying this case concludes that as far as the facts go the American action in Cuba was justified on the ground of humanity. *Supra*, note 101 at 75-76. Stowell points out the basis of the action as putting "an end to the shocking treatment which the military authorities were inflicting upon the non-combatant population in their futile efforts to suppress the insurrection".Stowell, *supra*, note 1 at 120. Von Glahn also cites the American action in Cuba as an instance of humanitarian intervention. Von Glahn, *Law Among Nations: An Introduction to Public International Law* (New York: MacMillan Publishing Co., 1992) at 165.

107 Quoted in Thomas & Thomas, *supra*, note 1 at 22.

108 The Joint Resolution stated, in part "that the people of the island of Cuba are and of right ought to be free and independent ... [and that] ... the United States hereby disclaims any disposition or intention to exercise sovereignty, jurisdiction, or control over said island, except for the pacification thereof,

nized that while the motives were not always pure (most often dictated by political advantage), the motivations of the intervening powers were in fact humanitarian.[109] In each of the examples considered, the sovereign authorities were either actively involved in committing atrocities or did nothing to prevent the killings of innocent individuals or groups within their territorial jurisdiction. In sum, the humanitarian motives, for example, behind the Concert of Europe's "recurrent interventions in Ottoman affairs [should] probably not ... be dismissed as bogus".[110]

By the early twentieth century there was less willingness to intervene for the sake of humanity.[111] Following World War I, the principles of humanitarian intervention as reflected in state practice, were mani-

---

and asserts its determination when that is accomplished to leave the government and control of the island to its people". *Ibid.* at 23. This statement hints at the altruistic nature regarding motives for undertaking the action in Cuba. Brownlie contends the "Joint Resolution of Congress approved on 20th April 1898 justified the intervention in terms of American interests". Brownlie, *supra*, note 63 at 46. Lillich opposes this contention by referring to the Preamble to the Resolution which mentions "abhorrent conditions which have existed for more than three years in the island of Cuba ... [and which] have shocked the moral sense of the people of the United States..". He relies on the similarity between the words "shocked the moral sense" in the text in the preamble and "shock the conscience of mankind" as descriptive of conditions which sanction humanitarian intervention. Lillich, "Humanitarian Intervention: A Reply to Ian Brownlie and a Plea for Constructive Alternatives" in Moore ed., *Law and Civil War in the Modern World* (Baltimore: Johns Hopkins University Press, 1974) at 234.

109 *Supra*, note 34 at 281.

110 *Ibid.* However, Brownlie, after examining the various instances of state practice relating to the doctrine asserts "the state practice justifies the conclusion that no genuine case of humanitarian intervention has occurred, with the possible exception of the occupation of Syria in 1860 and 1861." Brownlie, *supra*, note 63 at 340.

111 Earlier in the previous century, it was thought that the Treaties of Paris (1856) and Berlin (1878) which introduced the system of collective guarantees of certain rights for individuals by the European Powers would be likely to eradicate intervention for political purposes, under the guise of humanitarian intervention. In reality this did not work due to absence of machinery to deal with violations. Thomas & Thomas, *supra*, note 1 at 375.

fested in treaties protecting minority rights. Institutional guarantees of human rights and collective intervention were vested in the League of Nations as the principal organ to ensure the treaties were kept,[112] with ultimate recourse to the Permanent Court of International Justice (PCIJ) for interpretation.[113]

In the 1920s the minority system of the League worked quite well,[114] but broke down after 1931 in the face of the threat of totalitarian aggression.[115] States were either individually or collectively unwilling to intervene in the name of humanity. This unwillingness was shown by the Powers, for example, in the light of Hitler's bogus argument of oppression of Aryan minorities and consequent aggressive action, resulting in the incorporation of Austria into Germany, the disintegration of

---

112 The minority treaties concluded sought, among other things, to protect rights of linguistic and ethnic minorities within new state territories created by the Treaties of Versailles and St. Germain. Although the League's role regarding protection of minorities was not a great success, it paved the way for later concern to protect human rights. See, Robinson, *Were the Minorities Treaties a Failure?* (New York: Institute of Jewish Affairs, 1943); Sieghart, *The International Law of Human Rights* (Oxford: Clarendon Press, 1988) at 13; Shaw, *International Law* (Cambridge: Grotius Publications Ltd., 1986) at 29; Green, *supra*, note 99.

113 The PCIJ had occasion to interpret the significance of particular minorities Treaties and even the Minorities regime. See for example, *Treatment of Polish Nationals in Danzig*, P.C.I.J. (1932) 2 Hudson 789; *Minority Schools in Albania*, PCIJ (1935) 3 Hudson 485.

114 See Jones, "National Minorities: A Case Study in International Protection" (1949) 14 *Law & Contemporary Problems* 599.

115 Thomas & Thomas, *supra*, note 1 at 375. Green notes that "during the period between the accession to power of National Socialism in Germany and the outbreak of war in 1939, [t]he desire to maintain the balance of power was fundamental in European politics [thus playing] a major role in frustrating the work of the League of Nations as a protector of minorities.[This desire also] had much to do with the silent tolerance of atrocities being perpetrated in Germany [at the time]". Green, "The Intersection of Human Rights and International Criminal Law" in Cotler & Eliadis eds., *International Human Rights: Theory and Practice* (1993) 231 at 250.

Czechoslovakia and the partition of Poland.[116] Again, there was no intervention in the mass extermination of Jews in Europe in the 1930s and 1940s.[117] This unwillingness to intervene led H.A. Smith, then Professor of International Law at the University of London to complain that

> in practice we no longer insist that States shall conform to any common standards of justice, religious toleration and internal government. Whatever atrocities may be committed in foreign countries, we now say they are no concern of ours. Conduct which in the nineteenth century would have placed a government outside the pale of civilised society is now deemed to be no obstacle to diplomatic friendship. This means, in fact, that we have abandoned the old distinction between civilised and uncivilised states.[118]

In light of Nazi Germany's aggression and the arguments used to support it, Thomas and Thomas observed that the ideal of humanitarian intervention for protection of minorities "was twisted and warped into a cloak for illegal intervention".[119] Opponents of the doctrine have cited these instances of unjustified invasions of other nations as a fundamental reason why the doctrine should not be recognized by the international community. The problem here relates to discerning the credible exercise of the right from the non-credible.[120] These instances of misapplication

---

116 In justifying the German occupation of Bohemia and Moravia in 1939, Hitler referred to "assaults on the life and liberties of minorities, and the purpose of disarming Czech troops and terrorist bands threatening the lives of minorities". Brownlie, *supra*, note 63 at 340.

117 It should be noted that military intervention by the Allies in World War II was in response to Nazi Germany's external aggression and not to its commission of human rights atrocities against Jews living in Germany and other European nations under Nazi occupation. Scheffer, "Toward A Modern Doctrine of Humanitarian Intervention" (1992) 23 *University of Toledo Law Review* 253 at 255.

118 Smith, *The Listener*, Jan.26, 1938. Quoted in Green, "Institutional Protection of Human Rights" (1986) 16 *Israel Yearbook of Human Rights* 69 at 79.

119 Thomas & Thomas, *supra*, note 1 at 375.

120 Reisman & McDougal, *supra*, note 92 at 167.

of the doctrine, however, do not make it devoid of its inherent value as a safeguard for protection of humanity.

In sum, the discussion suggests that state sovereignty has coexisted with intervention for the cause of humanity since the inception of the state system. Humanitarian intervention is based on the notion that sovereign jurisdiction is conditional upon compliance with minimum standards of human rights.[121] Thus, an offending state which has abused its sovereign rights of protecting its inhabitants by violating all universal standards of humanity cannot invoke a claim of absolute sovereignty. The content of sovereign authority is not immune from state action to protect humanity. In situations of egregious violations or large-scale deprivations of the most fundamental rights members of the international community should step in and exercise the right of humanitarian intervention. These fundamental considerations and precedents in state practice motivated the writings of international scholars, to document the legality and instances in which the doctrine has been invoked.[122]

While the doctrinal writing is wider, state practice was limited to Conventions such as peace treaties and minority treaties. The precedents show in some instances a propensity to abuse the doctrine, or the presence of mixed motives in undertaking state action. However, the crucial underlying concern of the intervening States related to oppressive conditions and inhuman treatment suffered by populations under the jurisdiction of sovereign authorities who were supposed to protect their rights.

In conclusion, it seems clear that the argument supporting the doctrine has its underpinnings in recognized sources of international law as the views of international scholars and treaties indicate.[123] Addition-

---

121 *Ibid.*
122 But see, Michalska, "Humanitarian Intervention" in Mahoney & Mahoney eds., *Human Rights in the Twenty-First Century: A Global Challenge* (Dordrecht: Martinus Nijhoff Publishers, 1993), 393.
123 A minority view, however, argues that since most of these interventions were based on treaty provisions authorizing the European powers to intervene in the states of the Ottoman Empire to protect Christian minorities from atrocities, they do not support recognition of a broad right of humanitarian intervention. See for example, Brownlie, *supra*, note 63 at 342; *supra*, note 33 at 43. Sornarajah, however, concludes that an examination

ally, the many cases during the nineteenth and early twentieth century in which states invoked humanitarian grounds to justify intervention abroad constituted sufficient evidence of state practice to permit recognition of the right of humanitarian intervention. As Lillich tersely maintains, "the doctrine appears to have been so clearly established under customary international law that only its limits and not its existence is subject to debate".[124]

---

of state practice indicates that despite the invocation of treaty rights of intervention, states nonetheless "claimed the right of intervention on humanitarian grounds, attaching primacy to that principle over their treaty rights as the justification for the intervention". Sornarajah, "Internal Colonialism and Humanitarian Intervention" (1981) 11 *Georgia Journal of International and Comparative Law* 45 at 57.

124 Lillich, "Intervention to Protect Human Rights" (1969) 15 *McGill Law Journal* 205 at 210. Similarly, Shawcross asserts that "the rights of humanitarian intervention on behalf of the rights of man trampled upon by a state in a manner shocking the sense of mankind has long been considered to form part of the recognized law of nations". Speeches of the Chief Prosecutors at Nuremberg, Commd. Papers 6964 (1946) at 40, quoted in Thomas & Thomas, *supra*, note 1 at 374. Fonteyne, after an in-depth analysis of the doctrine and state practice, concludes that "while divergences certainly existed as to the *circumstances* in which resort could be had to the institution of humanitarian intervention, as well as to the *manner* in which such operations were to be conducted, the *principle* itself was widely, if not unanimously, accepted as an integral part of customary international law". *Supra*, note 40 at 235. See also, Sornarajah, *ibid.*, at 56 (noting "classical international law permitted intervention to protect the interests of minority groups subjected to violation of human rights by recognizing the doctrine of humanitarian intervention").

2

THE RIGHT OF HUMANITARIAN INTERVENTION IN
THE POST-CHARTER ERA (1945-1989)

1   INTRODUCTION

In the previous chapter, an attempt was made to show that the principle
of humanitarian intervention coexisted with the development of state
sovereignty, and that customary international law permitted intervention
in support of humanity under certain circumstances. The promulgation
of the United Nations (UN) Charter following World War II affirmed
a set of principles and norms that are directed towards governance of
the international system, or at least, aimed at influencing interactions
among states.[1] If the UN Charter, a document intended to be the primary

---

1   Robert Gilpin, for example, notes that a necessary "component of the gover-
     nance of an international system is a set of rights and rules that govern
     or at least influence interactions among states." He argues that these rules
     are negotiated at the conclusion of great wars, where the negotiated treaties
     serve as the constitution of the state system. See Gilpin, *War and Change
     in World Politics* (Cambridge: Cambridge University Press, 1981) at 34,
     36. In a similar vein, Goodrich, Hambro and Simons write: [i]t is necessary
     to think of the Charter not only as a treaty embodying the maximum limit-
     ations on a state's freedom of action, that nations at that stage of history
     and in light of experience were prepared to accept as consistent with their
     national interests, but also as a constitutional document setting forth the
     guidelines for future development. The exact nature of this development
     was to be determined not only by the Charter itself but also by the way
     in which the members of the United Nations interpreted these guidelines
     and made use of the organization in dealing with the ever-changing prob-
     lems of an ever-increasing world. The Charter thus provided the consti-
     tutional basis for achieving international peace, security, and well-being,
     and pointed the way – but the ultimate verdict was to rest with the actors

basis for postwar international relations, created a new international order, did the right of intervention for purposes of humanity survive into this order? The legal principles that guided the early evolution of the humanitarian intervention doctrine, according to some commentators, are no longer valid with the prohibition of the use of force under the Charter.[2] However, a school of thought holds that the institution of humanitarian intervention still exists.[3] This chapter investigates the

themselves." Goodrich, Hambro, and Simons, *Charter of the United Nations*, 3rd ed. (1969) at 1.

2   For a representative list of scholars who argue to that effect see for example, Brownlie, "Humanitarian Intervention" in Moore ed., *Law and Civil War in the Modern World* (Baltimore: John Hopkins Univ. Press, 1974) at 217; "Thoughts on Kind-Hearted Gunmen" in Lillich ed., *Humanitarian Intervention and the United Nations* (Charlottesville: Univ. of Virginia Press, 1973) at 139; Ronzitti, *Rescuing Nationals Abroad Through Military Coercion and Intervention on Grounds of Humanity* (Dordrecht: Martinus Nijhoff Publishers, 1985); Bowett, "The Interrelation of Theories of Intervention and Self-Defense" in Moore ed., *ibid.*, at 38; Asrat, *Prohibition of Force Under the UN Charter: A Study of Art.2(4)* (Uppsala: Iustus Forlag, 1991); Jhabvala, "Unilateral Humanitarian Intervention and International Law" (1981) 21 *Indian Journal of International Law* 208: Verwey, "Humanitarian Intervention under International Law" (1985) 32 *Netherlands International Law Review* 357; Hassan, "Realpolitik in International Law: After Tanzanian-Ugandan Conflict 'Humanitarian Intervention' Reexamined" (1980/81) 17 *Willamette Law Review* 859; Beyerlin, "Humanitarian Intervention" in Bernhadt ed., 3 *Encyclopedia of Public International Law* (Amsterdam: North-Holland Publishing Co., 1981) 2111; Michalska, "Humanitarian Intervention" in Mahoney & Mahoney eds., *Human Rights in the Twenty-First Century: A Global Challenge* (Dordrecht: Martinus Nijhoff Publishers, 1993) 393.

3   It should be noted that it is sometimes difficult to put scholars in straight jacket categories of proponents for and against the doctrine. Some advocates against the right of intervention for humanitarian purposes prefer collective humanitarian intervention by the UN as opposed to unilateral action by states. Still others opt for a limited right of humanitarian intervention. For a representative list of scholars favouring survival of the right of humanitarian intervention see for example, Lillich, "Humanitarian Intervention: A Reply to Ian Brownlie and a Plea for Constructive Alternatives" in Moore ed., *ibid.*, 229 [hereinafter cited as Lillich, "A Reply"]; Tesón,

evolution and strength of the principle of humanitarian intervention in the UN Charter during the era of the Cold War. Specific Charter provisions relating to nonintervention and human rights as well as international legal instruments beyond the Charter such as Conventions, Resolutions and Declarations are examined. It is argued that the international human rights regime, at least in principle, constitutes limitations on the sovereignty of states which have accepted the respective agreements. This, however, does not suggest the non-importance of sovereignty since the conclusion of these covenants are themselves acts of sovereignty. Thus a norm of justified intervention is grounded in the UN Charter, the human rights declarations, and covenants. In addition, the extent to which state practice recognised the legitimacy of humanitarian intervention is examined.

Humanitarian Intervention: An Inquiry into Law and Morality (Ardsley-on-Hudson, NY: Transnational Publishers, 1988); Fonteyne, "The Customary International Law Doctrine of Humanitarian Intervention: Its Current Validity under the UN Charter" (1974) 4 *California Western International Law Journal* 203; Bazyler, "Reexamining the Doctrine of Humanitarian Intervention in Light of Atrocities in Kampuchea and Ethiopia" (1987) 23 *Stanford Journal of International Law* 547; Reisman & McDougal, "Humanitarian Intervention to Protect the Ibos" in Lillich ed., *ibid.*, at 167; Green, "Rescue at Entebbe – Legal Aspects" (1976) 6 *Israel Yearbook on Human Rights* 312; Moore, "The Control of Foreign Intervention in Internal Conflict" (1969) 9 *Virginia Journal of International Law* 205 at 261-263, 338;Henkin, "Use of Force: Law and Policy" in Henkin, Hoffmann, Kirkpatrick et al. eds., *Right v. Might: International Law and the Use of Force* (New York: Council on Foreign Relations Press, 1991) 37;D'Amato, *International Law: Process and Prospect*, 2nd. ed., (Ardsley-on-Hudson, NY: Transnational Publishers, 1995) at 351; Behuniak, "The Law of Unilateral Humanitarian Intervention by Armed Force: A Legal Survey" (1987) 79 *Military Law Review* 157; Levitin, "The Law of Force and the Force of Law: Grenada, the Falklands and Humanitarian Intervention" (1986) 27 *Harvard International Law Journal* 612; Lillich, "Forcible Self-Help by States to Protect Human Rights" (1967) 53 *Iowa Law Review* 325 [hereinafter cited as Lillich, Self-Help]; Wright, "A Contemporary Theory of Humanitarian Intervention" (1989) 4 *Florida International Law Journal* 435.

2   EVOLVING NORMS

a.   *Principles of state sovereignty and non-intervention*

The UN Charter provides in Article 2(1) that the "Organization is based on the principle of the sovereign equality of all its Members".[4] This underlines the importance of the principle of sovereignty in the daily intercourse between states. The complementary principle of state sovereignty in international law is non-intervention. This principle provides that no state should be subject to interference in its internal affairs.[5] This

---

4   The sovereign equality of states is a concept of law that must be distinguished from the political equality of states. The concept is an umbrella category that includes within its scope the recognised rights and obligations which fall upon states. The 1970 Declaration on Principles of International Law which recognises this provides that:
"All states enjoy sovereign equality. They have equal rights and duties and are all equal members of the international community, notwithstanding differences of an economic, social, political or other nature. In particular, sovereign equality includes the following elements:
(a) States are juridically equal;
(b) Each state enjoys the rights inherent in full sovereignty;
(c) Each state has the duty to respect the personality of other states;
(d) The territorial integrity and political independence of the state are inviolable;
(e) Each state has the right freely to choose and develop its political, social, economic and cultural systems;
(f) Each state has the duty to comply fully and in good faith with its international obligations and to live in peace with other states". These are what Robert Jackson characterizes as the constitutive rules of the sovereignty game. See Jackson, "Quasi-states, dual regimes, and neoclassical theory: International Jurisprudence and the Third World" (1987) 41 *International Organization* 519.
5   As far back as 1749, Wolff articulated the principle of non-intervention by stating "[i]f the ruler of a state should burden his subjects too heavily or treat them too harshly, the ruler of another State may not resist that by force [...]. For no ruler of a State has a right to interfere in the government of another, nor is this a matter subject to his judgement". Wolff, Jus Gentium Methodo Scientifica Pertractum (1749), Secs.255-257. Quoted in Benneh, "Review of the Law of Non-Intervention" (1995) 7 *African Journal*

follows directly from the assumption that each state is a sovereign actor capable of deciding its own policies, internal organization, and independence. Thus, the principle has played a significant role in the evolution of the international order which now exists. However, the desirability of this order has come under increasing challenge during the twentieth century.[6] An international community of independent and sovereign states is no longer unquestioningly regarded as the most appropriate or even desirable mode of organisation for the future of humanity.[7] Given the significance of the non-intervention principle in sustaining this order, it is no wonder that the principle is now being placed under close investigation.

Support by states for adherence to a broadly formulated principle of non-intervention can be found in their reading of the UN Charter and

---

of International and Comparative Law 139 at 140. Both Wolff and Vattel recognized the observation of the non-intervention norm because acts of intervention necessarily infringe upon state sovereignty (although Vattel carved out an exception by allowing intervention in a civil war for a just cause). Their conclusion was reached by drawing an analogy between individuals and states. They argued that individuals have a right to their independence. By analogy, states have a similar right. Intervention was thus seen to be a violation of that right. On this basis Vattel identified an international legal order comprising independent states "closed or sealed off from one another". See Vincent, *Nonintervention and International Order* (Princeton: Princeton Univ.Press, 1974) 27-31;Carty, *The Decay of International Law? A Reappraisal of the Limits of Legal Imagination in International Affairs* (Manchester, 1986) at 89. The development of rules of non-intervention was historically linked to the response of Latin American states in the nineteenth century to intervention by the United States and European powers. For a comprehensive discussion of the evolution of the non-intervention principle see, for example, Vincent, *ibid.*; De Lima, *Intervention in International Law – With A Reference to the Organisation of American States* (Den Haag: Uitgeverij Pax Nederland, 1971) Thomas, *New States, Sovereignty and Intervention* (Aldershot: Gower Publishing Co.Ltd., 1985) at Chap.2.

6   Little, "Recent Literature on Intervention and No-intervention" in Forbes & Hoffman eds., *Political Theory, International Relations, and the Ethics of Intervention* (Hampshire: Macmillan Press Ltd., 1993) 13 at 14.

7   *Ibid.*

other international legal instruments. The most vigorous adherents of a policy of non-intervention have been weaker states, mostly third world states, apprehensive of severe limitation on their sovereign rights by the more powerful states in the international system.[8]

The starting points for analysing this principle have been Articles 2(4) and 2(7) of the Charter. Article 2(4) states:

> [a]ll members shall refrain in their international relations from the threat or use of force against the territorial integrity or political independence of any state, or in any manner inconsistent with the purposes of the United Nations. Whilst Article 2(7) provides that [n]othing in the present Charter shall authorize the United Nations to intervene in matters which are essentially within the domestic jurisdiction of any state or shall require the Members to submit such matters to settlement under the present Charter; but this principle shall not prejudice the application of enforcement measures under Chapter VII.[9]

This prohibition or apparent prohibition of the threat or use of force is subject to a number of limitations provided for in the Charter. Specific exemptions from Article 2(4) and other international instruments prohibiting the use of force, however, exist. These are actions taken or authorized by the UN in certain circumstances;[10] the use of force in

---

8   There is a general tendency here of Western states emphasizing the importance of human rights and Third World and former socialist states emphasizing a policy of non-intervention. See for example, Roberts & Kingsbury eds., *United Nations, Divided World: The UN's Roles in International Relations* (Oxford: Clarendon Press, 1988) at 16.

9   Incidentally, there has been considerable controversy surrounding the precise meaning of these provisions. Whilst a comprehensive discussion of the provisions is beyond the scope of this work, I shall adopt a viewpoint that, in my opinion, is consistent with the aims and purposes of the UN in light of the principle of humanitarian intervention. For further discussions of these articles see for example, Gordon, "Article 2(4) in Historical Context" (1985) 10 *Yale Journal of International Law* 279. But see Asrat, *supra*, note 2.

10   See Chap.VII of he Charter which contains provisions for self-defence or forceful measures authorized by the Security Council.

individual or collective defence;[11] military action against former enemy

---

11 Article 51 of the Charter states: "[n]othing in the present Charter shall impair the inherent right of individual or collective self-defence if an armed attack occurs against a member of the United Nations, until the Security Council has taken measures necessary to maintain international peace and security. Measures taken by Members in the exercise of this right of self-defence shall be immediately reported to the Security Council and shall not in any way affect the authority and responsibility of the Security Council under the present Charter to take at any time such action as it deems necessary in order to maintain or restore international peace and security". Whilst some commentators regard as questionable whether the protection of nationals abroad falls within the ambit of Article 51, others have argued humanitarian intervention should be seen as a legitimate category of self-defence. Thus, other states could act individually or in concert to protect individuals or groups against their own state. Commenting on this provision, Thomas and Thomas content that "a plea can be made that where it is legal to protect one's own nationals, it is an extension of this legality to protect the nationals of others. The so-called principle of nationality is not inflexible ..." For them, self-help to protect one's own nationals is included in the "inherent" right to self-defence preserved by Article 51. This concept is then extended to situations where the nationality link is missing. Thomas & Thomas, in Carey ed., *The Dominican Republic Crisis* (Dobbs Ferry: Oceana Publications Inc., 1967) at 20. Although Bowett admits that intervention for protection of a state's own nationals still exists as part of the traditional right of self-defence, he contends that its use must meet the normal conditions of self-defence. These requirements include failure by the territorial state to extend protection for aliens in accordance with international law;the existence of an actual or imminent danger requiring urgent action; and lastly, the actions taken must be proportionate and confined to the necessities of freeing the nationals from danger. However, he expresses doubt as to the validity of a right of intervention on behalf of aliens, grounded on purely humanitarian reasons as a category of self-defence in the absence of a link of nationality. *Supra*, note 2 at 45. See also, Bowett, "The Use of Force for the Protection of Nationals Abroad" in Cassese ed., *The Current Regulation of the Use of Force* (Dordrecht : Martinus Nijhoff Publishers, 1986) at 39-55. Hassan holds the conviction that "even if the protection of nationals was guaranteed under self-defense, extending this rationale to the protection of foreigners is a distortion of the Charter's language". *Supra*, note 2 at 888. Scheffer however, laments the "paradox of international law that while this customary rule to permit missions to

states; and certain actions taken pursuant to regional arrangements or agencies authorized by the Security Council.[12] It is sufficient to note for now that, leaving aside the exceptions mentioned, the interpretation of Article 2(4) for some scholars indicates a total and complete prohibition of force in international relations.[13] The majority of states during United Nations debates favoured an absolute interpretation of the Charter prohibition of intervention.[14] This view appeared to have been articulated in other international legal instruments. The Declaration on the Inadmissibility of Intervention in the Domestic Affairs of States and the Protec-

---

rescue endangered nationals has been recognized, armed intervention to rescue thousands or even millions of people whose lives are at stake because of a governments's repressive conduct somehow has not met the test of legitimacy under the UN Charter..." He argues the "conventional characterization of rescue operations as acts of self-defense or self-help is an artificial distinction that should be scrapped. Interventions to rescue nationals from life-threatening dangers in another country are humanitarian in character and should be recognized strictly for that purpose, and not as some extended application of national self-defense". Scheffer, "Toward a Modern Doctrine of Humanitarian Intervention"(1992) 23 *University of Toledo Law Review* 253 at 272. Although Tesón does not explore the inter-relationship between the principles of self-defence and intervention for the protection of a state's nationals abroad, he notes since "the law of human rights has a universal reach, ...it extends to nationals and aliens" and that "there is no reason in principle why protection of nationals of the intervening state should be, by definition, less humanitarian than the action undertaken to protect nationals of the target state". *Supra*, note 3 at 6. The distinction between rescuing nationals abroad as flowing from the right of self-defence on one hand which is considered legal, and humanitarian intervention on the other, which some writers consider illegal, should be scrapped since humanitarian considerations are involved in both situations. There would have been a row if, for example, as in the Entebbe case, both nationals and aliens were affected and only Israel's own nationals were rescued, leaving behind Jewish nationals of other countries.

12 See Chap. VIII of the Charter.
13 See for example, Brownlie, *International Law and the Use of Force by States* (Oxford: Clarendon Press, 1963) at 265-270.
14 See Fonteyne, "Forcible Self-Help to Protect Human Rights: Recent Views from the United Nations" in Lillich ed., *supra*, note 2 at 209-211.

tion of their Independence and Sovereignty,[15] adopted by the General Assembly in 1965, it has been argued, did not only outlaw "armed intervention" but went beyond, condemning also "all other forms of interference or attempted threats against the personality of the State".[16] In addition to that declaration there is the more fundamental Declaration of Principles of International Law concerning Friendly Relations and Cooperation among States in Accordance with the Charter of the United Nations.[17] This resolution, whilst approving the principles enunciated

---

15 The Declaration reads in part:

No State has the right to intervene, directly or indirectly, for any reason whatever, in the internal or external affairs of any State. Consequently, armed intervention and all other forms of interference or attempted threats against the personality of the State or against its political, economic, or cultural elements are condemned.

No State may use or encourage the use of economic, political or other type of measure to coerce another state in order to obtain from it the subordination of the exercise of its sovereign rights, or to secure from it advantages of any kind. Also no state shall organize, assist, foment, finance, invite or tolerate subversive terrorist or armed activities directed towards violent overthrow of the regime [government] of another state or interfere in civil strife in another state.

See, Res.2131 (XX) 20 UN GAOR Supp. (No.14), (UN Doc. A/6014 (1965).
16 Fairley, "State Actors, Humanitarian Intervention and International Law: Reopening Pandora's Box" (1980) 10 *Georgia Journal of International and Comparative Law* 29 at 43.
17 G.A. Res.2625, 25 UN GAOR, Supp.(No.28) at 121, UN Doc. A/8028 (1970). Reproduced in (1970) 9 *International Legal Materials* 1292. See also, The 1974 UN Definition of Aggression, G.A. Res.3314, UN GAOR, Supp. No.31, at 142, UN Doc. A/9631 (1974). Reprinted in (1975) 69 *American Journal of International Law* 480. This document defines "aggression" as "the use of armed force by a State against the sovereignty, territorial integrity or political independence of another State". It further specifies "[n]o consideration of whatever nature, whether political, economic, military or otherwise, may serve as a justification for aggression". Opponents of humanitarian intervention have also used this resolution as a springboard to argue any first use of force is 'aggression' unless the Security Council (and not the state actors) removes this label.See Verwey, *supra*, note 2 at 389.

in the 1965 Declaration as the "basic principles" of international law, and laying down a broad non-intervention principle, perhaps merely restating Article 2(7) in detail, ended with the usual caveat that [n]othing in the foregoing paragraphs shall be construed as affecting the relevant provisions of the Charter relating to the maintenance of international peace and security".[18] It should be noted that despite the general pronouncements of non-intervention both in the General Assembly and in statements of the various state delegations, there were fewer opinions expressed and little condemnation of humanitarian intervention during the course of the UN debates. At the General Assembly debates on the Question of Defining Aggression, and on Principles Concerning Friendly Relations and Cooperation Among States, representatives of Mali, Jamaica, Senegal, Chile and the Netherlands spoke out in favour of intervention to remedy gross human rights violations such as genocide.[19] Opposed to such a doctrine were China, Israel, Panama, Mexico, Romania and a handful of others.[20]

Similarly general proscriptions of intervention have been written into the Charter of the Organization of African Unity, Article 18 of the Charter of the Organization of American States, and in the Principles of the Final Act of the Helsinki Conference in 1975 (the Helsinki Accord), following from the Conference on Security and Cooperation in Europe process.[21]

These declarations, however, are not ordinary treaties or conventions, and like general assembly resolutions do not create obligations binding

---

18 Franck and Rodley argue that the Resolution "brooks no exceptions, not even for the protection of human rights" and that its clarity is not obscured by the addition of a paragraph reiterating the obligation of states to respect the right of self-determination and human rights" Franck & Rodley, "After Bangladesh: The Law of Humanitarian Intervention by Military Force" (1973) 67 *American Journal of International Law* 275 at 299-300.

19 See, *supra*, note 14 at 216;Ronzitti, *supra*, note 2 at 106-107.

20 *Ibid.*

21 See Farer, "Intervention and Human Rights: The Latin American Context "(1982) 12 *California Western International Law Journal* at 503-507; Van Dijk & Bloed, "Conference on Security and Cooperation in Europe, Human Rights and Non-intervention" (1983) 8 *Liverpool Law Review* at 117-42.

on states. Nevertheless, Fairley argues "there is a wide consensus that these declarations actually established new rules of international law binding upon all [s]tates"[22] and that the support generated for this idea certainly enhances its persuasive value...".[23]

However, it is impossible to identify in a set of comprehensive rules the difference between permissible and impermissible acts of intervention.[24] Most interactions between states occur under pressure and inducement, thus the non-intervention norm stands little chance of affecting behaviour if it excludes what occurs everyday as normal world politics.[25] Indeed, the inconsistency between states' pronouncements on the prohibition of intervention and their actual responses to the use of force is evident. Indian use of force in East Pakistan (Bangladesh) in 1971, Tanzanian intervention in Uganda in 1978, Vietnam's intervention in Cambodia in 1979, and India's use of its air force to drop supplies to Tamils in 1987 are but some examples. There is clearly a longstanding contrast between what is preached (ie non-intervention), but not practised.

---

22 *Supra*, note 16 at 44, quoting Sohn, "The Shaping of International Law" (1978) *Georgia Journal of International and Comparative Law* 16.

23 *Ibid.*

24 Pease & Forsythe, "Human Rights, Humanitarian Intervention, and World Politics" (1993) 15 *Human Rights Quarterly* 290 at 293.

25 *Ibid.* Vaughan Lowe, for example, asks why on earth anyone should suppose that the principle of non-intervention exists. He writes; "[f]rom the most cursory review of the international history of the past two centuries it is apparent that intervention in foreign States is quite normal. Indeed, if international history is thought of as the analysis of the influences of nations upon each other, it is arguable that the very terrain of history is mapped out on the grid of intervention...[although this] presuppose[s] a wide conception of what intervention might be". Lowe, "The Principle of Non-intervention: Use of Force" in Lowe & Warbrick eds., *The United Nations and the Principles of International Law – Essays in Memory of Michael Akehurst*(London: Routledge, 1994) 64 at 67.

Beyond state rhetoric and practice this complex subject matter has yielded little scholarly consensus.[26] The issue of what is permissible and impermissible intervention, however, is a relative one. As far back as 1923 the Permanent Court of International Justice, in its advisory opinion in the *Nationality Decrees* case, pointed out

> the question whether a certain matter is or is not solely within the juris-
> diction of a State is an essentially relative question; it depends on the
> development of international relations "... it may well happen that, in
> a matter which...is not, in principle, regulated by international law, the
> right of a State to use its discretion is nevertheless restricted by obli-
> gations which it may have undertaken towards other States. In such
> a case, jurisdiction which, in principle, belongs solely to a State is
> limited by the rules of international law.[27]

Therefore what was once an internal matter for states may become issues subject to international inquiry and thus of international concern. This is the case with the internationalization of human rights issues.

It is pertinent to rethink the prevailing assessment of the non-inter-vention principle due to its unsatisfactory nature. The context of inter-ventionary practice has changed; thus, the principle needs reformulation and some coherence to take account of developments in international relations. The identification of international law with society conceived in terms of states emerged largely with the growth of positivist theories and the ascendance of the nation-state as the predominant actor in the global arena. This development is rapidly changing with the emergence and influence of non-state actors in international relations. Modern prac-tice does demonstrate that individuals have become increasingly recog-nized as participants and subjects of international law. They possess cer-tain rights as against their states, and states are subject to international

---

26   See for example the different perspectives on intervention in Bull ed.,
     Intervention in World Politics (Oxford: Clarendon Press, 1984); Damrosch,
     "Politics Across Borders: Nonintervention and Nonforcible Influence over
     Domestic Affairs" (1989) 83 *American Journal of International Law* 1.
27   *Nationality Decrees in Tunis and Morocco* (1923) PCIJ, Series B no.4, 24,
     27.

scrutiny regarding their human rights practices. If the increase in and growing concern about violations of human rights is taken into account, which the principle of non-intervention fails to take into account, then a justification for reformulating the principle will be in order and of the utmost importance.

Also, it has been argued that the major preoccupation of the UN in 1945 was to identify ways of prohibiting the use of force which in large measure accounted for the significance attached to the principle of non-intervention. But the consequence of this blanket prohibition of the use of force is that there is no possibility of discriminating on a normative basis between divergent uses of force. For example, as currently consti-tuted, it is difficult to distinguish between the Soviet intervention in Czechoslovakia in 1968 or the Tanzanian intervention in Uganda in 1977. In the former case, the human rights of the citizens were clearly violated by the intervention, whereas in the latter case, the effect of the intervention was to promote the human rights of the citizens.[28] From this perspective therefore, the principle of non-intervention is becoming increasingly irrelevant.[29] According to Levitin, the concern with war was legitimate after the Second World War; today, however, the danger of world war has receded, while egregious violations of human rights have become a routine feature of international politics. Therefore, the principle of non-intervention ought to be revised. If international law is to be more relevant in these circumstances, it must become "more nearly congruent with its moral bases".[30]

An argument to a similar effect is also made by Tesón, who, how-ever, identifies a "congenital tension between the concern for human rights and the notion of state sovereignty – two pillars of international law".[31] This tension generates a major dilemma for all concerned about the normative dimensions of international relations, because if interven-

---

28 Little, *supra*, note 6 at 24.
29 Levitin, "The Law of Force and the Force of Law: Grenada, The Falklands and Humanitarian Intervention" (1986) 27 *Harvard International Law Journal* 621 at 651.
30 *Ibid.*
31 Tesón, *supra*, note 3 at 3.

tion is prescribed to promote human rights, then the floodgates will be opened to "unpredictable and serious undermining of world order". But if intervention is prohibited even to check human rights violations, then the principle of non-intervention involves a "morally intolerable proposition whereby the international community is impotent to combat massacres, acts of genocide, mass murder and widespread torture".[32] He asserts that it is only individuals who have rights. Sovereignty, therefore does not constitute an inherent right of the state. In other words, a sovereign derives its rights from its citizens and has no separate identity. He associates international legal theories that attempt to defend the autonomous moral standing of states and government with the "Hegelian Myth" that states have inalienable rights. For him, the legitimacy of the state can only be justified if it promotes the rights of all its citizens. Where the state fails to perform this duty, it loses its legitimacy and the protection afforded by the principle of non-intervention. Other states under these circumstances are entitled to intervene in order to remedy the human rights violations which have taken place. Tesón's argument can be viewed in two ways: either opening up an exception to the non-intervention norm, or returning to the Grotian position of permitting intervention provided the cause is just.[33] This builds on other theorists who have taken an increasingly permissive attitude on intervention, and who are not concerned about the traditional justification underlying the non-intervention principle.[34]

---

32 *Ibid.*, at 4.

33 Little, *supra*, note 6 at 25.

34 See, for example, the articles cited in *ibid.*, at 30-31, footnote 47. Little notes Tesón contests the views of theorists such as Walzer who acknowledge that state sovereignty and legitimacy derive ultimately from the rights of individuals, but caution against the open-ended consequences of this viewpoint. Walzer argues there are few, if any, states which could put forward the claim that none of their citizens' rights have been violated. Taken to the extreme, non-intervention is rendered void by such a principle of just intervention. Therefore, intervention can only be justified in extreme situations where massacre, genocide, or enslavement occur. See Walzer, *Just and Unjust Wars: A Moral Argument with Historical Illustrations* (New York: Basic Books Publishers, 1977) at 53. Slater and Nardin however suggest that once Walzer has accepted the legitimacy of humanitarian interven-

b.   The internationalization of human rights

One of the goals of the allied powers during World War II was the realization that only international protection and promotion of human rights
can achieve international peace and progress.[35] This was a reaction
to the atrocities of the Holocaust which provided the impetus for the
struggle for human rights. The Charter thus provided initial principles
for the protection of human rights. One of its basic purposes, as stated
in Article 1(3), is "promoting and encouraging respect for human rights".
Similarly, by Article 55, [36]the members of the UN reaffirm a commitment to promoting universal respect for and observance of human rights
and fundamental freedoms for all. Under Article 56, all members of the
UN "pledge themselves to take joint and separate action in cooperation

---

tion "he can provide no plausible argument for drawing the line restrictively
as he does". See Slater & Nardin, *"Nonintervention and Human Rights"*
(1986) 48 Journal of Politics 91.

35   The preamble of the Charter declares the determination of the peoples of
the world "...reaffirm[ing] faith in fundamental human rights, in the dignity
and worth of the human person, in equal rights of men and women..." and
a commitment "to ensure, by the acceptance of principles and methods,
that armed force shall not be used, save in the common interest". In finding
the connection between the maintenance of peace and security and the
protection of fundamental human rights, Lauterpacht notes "[t]he correlation
between peace and observance of fundamental human rights is now a
recognized fact. The circumstance that the legal duty to respect fundamental
human rights has become part and parcel of the new international system
upon which peace depends, adds emphasis to that intimate connection".
Lauterpacht, *International Law and Human Rights* (London: Stevens, 1950)
at 186.

36   Article 55 provides: "[w]ith a view to the creation of conditions of stability
and well-being which are necessary for peaceful and friendly relations
among nations based on respect for the principle of equal rights and self-
determination of peoples, the United Nations shall promote: [among con-
ditions] (c) universal respect for, and observance of human rights and
fundamental freedoms for all without distinction as to race, sex, language,
or religion".

with the Organization for the achievement of the purposes set forth in
Article 55".

In spite of differing opinions on their legal effect, the actual practice
of the UN has been that it has not been prevented from investigating,
discussing and evaluating human rights abuses and today even taking
action despite the numerous constraints which the Organization faces.
It would seem that the Charter provisions regarding human rights represent binding legal obligations for all states.[37] The cumulative effect
of these provisions is that intervention to prevent human rights abuses
is still valid.[38] While it may be doubtful whether states can be called
to account for every alleged violation of the general Charter provisions,
there is little doubt that "responsibility exists under the Charter for any
substantial infringement of the provisions, especially when a class of
persons, or a pattern of activity are involved".[39]

Elaborating and supplementing the Charter provisions on human
rights is the Universal Declaration of Human Rights which was adopted
by the General Assembly on 10th December 1948. It proclaims a whole
gamut of civil and political rights and economic, social and cultural
rights pertinent to human existence. The Declaration at the very least

---

37 See for example, Ramcharan, *The Concept and Present Status of the Inter-
    national Protection of Human Rights – Forty Years after the Universal
    Declaration* (Dordrecht: Martinus Nijhoff Publishers, 1988) at 59.

38 Reisman and McDougal conclude that the effect of these Articles "in regard
    to the customary institution of humanitarian intervention is to create a
    coordinate responsibility for the active protection of human rights: members
    may act jointly with the organization in what might be termed a new
    organized, explicitly statutory, humanitarian intervention or singly or collec-
    tively in the customary or international common law humanitarian interven-
    tion" They add that "[i]n the contemporary world there is no other way
    the most fundamental purposes of the Charter in relation to human rights
    can be made effective". Reisman & McDougal, *supra*, note 3 at 175. Tesón
    also argues "the promotion of human rights is a main purpose of the United
    Nations...[T]he use of force to remedy serious human rights deprivations,
    far from being 'against the purposes of the UN serves one of its main
    purposes". Tesón, *supra*, note 3 at 131.

39 Brownlie, *The Principles of Public International Law*, 4th ed. (Oxford:
    Clarendon Press, 1990) at 570.

serves as a yardstick in measuring the degree of respect for, and compliance with international standards of human rights.

The International Covenant on Civil and Political Rights,[40] and the Optional Protocol on communication (petitions), was adopted by the General Assembly, and entered into force on March 23, 1976. The Covenant defines and sets out in much greater detail than the Universal Declaration a variety of rights and freedoms. In addition it contains a number of rights that are not listed under the Declaration. It imposes an absolute and immediate obligation on each of the states parties in Article 2(1) to "respect and to ensure to all individuals within its territory and subject to its jurisdiction the rights recognized in the present Covenant without distinction of any kind...". Under Article 2(2) each Party "undertakes to take the necessary steps...to give effect to the rights recognized in the present Covenant" where a right is not already protected by existing legislation.

The International Covenant on Economic, Social and Cultural Rights adopted in 1966 entered into force in 1976. It contains 31 Articles and is divided into five parts. It elaborates upon most of the economic, social and cultural rights provided for under the Universal Declaration, and frequently sets out measures that should be undertaken to achieve their realization. Under the Covenant, the duties of states parties is merely to take steps "to the maximum of its available resources" aimed at achieving "progressively the full realization" of these rights. This provision seems realistic given the fact that economic constraints on states, (especially third world countries) may prevent the immediate enjoyment of those rights.[41] However, the question is whether it is within the dis-

---

40   999 United Nations Treaty Series 171. Reprinted in Newman & Weissbrodt, *Selected International Human Rights Instruments* (Cincinnati: Anderson Publishing Co., 1990).

41   It is worthwhile noting a general argument can be made to the effect that the richer parties are obligated to aid poorer countries' economic, social and cultural efforts. This argument can be maintained, if the Economic Covenant is read in conjunction with Articles 55 and 56 of the UN Charter which creates an obligation on all members of the UN to assist in these efforts; although no specific provision can be found in the text of the Covenant or in its legislative history. See Trubek, "International Protection

cretion of states parties to determine when available resources permit their realization. It has been suggested that

> the principle of progressive realization ...really means that a state is obligated to undertake a programme of activities – including but not limited to specific measures listed in the Covenant – to realize those rights. While this obligation is limited by resource constraints, the Covenant indicates that priority should be given to this area and that the level of effort should increase over time.[42]

On the issue of standards to be applied under the Covenant, it is maintained that different measures would have to be adopted as a matter of practical reality, since no two states are likely to have the same "available resources".[43]

Apart from these instruments, there are also a host of declarations, conventions and instruments adopted by the General Assembly elucidating specific obligations pertaining to particular human rights.[44] The UN by and large plays only a supervisory role in implementation and enforcement action. One writer suggests it may be classified as "weak" to "strong" depending upon how directly and quickly it acts in response to complaints.[45]

---

of Social Welfare in the Third World: Human Rights Law and Human Needs Programs" in Meron ed., *Human Rights in International Law*, Vol.1 (Oxford: Clarendon Press, 1984) at 216.

42 *Ibid.*, at 217.

43 Buergenthal, *International Human Rights* (St.Paul, Minn: West Publishing Co., 1988).

44 These instruments address a broad range of concerns that include: the prevention and punishment of the crime of genocide; the humane treatment of military and civilian personnel in time of war;the status of refugees; the protection and reduction of statelessness;prevention of discrimination and the protection of minorities; the promotion of the political rights of women; the elimination of all forms of discrimination against women; the rights of children; rights of indigenous peoples; and, the promotion of equality of opportunity and treatment of migrant workers, among others.

45 See, Claude & Weston, *Human Rights in the World Community – Issues and Action* (Philadelphia: Univ.of Pennsylvania Press, 1989) at 186-187.

A number of institutional arrangements have been established designed to deal with the promotion and protection of human rights. These arrangements constitute the international human rights regime. The UN's efforts in this regard have been through the use of committees, commissions, sub-commissions, specialized agencies, and working groups. The main techniques employed in their enforcement measures have been communications, inquiries, investigations, periodic reports, advisory services, global studies of specific rights or groups of rights, and recommendations. It uses global and regional conferences and seminars on various specialized topics, open to individuals and organizations, to make them aware of human rights values enshrined in international instruments.[46]

The Human Rights Committee is the principal organ responsible for implementing the International Covenant on Civil and Political Rights.[47] It has adopted a dynamic approach to protection by reminding states parties that the obligation under the Covenant is not only limited to respect for human rights, but also to ensure the enjoyment of those rights.

The Commission on Human Rights under Article 68 of the Charter is mandated to establish "commissions in economic and social fields

---

46   Topics covered in such conferences have included: human rights in developing countries; the participation of women in the economic life of their states; human rights and scientific and technological development; women, equality, development and peace; and human rights teaching. The significance of these topics help to promote penetrating discussions of deeper issues of injustice underlying human rights violations.

47   See part IV of the Civil and Political Covenant. For detailed insights into measures of implementation under the Covenant see for example, Schwelb "International Measures of Implementation of the International Covenant on Civil and Political Rights and the Optional Protocol" (1977) 12 *Texas International Law Journal* 141. See also Procedure for Dealing with Communications Relating to Violations of Human Rights and Fundamental Freedoms, May 27, 1970, ECOSOC Res 1503 (XLVIII), 48 UN ESCOR, Supp. (No. 1A) 8, UN Doc. E/4832/Add.1 (1970). This procedure involves the entire UN Human Rights organs i.e. The General Assembly, the Economic and Social Council, the Commission on Human Rights, and its Sub-Commission on Prevention of Discrimination and Protection of Minorities.

and for the promotion of human rights". The commission is instructed
to report its recommendations on violations to the Economic and Social
Council. The commission has created various programs for the promotion
of human rights, as well as developing international machinery to deal
with violations, such as the special rapporteurs and working groups.[48]

Despite efforts of the UN aimed at promotion and protection there
are still widespread human rights violations.[49] Apart from weaknesses
in the implementation procedures, the main problems encountered relate
to: governmental commitment; problems of perspectives and priorities;
problems in the field of fact-finding; problems stemming from institutional structure; the primitiveness of remedial responses, methods and
procedures; responsibilities in the information process and problems of
resources.[50] As presently constituted, these mechanisms fail to deal

---

48 For details of the work of the Commission since its inception see Report
    of the Commission on Human Rights (Annual). See also Meron, *Human
    Rights Law-Making in the United Nations* (Oxford: Clarendon Press, 1986);
    Tolley, "Decision-Making in the United Nations Commission on Human
    Rights" (1977-82) *Human Rights Quarterly* 27.
49 See, for example, the volumes of the *Human Rights Internet Reporter*.
50 For a detailed discussion of these problems see for example, Gotlieb,
    "Global Bargaining: The Legal and Diplomatic Framework" in Onuf ed.,
    *Law-Making in the Global Community (Durham, NC: Carolina Academic
    Press, 1982)* at 267-273. With regard to criticisms relating to efforts at
    implementation, Haas notes that UN efforts to implement human rights
    standards "do not work". Haas, "Human Rights: To Act or not to Act?"
    in Oye et al. eds., *Eagle Entangled: US Foreign Policy in a Complex World*
    (New York: Longman, 1979) at 188. van Boven writes: "[i]n global and
    general terms the United Nations defends the rights and interests of the
    weaker nations, of under-privileged groups and persons. In actual practice
    the United Nations is, however, unable and powerless to bridge the gap
    between profession and practice. This is largely due to the fact that the
    Member States which make up the United Nations are more guided by their
    own political, economic and military interests than by the standards of the
    Organization. In this respect the nations that criticize the United Nations
    for its human rights record do not form an exception to the rule". van
    Boven, "United Nations and Human Rights: A Critical Appraisal" in Cas-
    sese, *UN Law/Fundamental Rights – Two Topics in International Law* (Sijt-
    hoff & Noordhoff, 1979) 119 at 127; Ullman states "the UN human rights

with situations involving massive human rights violations, as past practice has shown.

In their survey of the UN Human Rights machinery, Pease and Forsythe indicate most states not only allowed these treaties to originate from UN bodies, but also that more than half of the international community became legal parties to them. About a quarter of the international community have accepted monitoring systems of differing strength for the supervision of the implementation of these internationally recognized norms. Although few states objected to the overall process, "[t]here is an overwhelming official consensus that at least the discussion of human rights is a proper international subject matter, even if many disagreements remain over definition and implementation".[51]

Apart from the UN Human Rights machinery, it is also worthwhile noting that most of the world's regional organizations have enacted treaties bolstering the protection of human rights. Examples of these treaties are the European Convention for the Protection of Human Rights, the American Convention of Human Rights and the African Charter on Human and Peoples Rights.[52] The accumulation of these instruments has helped in crystallizing legal norms in favour of human rights so that

---

machinery has become so politicized as to be almost completely ineffective for either monitoring or for enforcement". Ullman, "Human Rights: Toward International Action" in Dominguez et al. eds., *Enhancing Global Human Rights* (New York: McGraw Hill, 1979) at 10. See also, Moskowitz, "Implementing Human Rights: Present Status and Future Prospects" in Ramcharan ed., *Human Rights: Thirty Years After the Declaration* (Dordrecht: Martinus Nijhoff, 1979) at 109-130; Anderson, Human Rights and the Structure of International Law" (1991) 12 *New York Law School Journal of International and Comparative Law* 1.

51 Supra, *note* 24 at 295.

52 For a detailed discussion of these treaties see for example, Weston, Lukens, & Hnatt, "Regional Human Rights Regimes: A Comparison and Appraisal" (1987) 20 *Vanderbilt Journal of Transnational Law* 585.

"...everyone is now entitled to certain basic human rights under UN Conventions, regional treaties, and bilateral agreements".[53]

The various developments on human rights outlined above have had a significant effect on the status of individuals in international law. Each progress made in terms of concepts, standard setting, procedures and mechanisms leads to a realignment of the position of individuals in relation to states.[54] If the above examination, broadly speaking, is correct, then it portends or indicates a gradual shift in thinking about absolute notions of state sovereignty and its corollary principle of non-intervention.[55] It is increasingly becoming accepted that human rights violations within states will not preclude the taking of international action to redress those situations of abuse. Gross systematic violations of human rights have become a concern of the whole international community and not just a matter exclusively within the domestic purview of states, constituting infringement on their sovereign rights. These human rights treaties not only create binding legal obligations among states parties, but they also provide evidence of state practice and new attitudes regarding human rights. Particularly significant is the trend reflected in the Preamble to the Additional Protocol to the American Convention on Human Rights, which suggests that human rights treaties merely codify what is intrinsic in the human condition. It

> recogniz[es] that the essential rights of man are not derived from one's being a national of a certain state, but are based upon attributes of the human person, for which reason they merit international protection in the form of a convention reinforcing or complementing the protection provided by the domestic law of the American States.[56]

---

53 Kartashkin, "Human Rights and Humanitarian Intervention" in Damrosch & Scheffer eds., *Law and Force in the New International Order* (Boulder: Westview Press, 1991) at 202.

54 McGoldrick, "The Principle of Non-intervention: Human Rights" in Lowe & Warbrick eds., *supra*, note 25 at 106.

55 See for example, Reisman, "Sovereignty and Human Rights in Contemporary International Law" (1990) 84 *American Journal of International Law* 866-876.

56 (1989) 28 *International Legal Materials* 161.

The extension of this principle into the international arena suggests a theoretical shift in the conception of human rights.[57]

Although there were significant developments regarding human rights prior to the Charter, the human rights provisions of the Charter and the international human rights instruments discussed above were a watershed. Since the inception of the UN human rights regime, human rights issues have become important, and their internationalization has been increasingly recognized. Even though this is the case, and one finds an ethos of moral universalism underlying the international human rights instruments, one does not find any explanation why the human rights provided for are in fact human rights and why they should be accepted as universal. Taking action in support of human rights necessarily confronts objections of cultural relativism. Supporters of cultural relativism point out that it is impossible in a culturally diverse world to have universal notions of human rights. While the objective here is not to resolve the debate one way or the other, although a universal conceptualization of human rights is preferred, it tends to elucidate the issues at stake in the international human rights discourse. The significance of arguments about moral universalism should therefore serve to support the examination of the universality of the UN human rights instruments. Thus, some remarks about the concept of human rights and the debate it engenders will be appropriate.

The concept of "human rights"[58] does not lend itself easily to any

---

57 See, for example, *ibid*.

58 On the application of rights theory in the international context, even the term "rights" as postulated by Hohfeld, is a 'chameleon-hued' word. According to Hohfeldian analysis, "rights" is an ambiguous term used to describe different legal relationships. A right can be used in a sense to denote a right-holder being entitled to something with a correlative duty in another. It can be used to indicate an immunity from having a legal status altered. Sometimes it can refer to a power to create a legal relationship. See Hohfeld, "Fundamental Legal Conceptions as Applied to Judicial Reasoning" (1913) 23 *Yale Law Journal* 16. It should be pointed out that although all of these terms have sometimes being identified as rights, each concept conjures different protection and produces different results. On the confusion

precise definition.[59] Although the concept eludes any precise definition,

---

that can arise from definitional problems as applied to some provisions of
the UN Covenants on Civil and Political Rights and the Economic, Social
and Cultural Rights, see for example, Shestack, "The Jurisprudence of
Human Rights" in Meron, ed., *supra*, note 41 at 71-74. It should also be
noted that the expression "Human Rights" is relatively recent. It gained
currency from World War II and the establishment of the United Nations
in 1945. They have been traditionally known as "the rights of man" or
"natural rights", intimately linked to the concept of natural law. See
Cranston, *What are Human Rights?* (London: Bodley Head, 1973) at 1.
Natural rights theory regarded as a product of Western liberal thought
played a prominent role in elevating human rights to the international plane.
See Donnelly, "Human Rights and Human Dignity: An Analytic Critique
of Non-Western Conceptions of Human Rights" (1982) 76 *American
Political Science Review* 303. The most significant human rights doctrines
today, from an international point of view, are to be found in protection
of minorities, humanitarian intervention, state responsibility for injuries
to aliens, the League of Nations mandates and minority systems.

59   A detailed discussion of definitional problems as well as philosophical
underpinnings of human rights is, however, beyond the scope of this work.
It is sufficient to draw attention to some of the problems inherent in the
concept of human rights. One of the most significant of the many conditions
affecting the international community's inability in securing the protection
of human rights relates to simple intellectual confusion. This is largely due
to lack of any comprehensive agenda of the totality of human rights and
the lack of clarity in the detailed examination of the content of particular
rights. Bilder aptly notes that "[t]he issue of definition is not trivial. For
what we think human rights really are will inevitably influence not only
our judgement as to the types of claims to recognize as human rights, but
also our expectations and programs for implementation and compliance
with these standards". Bilder, "Rethinking International Human Rights:
Some Basic Questions" (1969) *Wisconsin Law Review* 170 at 174. See also
McDougal, Laswell & Chen, *Human Rights and World Public Order: The
Basic Policies of an International Law of Human Dignity* (New Haven:
Yale University Press, 1980) at 63-64; Ganji, *International Protection of
Human Rights* (Geneve: E. Droz, 1962); D'Amato, The Concept of Human
Rights in International Law (1982) 82 *Columbia Law Review* 1110; For-
sythe, *The Internationalization of Human Rights* (Lexington, Mass.:
Lexington Books, 1991) Chp.1. Fields and Narr, for example, argue that
a theory of human rights must be based upon real human beings rooted

it can be argued that human rights are our entitlements as human beings, which we may demand from one another and from our societies.[60] The idea of human rights is tied to the idea of human dignity: rights are essential for the maintenance of human dignity. They are based on elementary human needs as imperatives.[61] Human rights are universal and inalienable. They exist by virtue of the right-holder's existence. They are not created or granted by the state or some agent and therefore cannot be taken away. The practical effect of this would be that rights are not creations of society, state, or any political authority, legitimate or not, and thus cannot be limited or taken away by them. If this were the case, then, it would follow that all human beings have rights in the same way and to the same extent regardless of race, culture, political system or any other distinction.[62] The conviction that human beings have certain rights, which governments have a duty to respect, essentially, is

---

in their social contexts. Thus human rights must be conceived of in a holistic way; finding legitimate criteria in the historical experiences of real people struggling to overcome domination rather than being caught in the trap of searching for abstract normative criterion. See, generally, Fields & Narr, "Human Rights as a Holistic Concept" (1992) 14: 1 *Human Rights Quarterly* 1.

60 Puchala, *The Ethics of Globalism* (Providence: Academic Council on the United Nations System Reports and Papers No.3, 1995) at 4.

61 Humphrey, *No Distant Millennium: The International Law of Human Rights* (Paris: UNESCO, 1989) at 20-21; Agarwal, *Implementation of Human Rights Covenants: With Special Reference to India* (Allahabad: Kitab Mahal, 1983) at 1. Cranston considers human rights as a moral claim which is universal, paramount and practical. It is an entitlement which belongs to every human being in the world as a human being; taking precedence over all competing claims that are based on 'mere' public policy concerns. It must be practically feasible to secure protection for its entitlement in the present social and world order. See Cranston, *supra*, note 58 at Chap. VIII. Humanistically conceived, "a human right is a universal entitlement founded on a basic human need; an entitlement in principle possible in the kind of world that we must struggle to build" Bay, *Toward a Postliberal World Order of Human Rights* (Dept. of Pol.Sci. University of Toronto; Working Paper A7, 1983) at 5.

62 O'Manique, "Universal and Inalienable Rights: A Search for Foundations" (1990) 12 *Human Rights Quarterly* 465 at 467.

a reaction or response to a feeling of revulsion occasioned by acts of
political, religious or economic repression. The universality of human
rights is a feeling of moral outrage. This consciousness draws on the
moral resources of humankind's belief that there is an underlying universal humanity, and that it is possible to achieve or strive to achieve a
type of society that ensures that fundamental human needs and reasonable aspirations of human beings all over the world are effectively realized.[63]

The renaissance of natural rights and its consequent influence upon
international human rights is regarded as a product of Western liberal
thought and its justifications for claims about the truth, immutability,
and universality of rationally accessed moral dictums.[64] This conceptual
approach, however, does not necessarily have universal acceptance
throughout the world. The concept of human rights can assume different
meanings to different societies, and is influenced depending on a particular society's perception by culture, economics, politics and religion,
among other factors.[65] Polis and Schwab, for example, criticized the

---

63   Nariman, "The Universality of Human Rights (1993) 50 *The Review -
     International Commission of Jurists* 8.
64   *Supra*, note 60 at 8.
65   For a discussion of the Islamic perspective see for example, Haka, *Human
     Rights in Islam vis-à-vis Universal Declaration of Human Rights of the
     United Nations* (Washington, D.C.: World Peace through Law Center, 1981)
     at 19-20; Nasr, "The Concept and Reality of Freedom in Islam and Islamic
     Civilization" in Rosenbaum ed., *The Philosophy of Human Rights: Inter-
     national Perspective* (Westport Conn.: Greenwood Press, 1980) at 96; Sajoo,
     "Islam and Human Rights: Congruence or Dichotomy?" (1989) 4 *Temple
     International and Comparative Law Journal* 24. For an exposition of the
     traditional African perspective see for example, Njoya, "African Concept"
     in UNESCO ed., *International Dimension of Humanitarian Law* (Paris: Marti-
     nus Nijhoff Publishers, 1988) at 9; Cobbah, "African Values and Human
     Rights Debate: An African Perspective" (1987) 9 *Human Rights Quarterly*
     320; Howard, "Group versus Individual Identity in the African Debate on
     Human Rights" in Na'im & Deng eds., *Human Rights in Africa* (Washing-
     ton, D.C.: The Brookings Institution, 1990) at 166. For the traditional Asian
     view see, for example, Khushalani, "Human Rights in Asia and Africa"
     (1983) 4 *Human Rights Law Journal* 408;Buultjens, "Human Rights in

established human rights norms by expressing an objection to ethno-centrism thus:

> Unfortunately not only do human rights set forth in the Universal De-claration reveal a strong western bias, but there has been a tendency to view human rights ahistorically and in isolation from their social, political, and economic milieu.[66]

This particular moral/cultural relativist position which presents theoretical obstacles to human rights activism essentially asserts, firstly, that rules about morality vary from one place to another. Secondly, the way to understand this heterogeneity is to place it in its cultural context. Thirdly, it asserts that moral claims derive from, and are enmeshed in, a cultural context which is itself the source of their validity. There is no universal morality because the history of the world is the history of the plurality of cultures. The attempt to assert universality is a more or less well-dis-guised account of the imperial practice of making the values of a parti-cular culture general.[67] In this respect, the United Nations human rights regime as enshrined in such documents as the Universal Declaration of Human Rights, are futile proclamations derived from the moral prin-ciples valid in one culture and thrown out into the moral void between cultures.[68] In effect the particular is presented as the universal.

Indian Political Culture" in Thompson, ed. *The Moral Imperatives of Human Rights: A World Survey* (Washington, D.C.: University Press of America, 1980) 112-113; Woo, "A Metaphysical Approach to Human Rights from a Chinese Point of View" in Rosenbaum ed., *ibid.*, at 113-124; Nitobe, *Bushido: The Soul of Japan* (Rutland, Vermont: Charles Tuttle Co., 1969) at ix; Adachi, "The Asian Concept" in UNESCO ed., *ibid.*, at 14-15. See also (1981) 3: 3 *Human Rights Quarterly* (which contains a symposium on South Asian Perspectives on Human Rights).

66 Polis and Schwab, "Human Rights: A Western Construct with Limited Ap-plicability" in Polis and Schwab eds., *Human Rights: Cultural and Ide-ological Perspective* (New York: Praeger, 1979) at 17.

67 See Vincent, *Human Rights and International Relations* (Cambridge: Cam-bridge Univ.Press, 1986) at 38.

68 *Ibid.* See also the literature cited in *supra*, note 65.

In practice, most governments accused of human rights violations often resort to the doctrine of state sovereignty to deny the legitimacy of external criticism. This defence, however, is commonly strengthened by some form of cultural relativism. This relativism underlies the assertion of noninterference in the internal affairs of states. The argument usually goes that outsiders are not competent in matters relating to solving problems internal to another culture. Thus, a particular interpretation or even the basic idea of human rights may be alien to a particular culture, so that such a culture should not be judged by standards emanating from external sources.[69]

There are few relativists, however, who advocate the extreme position that whatever is, is right, reducing relativism to subjectivism where, in the absence of grounded criteria every individual may determine what is right or wrong, good or bad, for him or herself.[70] According to Puchala, the most readily defendable moral relativist position is the one provided for in the Bangkok Declaration, adopted at the World Conference Regional Preparatory Meeting in April 1993. In that Declaration, the Asian states agreed that human rights need to be considered in a context that takes into consideration "the significance of national and regional particularities and various historical, cultural and religious backgrounds". He succinctly argues that the moral relativist position turns out to be unsustainable for the following reasons:

> First, relativism tends to confuse empirical facts of differences in moral codes with philosophical justification for differences. Simply because there are differences does not mean that all the alternatives are right or acceptable. Second, the justification for relativism itself has to be philosophically located beyond relativism. That is, moral relativism can only be right if we all accept the *universality* of dictums such as mutual tolerance and noninterference in one anothers' affairs. Third, and at a more practical level, even the relativists balk in the face of the morally atrocious – human sacrifice, ritualistic mutilation, slavery, genocide, apartheid, concentration camps, gulags, and gas chambers.

---

69 Freeman, "The Philosophical Foundations of Human Rights" (1994) 16 *Human Rights Quarterly* 491 at 495.

70 Supra, *note* 60 at 9.

To explain why such atrocious behavior is immoral invariably requires reaching for universals, and when presented with such behavior most relativists accordingly reach out. Finally, there also exists the damning assertion that relativism is itself immoral because, in the name of community standards, noninterference, political correctness, or the like, it leads to the condoning of principles and practices that are widely distasteful.[71]

He argues for the reassertion of moral universalism by pointing out that if it is unjustifiable and moral relativism is unsustainable, then it would seem that the contemporary debate about the universality of human rights, if engaged philosophically, would result in an impasse. And if this were the case, the question of whether the UN human rights regime is to remain intact or be done away with would become an issue of politics, power, and money only, which could well be for the benefit of Western countries.[72]

A strong case for moral universalism, according to Puchala, can be made which does not depend for its justification upon either the will of God or the immutability of natural law. He employs the aid of anthropologists who argue that scholars usually find what they seek. Those who have sought differences among cultures have found them. By the same token, those who have sought similarities among cultures in recent works have also found many, especially in realms of morality.[73]

Furthermore, studies in contemporary psychology have reinforced the proposition that "human beings are genetically wired and cognitively

---

71   *Ibid.*, at 10-11. See also, Bayefsky, "Cultural Sovereignty, Relativism, and International Human Rights: New Excuses for Old Strategies" (1996) 9 *Ratio Juris* 42.

72   *Ibid.*

73   One scholar, for instance, has found twenty-two moral dictums that appear empirically transcultural. These dicta include: the prohibition of murder or maiming without justification; economic justice; reciprocity and restitution; provision for the poor and destitute; the right to own property; and priority for immaterial goods. See Bies, "Some Contributions of Anthropology to Ethics" *Thomist* 28, 1964. Cited in *supra*, note 60 at 12.

equipped to behave morally".[74] These studies conclude that all human beings are similarly constituted regarding their moral capacities. The differences among them have only to do with different attainments of moral maturity. Accordingly, human beings achieving similar levels of moral maturity, irrespective of culture, have similar conceptions about the bases of right and wrong.[75] Also, sociologists of religion have found out that the ethical contents of the major religions of the world are similar in their emphases upon such ideals as charity, civility, humility, piety, and nonviolence.[76]

Perhaps the international community's inability to agree on a universal conceptualization of human rights stems from the failure of perceiving what the most basic human needs are according to just priorities of each society. Individual and societal needs may vary from one environment to another at any given period of time. It is probably best that the international community perceives and recognises this. However, concerns of humanity as a whole should outweigh any cultural preferences of different societies. As Puchala poignantly points out:

> [o]ur entitlement is not a claim on God or nature, but a claim on one another. The basis of our morality is in our obligation as human beings – individuals and in our societies – to allow and help one another to flourish as human beings. And since the human essence is universal, requirements for human flourishing are universal, obligations to promote such flourishing are universal, and therefore, so is human morality.[77]

In sum, the status of humanitarian intervention is inextricably linked to the status of human rights. Greater respect for human rights will make the international community more likely to engage in actions to protect those rights when violated.

---

74 See Kohlberg, *The Philosophy of Moral Development: Moral Stages and the Idea of Justice* (Notre Dame Press, 1989). Cited in *ibid.*, at 12.
75 *Ibid.*, at 12-13.
76 *Ibid.*
77 *Ibid.*, at 14.

3   THE UN CHARTER'S EFFECT ON HUMANITARIAN INTERVENTION

A consideration of the relevant principles of the Charter will now be undertaken to determine the justification for humanitarian intervention.[78] In arguing the survival of the right of humanitarian intervention, the domestic jurisdiction norm becomes pertinent. The starting point is the interpretation of Article 2(4). According to some scholars, emphasis must be placed on the need to interpret that provision broadly and consistently with its plain language. It is the fundamental provision of an organization established 'to save succeeding generations from the scourge of war'. It cannot therefore be subject to an interpretation that would negate its true meaning and content.[79] The conclusion reached for an absolute prohibition of use of force in any manner, it is argued, is further reinforced by an examination of the *travaux préparatoires* that led to drafting of Article 2(4).[80]

Support has also been found by commentators in international case law such as in the *Corfu Channel Case*.[81] While this case can be distin-

---

78 Although the Charter does not expressly mention unilateral or collective humanitarian intervention by states, at the same time it does not specifically invalidate the doctrine. Lillich, "A Reply", *supra*, note 3 at 236.

79 Skubiszewski, "Use of Force by States" in Sorensen ed., *Manual of Public International Law* (London, 1968) 732 at 746. See also *supra*, note 13; Schwarzenberger & Brown, *A Manual of International Law* (Milton: Professional Books, 1976) at 151-152; Akehurst, *A Modern Introduction to International Law* (London: George Allen & Unwin, 1985) at 219-220.

80 A reference to the travaux préparatoires is permitted by Article 32 of The Vienna Convention on the Law of Treaties of 1969. UN Conference on the Law of Treaties, Official Records, Documents of the Conference (UN Publ. E70.V.5) It should be noted that Brownlie for example, does not subscribe to any attempt to find in the words "against the territorial integrity or political independence of any state" a qualified prohibition leaving open a resort to force not infringing these rights. See, Brownlie, *ibid.*, at 267.

81 [1949] ICJ Report 4. In that case, the United Kingdom government argued that its use of force in Albanian territorial waters was consistent with its Charter obligations because it "threatened neither the territorial integrity nor the political independence of Albania". The court in rejecting this argument, stated: "To ensure respect for international law, of which it is

guished on the ground that it did not touch directly on the principle of humanitarian intervention, arguments have been made to the effect that the Court's "judgement should be interpreted as condemning *all* intervention, self-protection, or self-help involving the use of force – including ... humanitarian intervention".[82] Therefore, according to this interpretation of the Charter, the ban on the use of force was provided to preserve territorial integrity and political independence of states, its col-

---

the organ, the Court must declare that the action of the British Navy constituted a violation of Albanian sovereignty". It went on further to state "the alleged right of intervention as the manifestation of a policy of force, such as has, in the past, given rise to most serious abuses and such as cannot, whatever be the present defects in international organization, find a place in international law". *Ibid.* at 35. It is claimed that this case reaffirms the unassailability of state sovereignty as an essential foundation of international relations. See Hassan, *supra*, note 2 at 883; Oglesby, "A Search for Legal Norms in Contemporary Situations of Civil Strife" (1970) 3 *Case Western Reserve Journal of International Law* 30.This view is also shared in the *United States* v. *Nicaragua* decision. In that case the Court inquired whether there was a "general right of States to intervene, directly or indirectly, with or without force, in support of an internal opposition in another state, whose cause appeared particularly worthy by reason of the political and moral values with which it was identified". In answering this question in the negative the Court stated: "no such general right of intervention, in support of the opposition within another country, exists in contemporary international law". See, *Military and Paramilitary Activities in and Against Nicaragua* (US v. Nicaragua) 1986 ICJ 14 (Judgement of June 27).at para.208. Whilst this statement did not deal with humanitarian intervention, it has been suggested that it is broad enough to preclude any right of humanitarian intervention under international law. For a detailed discussion of the decision in this case see, for example, "Appraisals of the ICJ Decision: Nicaragua v. United States (Merits)" (1987) 81 *American Journal of International Law* 77; Tesón, *supra*, note 3, at Chap.9; Rodley, "Human Rights and Humanitarian Intervention: The Case of the World Court" (1989) 38 *International and Comparative Law Quarterly* 321 at 327-330.

82 [In original]. Akehurst, "Humanitarian Intervention" in H. Bull ed., *supra*, note 26 at 110.

lective security measures were to ensure peace, and therefore unilateral humanitarian intervention is rendered illegal.[83]

However, a qualification must be placed on the prohibition of use of force under Article 2(4).[84] Intervention for human rights purposes would not contravene that provision if it is confined within the conditions for its exercise.[85] It is argued that Article 2(4) is not an absolute

---

83 Verwey, *supra*, note 2 at 377. Bowett notes that quite apart from the legal incompatibility of humanitarian intervention with Article 2(4), policy considerations suggest allowing the institution under that provision will "introduce a dangerous exception to these prohibitions". *Supra*, note 2.

84 The Article 2(4) norm does not proscribe all kinds of use of force. But see Brownlie, who argues on the contrary that "[t]he conclusion warranted by the travaux préparatoires is that [it] was not intended to be restrictive but, ...to give more specific guarantees to small states and that it cannot be interpreted as having a qualifying effect". *Supra*, note 13 at 267.

85 Reisman and McDougal, relying upon a major-purposes interpretation of the Charter, indicate that Article 2(4) "is not against the use of coercion per se, but rather the use of force for specified unlawful purposes". They further argue: "[s]ince a humanitarian intervention seeks neither a territorial change nor a challenge to the political independence of the state involved and is not only not inconsistent with the Purposes of the United Nations but is rather in conformity with the most fundamental peremptory norms of the Charter, it is distortion to argue that it is precluded by Article 2(4). In so far as it is precipitated by intense human rights deprivations and conforms to the general international legal regulations governing the use of force – economy, timeliness, commensurance, lawfulness of purpose and so on – it represents a vindication of international law, and is, in fact, substitute or functional enforcement". *Supra*, note 3 at 177. In a similar vein, Mullerson argues that even though humanitarian intervention may constitute a threat to the survival of the government of the target state, "it does not necessarily mean that it constitutes a threat to the independence of the target state. Government is only one of the three elements (government, population and territory) of statehood. He continues: "[w]hen the government and the population are fighting each other, or the government is trying to exterminate a part of the population and the survival of the latter is at stake, an outside intervention on behalf of the population does not violate the independence of the target state. To think otherwise would be to equate the state and the government, leaving other components out of the equation". Mullerson, *Human Rights Diplomacy* (London: Routledge,

proscription of use of force; for, if force is used in a manner which does not threaten the "territorial integrity or political independence of a state, it escapes the restriction of the first clause".[86] Thus, Schachter observes that "if these words are not redundant, they must qualify the all-inclusive prohibition against force".[87]

In essence, Article 2(4) does not cover territorial inviolability so that a state's territorial integrity may be preserved even though there is a limited armed foray into that state's territory.[88] On the contrary, views have been expressed to the effect that even in situations where a rapid withdrawal by the intervenor takes place when its mission is accomplished without a dissolution of the existing authoritative structure, that intervention will still temporarily violate the target state's territorial integrity and political independence. Akehurst argues: "[a]ny humanitarian intervention, however limited, constitutes a temporary violation

---

1997) at 156.

86 Jessup, *A Modern Law of Nations* ((New York: MacMillan, 1948) at 162. According to Stone, "Article 2(4) does not forbid the threat of use of force *simpliciter*;it forbids it only when directed against the territorial integrity or political independence of any State, or in any manner inconsistent with the purposes of the United Nations". Stone, *Aggression and World Order* (London: 1958, reprinted 1976) at 95. Tesón also argues: "[a] genuine humanitarian intervention does not result in territorial conquest or political subjugation". Tesón, *supra*, note 3 at 131. See also, Fonteyne, *supra*, note 3 at 253-254. Such an interpretation of Article 2(4) has been questioned by those who view any act of armed intervention as at least a temporary violation of the target state's territorial integrity. See Brownlie, *supra*, note 2 at 222-223; Bowett, *supra*, note 2 at 44-45.

87 Schachter, "The Right of States to Use Force" (1984) 82 *Michigan Law Review* 1620 at 1625. In this context, Green also shares the view that "..*ipso verba* the Charter is referring to threats against or attacks upon the territorial integrity or political independence of a state and not to exercises which may be necessary but not directed to this end".Green, "Humanitarian Intervention – 1976 Version" (1976) 24 *Chitty's Law Journal* 217 at 222; See also, Stone, *ibid.*, at 95; Moore, "The Control of Foreign Intervention in International Conflict" (1969) 9 *Virginia Journal of International Law* 205 at 262.

88 See D'Amato, *International Law: Process and Prospect* (New York: 1987) at 37.

of the target State's political independence and territorial integrity if it is carried out against that State's wishes".[89] On the same subject-matter, Higgins notes: "even temporary incursions without permission into another state's air space constitute a violation of its territorial integrity".[90] Levitin opines that a more sensible reading of Article 2(4) is that "a state's political independence is compromised whenever another state attempts through armed force to coerce it, to limit its choices on the international plane, or to interfere with its domestic political regime".[91] Nanda, however, advocates a cautious approach by arguing for a limited use of force for humanitarian purposes which he suggests is permissible in international law, even though a temporary breach of a state's territorial integrity is occasioned.[92]

In any case, it is argued that provided conditions and limits set out under international law are met, there would be no violation of the territorial integrity or political independence of the target state.[93] Since humanitarian intervention does not seek to challenge attributes of sovereignty, territorial integrity or political independence of a state, it will not fall within the scope of the Article 2(4) prohibition of force norm.

The other Charter provision meriting consideration in dealing with the right of humanitarian intervention is Article 2(7) which, as noted earlier, establishes the principle of non-intervention in the internal affairs of states. This Article, it seems, protects states against international

---

89 In Bull ed., *supra*, note 26 at 95, 105.

90 Higgins, *The Development of International Law Through the Political Organs of the United Nations* (London: Oxford University Press, 1963) at 183.

91 *Supra*, note 3.

92 Nanda, "Tragedies in Northern Iraq, Liberia, Yugoslavia, and Haiti – Revisiting the Validity of Humanitarian Intervention Under International Law – Part I" (1992) 20 *Denver Journal of International Law and Policy* 305 at 311. See also, Hassan, *supra*, note 2 at 887.

93 See, D'Amato, *supra*, note 88. See also, O'Connell, *International Law* (London: Stevens, 1970) at 304; D'Angelo, "Resort to Force by States to Protect Nationals: The US Rescue Mission to Iran and its Legality under International Law" (1981) 21 *Virginia Journal of International Law* 485 at 487;Bowett, *supra*, note 11 at 40.

action and activities occurring strictly within their territorial boundaries. Thus, it becomes significant to determine whether human rights issues and their protection are matters lying essentially within the domestic jurisdiction of states. For, if they are, then any right of intervention for whatever purpose would appear to be precluded.

The interpretation of this clause has been qualified despite its assertive nature.[94] In the past, the UN has found that matters lying within a state's domestic jurisdiction provided no impediment to de-colonization[95] or anti-apartheid actions.[96] In the same vein, some state treaty obligations affecting sovereignty and territorial boundaries cannot be regarded as matters "within domestic jurisdiction".[97] As states make commitments "to a larger and more intrusive regime of international

---

94 See for example, Brownlie, *supra*, note 39 at 553-554; *Supra*, note 90 at 64-90, 118-130. Falk, for instance, argues that states have not exercised the autonomy which is traditionally attributed to them: "in fact, the domestic order has never enjoyed autonomy in any strict sense. It is now commonplace to accept the interdependence of economic, cultural, and military affairs. In fact, nations have always had a vital concern with what goes on elsewhere, even if elsewhere is a foreign state. Sovereignty only confers a primary competence upon a nation; it is not, and never was, an exclusive competence". Falk, "The Legitimacy of Legislative Intervention by the United Nations" in Stanger ed., *Essays on Intervention* (Cleveland: Ohio State University Press, 1964) at 36.

95 See for example, Declaration on the Granting of Independence to Colonial Countries, G.A. Res. 1514, (1960); G.A. Res.1805, (1962). There are in addition other Declarations on the subject-matter, culminating in General Assembly Resolution 2288 (1967) which called for global decolonization.

96 See for example, Res. 1904 (XVIII), Nov. 20, 1963; Res. 3068 (XXVIII), Nov. 30, 1973; U.N S.C.Res.418, S/RES/418 (1977) (Security Council action imposing a mandatory arms embargo against South Africa's government-imposed policy of apartheid).

97 Article 27 of the Vienna Convention on the Law of Treaties of 1969 affirms the principle recognized by several international tribunals that a "party may not invoke the provisions of internal law as justification for its failure to perform a treaty". Brownlie points out that "the reservation [in Article 2(7)] is inoperative when a treaty obligation is concerned" and that "[t]he extent to which...states can now rely on some type of formal interpretation [of the provision], is in doubt. *Supra*, note 39 at 552-553.

treaties and conventions and as customary international law expands its reach, the concept of "domestic jurisdiction" shrinks.[98] If the further condition of essentiality mentioned in Article 2(7) is taken into account, issues subject to international inquiry become considerable,[99] and call for reorientation of priorities. Fundamental human rights must take precedence over any norms of non-intervention in the internal affairs of states.

In stressing the need for balancing the rights of States (as mentioned in the Charter) against individual rights affirmed by the Universal Declaration of Human Rights and other human rights Conventions, Javier Perez de Cuellar, as Secretary-General of the UN, challenged the traditional construction placed on Article 2(7). He maintained that a new balance must be struck between sovereignty and the protection of human rights.[100]

---

98 Scheffer argues "'[d]omestic jurisdiction' does not exempt everything within sovereign borders from scrutiny of the international community any more than the domestic jurisdiction of the city of Toledo shields its government and residents from the reach of Ohio state law, federal law, or, for that matter international law". Scheffer, *supra*, note 11 at 261. See also, *supra*, note 27.

99 *Ibid.*

100 He writes: "I believe that the protection of human rights has now become one of the keystones in the arch of peace. I am convinced that it now involves more a concerted exertion of international influence and pressure through timely appeal, admonition, remonstrance or condemnation and, in the last resort, an appropriate United Nations presence, than what was regarded as permissible under traditional international law.
It is now interestingly felt that the principle of non-interference within the essential domestic jurisdiction of States cannot be regarded as a protective barrier behind which human rights could be massively or systematically violated with impunity. The fact that, in diverse situations, the United Nations has not been able to prevent atrocities cannot be cited as an argument, legal or moral, against the necessary corrective action, especially where peace is also threatened. Omissions or failures due to a variety of contingent circumstances do not constitute a precedent. The case for not impinging on the sovereignty, territorial integrity or political independence of States is by itself indubitably strong. But it would only be weakened if it were to carry the implication that sovereignty, even in this day and

As already noted, it is now increasingly accepted that human rights
issues are no longer strictly within the domestic purview of states. It
is a matter of concern for the whole world community.[101] Consequent-

---

age, includes the right of mass slaughter or of launching systematic campaigns of decimation or forced exodus of civilian populations in the name
of controlling civil strife or insurrection. With the heightened international
interest in universalizing a regime of human rights, there is a marked and
most welcome shift in public attitudes. To try to resist it would be politically unwise as it is morally indefensible. It should be perceived as not so
much a new departure as a more focused awareness of one of the requirements of peace". J Perez De Cuellar, *Report of the Secretary-General on
the Work of the Organization: 1991* (1991) at 11-13. Quoted in Scheffer,
supra, note 11 at 262-263.

101 See, Fonteyne, *supra*, note 3 at 241. According to Lauterpacht, "human
rights and freedoms having become the subject of a solemn international
obligation and of one of the fundamental purposes of the Charter, are no
longer a matter which is essentially within the domestic jurisdiction of the
Members of the United Nations...". Lauterpacht, *International Law and
Human Rights* (Praeger: New York, 1950) at 178. Another writer has also
concluded that massive human rights violations "are no longer essentially
within the domestic jurisdiction of States, and therefore the principle of
nonintervention is not applicable". F. Ermacora, "Human Rights and Domestic Jurisdiction (Article 2(7) of the Charter) "(1968) 124 *Recueil Des Cours*
bk.II, 371 at 436. Beyerlin states that although this issue is still highly
debatable, "...the scope of domestic jurisdiction in human rights matters
seems to be narrowing". See, *supra*, note 2 at 214-215. Asrat contends that
while unilateral humanitarian intervention does not appear to be valid under
contemporary international law, it does not mean states do not have the
legal option of compelling governments to redress human rights abuses.
They could resort to non-violent reprisals since respect for basic human
rights has been held to be the "concern of all [s]tates and to constitute an
obligation *erga omnes*". He cites the International Court of Justice decision
in the *Barcelona Traction Case* to support this position. Asrat, *supra*, note
2 at 185. The Court stated in that case that obligations of this type "derive,
for example, in contemporary international law, from the outlawing of acts
of aggression, and of genocide, as also from the principles and rules concerning the basic rights of the human person, including protection from slavery
and racial discrimination...". See, Barcelona Traction (Judgement) (1970)
International Court of Justice Reports 3 at para.33. This case therefore lays
down the proposition that obligations of a state towards the international

ly, human rights abuses prompting humanitarian action are no longer "matters essentially within the domestic jurisdiction of a state", and so will not amount to a violation of the non-intervention principle. It should also be noted that Article 2(7) ends with a critical proviso: "this principle shall not prejudice the application of enforcement measures under Chapter VII" which deals with enforcement actions to maintain international peace and security. As we will see in the next Chapter, the Security Council is now engaging in more Chapter VII enforcement actions in matters that were previously considered within the domestic jurisdiction of states.

Article 2(7) does not affect the right of humanitarian intervention.[102] For, if the most basic rights are not protected, governments will engage in gross violations of human rights without fear of punishment. Attempts by other states aimed at protesting the occurrence of human rights violations will only meet with rebuff under the cloak of non-intervention in domestic matters.

In addition to the above considerations, some proponents express their concern over the preservation of humanity, arguing that the value of human life takes precedence over legal principles.[103] Thus, basic

---

community as a whole derive from, among others, the principles and rules concerning the rights of the human person.

102 Ganji states "with regard to action pertaining to the international protection of [human rights and fundamental freedoms that]...the provisions of Article 2, paragraph 7 cannot be invoked". Ganji, *supra*, note 59 at 135. Lillich asserts the UN definitely has the legal right to intervene for humanitarian reasons if a state violates fundamental human rights causing an actual threat to the peace. Lillich, "Intervention to Protect Human Rights" (1969) 15 *McGill Law Journal* 205 at 212. It has been further suggested that human rights concerns have been placed outside the scope of Article 2(7) even in cases not amounting to a threat to the peace. See Reisman & McDougal, *supra*, note 3 at 189, 190-191.

103 Lillich writes: "...to require a state to sit back and watch the slaughter of innocent people in order to avoid violating blanket prohibitions against the use of force is to stress blackletter at the expense of far more fundamental values". Lillich, "Self Help", *supra*, note 3 at 344.

humanitarian feelings lend credence to the view that states cannot remain indifferent whilst massive human rights violations take place.[104]

Another reason for continued justification of the right of humanitarian intervention lies in the failure of the UN realizing its original aims. The founding fathers of the Organization expected states would take collective action under the aegis of the UN in situations of "threats to the peace", "breaches of the peace", or "acts of aggression", rather than rely on unilateral state action.[105] The Security Council under Chapter VII of the Charter is seized with mandatory jurisdiction to take action in those situations.[106] This machinery for collective security and enforcement has, however, proved to be largely ineffective.[107] Thus, if the

---

104 Leff, "Food for the Biafrans" *New York Times*, October 4, 1968 at A46, Col.3, quoted in Farer, "Humanitarian Intervention: The View from Charlottesville" in Lillich, ed., *supra*, note 2 at 151. Leff puts it tersely in context of the Biafran war thus: "I don't care much about international law, Biafra or Nigeria. Babies are dying in Biafra....Forget all the blather about international law, sovereignty and self-determination, all that abstract garbage: babies are starving to death". *Ibid.*

105 See Articles 39-51 of the Charter. On the issue of the appropriateness of unilateral intervention by a state in the interest of humanity see Westlake, *International Law, Part I;Peace* (London: Cambridge University Press, 1910) at 318-320.

106 Articles 39-44 of the Charter. Also, by the "Uniting for Peace" Resolution, where the Council is unable to function, the secondary authority of the General Assembly becomes operative.The Assembly may thus perform duties and powers of the Council. See, Uniting for Peace, G.A. Res. 377(v), UN GAOR Supp. No. 20 (A/1775) at p.10. See also Green, "The Little Assembly" (1949) 3 *The Yearbook of World Affairs* 169.

107 Soon after the Charter regime came into effect, Jessup observed, "[i]t would seem that the only possible argument against the substitution of collective measures under the Security Council for individual measures by a single state would be the inability of the international organization to act with the speed requisite to preserve life. It may take sometime before the Security Council, with its Military Staff Committee, and the pledged national contingents are in a state of readiness to act in such cases, but the Charter contemplates that international actions shall be timely as well as powerful". Jessup, *supra*, note 86 at 170. McDougal and Behr, in a comment that is still valid today, note "the most difficult problem still confron-

Security Council failed to act under such circumstances, "the cumulative effect of articles 1, 55 and 56 [would] be to establish the legality of unilateral self-help". In effect, "[t]he deterioration of the Charter security regime has stimulated a partial revival of a type of unilateral *jus ad bellum*".[108] This "contemporary doctrine relates only to the vindication of rights which the international community recognizes but has, in general or in a particular case, demonstrated an inability to secure or guaran-

---

ting the framers of the United Nations' Human Rights Program is that of devising effective procedures for enforcement". McDougal and Behr, "Human Rights in the United Nations" (1964) 58 *American Journal of International Law* 603 at 629. Lillich points out the UN's inability to function effectively in intervening for humanitarian purposes by citing Friedmann's comments that "[a] combination of the failure to establish a permanent international military force and the existence of the veto power, has effectively destroyed the power of the United Nations to act as an organ of enforcement of international law against a potential lawbreaker" and concludes: "the effective power of using military or lesser forms of coercion in international affairs essentially remains with the nation [s]tates". *Supra*, note 3 at 170-171. Bazyler observes that "[w]hen mass slaughters occur, and the United Nations fails to act, the possibility of individual state action must remain open". Bazyler, *supra*, note 3 at 577, footnote 130. Examples of the UN's inability to act swiftly abound in state practice, which will be discussed in the next section. An examination of the UN's role in the 1990s in so far as humanitarian purposes are concerned will also be undertaken in the next chapter.

108 Reisman, "Criteria for the Lawful Use of Force in International Law (1985) 10 *Yale Journal of International Law* 279 at 281.

tee".[109] Included in this category of rights is humanitarian intervention.[110]

Thus, individual states may undertake humanitarian interventions, for there exists "a coordinate responsibility for the active protection of human rights: members may act jointly with the Organization ... or singly or collectively".[111] Were this not the case, as McDougal and Reisman contend, it "would be suicidally destructive of the explicit purposes for which the United Nations was established".[112]

In sum, the argument here is that the provisions of the UN Charter, declarations and covenants constitute an elaborate international human rights regime that provide justification for intervention in protection of those rights.

4   CASE STUDIES OF STATE PRACTICE FROM 1945-1989

The competing arguments will be examined in relation to state practice in cases where intervention by a state ended gross violations of human rights and the international community's responses to such interventions. Since the promulgation of the UN Charter, states have undertaken a number of interventions which have been justified on the basis of humanitarianism or characterized as humanitarian interventions. In examining the extent to which state practice supports the doctrine or otherwise, it is

---

109 *Ibid.* Ronzitti writes that: "a simple truth [must be] taken into account: the absence of – or partial-implementation of the United Nations collective security system. This factor has mounted a process which has led States to try and resurrect-albeit with necessary modifications – part of the law which existed before the entry into force of the United Nations Charter. This can explain why a number of States, while verbally abiding by the prohibition of force, are at the same time rediscovering such pre-Charter law as...the time honoured institution of humanitarian intervention". Ronzitti, *supra*, note 2 at xi.

110 *Ibid.*

111 McDougal and Reisman, "Response by Professors McDougal and Reisman" (1969) 3 *International Lawyer* at 438, 444.

112 *Ibid.*, at 444.

important, however, to keep in mind the facts relating to egregious human rights violations, the extent to which humanitarian considerations were a factor in the decision of one state's intervention in another, and the humanitarian outcomes achieved by the intervention. Examples of these interventions constitute relevant state practice in so far as they involve making a compelling case for humanitarian intervention. Force has been used, arguably, for humanitarian purposes in the following instances: the Congo intervention of 1964;the Dominican Republic intervention of 1965;the East Pakistani intervention of 1971; the Tanzanian intervention in Uganda, 1979; and, Vietnam's intervention in Cambodia (Kampuchea) in 1978. These cases have been frequently cited as confirming the right of humanitarian intervention. Due to the level of human rights violations which had occurred, the reasons proffered, and the humanitarian outcomes achieved, it appeared that a case for unilateral humanitarian intervention could be made.

a. The Congo Intervention of 1964

In September 1964, insurgents fighting the Congolese government took over two thousand foreign residents as hostages in Stanleyville and Paulis, with the objective of extracting certain concessions from the central government. When the government rejected their demands, the insurgents killed forty-five of the hostages within a period of weeks. The situation was worsened by threats of further executions.[113] Efforts to secure the release of the hostages proved futile. As a result, Belgian forces with the aid of United States airplanes and using British military facilities intervened in the Congo, evacuating the endangered persons

---

113 A telegram from a rebel general to an officer in charge of the hostages was allegedly intercepted which read; "[i]n case of bombing region, exterminate all without requesting further orders". *United States Department of State Bulletin* (1965), at 18. Quoted in Lillich, "Self-Help", *supra*, note 3 at 339. See also, *ibid.*, at 185.

on a rescue mission that lasted four days.[114] The interventionary force withdrew from the country upon completion of their mission.

The intervention was condemned in the Security Council by many African states, as well as the Soviet Union. The African states insisted at the time that even as the operation went on – with the rescue of the white foreign residents – innocent blacks were being killed in the process, which smacked of racism.[115] Perhaps this point was driven home to emphasize the idea that the rescuers valued the lives of one particular group of people (whites) more than another (i.e. blacks). Whilst an accurate account of whatever took place during the operation is still lacking, [116]there is some degree of certainty that its fundamental purpose was aimed at saving lives given the dangerous situation posed by rebel activities in the region. This was evident in the fact that Congolese (including other Africans) as well as people of other nationalities were rescued.[117]

---

114 Lillich, *ibid*.

115 *Supra*, note 18 at 288. Some African delegates expressed their dislike for the whole operation at the UN. The Congo Brazzaville delegate for example had this to say: "why, in a conflict in which the Congolese are fighting between themselves, should there be no concern for the safety of the civilian population in general and why should the fate of the whites be the sole consideration?". 19 UN SCOR, 117th meeting 14 (1964). Quoted in Weisberg, "The Congo Crisis 1964: A Case Study in Humanitarian Intervention" (1972) 12 *Virginia Journal of International Law* 261 at 267.

116 Franck and Rodley, *ibid*. It has been pointed out that whilst the facts are unclear as to responsibility for the deaths of several blacks, the circumstances indicated an active role played by the white mercenaries of the Tshombe army. Weisberg, *ibid*.

117 Whilst the primary aim of the intervening forces was to rescue their own nationals, the overall humanitarian consideration was not absent. This is evident, for example, from the statement of the US ambassador to the UN that "while our primary obligation was to protect the lives of American citizens, we are proud that the mission rescued so many innocent people of 18 other nationalities from their dreadful predicament". United States Department of State Bulletin (1965) at 17. Quoted in Lillich, "Self-Help", *supra*, note 3 at 340.

In justifying their action, the intervening states pointed to the humanitarian aspect of their mission. A statement from the US Department of State read:

> This operation is humanitarian – not military. It is designed to avoid bloodshed – not to engage the rebel forces in bloodshed. Its purpose is to accomplish its task quickly and withdraw – not to seize or hold territory. Personnel engaged are under orders to use force only in their own defense or in the defense of the foreign and Congolese civilians. They will depart from the scene as soon as their evacuation mission is accomplished.[118]

Similarly, the Belgian official statement pointed out that

> [i]n exercising its responsibility for the protection of its nationals abroad, [the Belgian] government found itself forced to take this action in accordance with the rules of international law, codified by the Geneva Conventions. What is involved is the legal, moral and humanitarian operation which conforms to the highest aims of the United Nations: the defence and protection of fundamental human rights and respect for national sovereignty.[119]

A point worth noting about the mission is that it was undertaken with express authorization of the Congolese government. It was understood that the intervening forces would withdraw as soon as the operation was completed, which was done.[120] Thus, it could be argued that this satisfied the requirement of consent by the *de facto* government of the target state in a situation in which it was unable to protect the lives of the endangered nationals. Whilst this consent factor adds to the legitimacy of the intervention, it should, however, not be treated as the necessary prerequisite in the circumstances of this case.

---

118 *United States Department of State Bulletin* (1964), at 842. Quoted in *ibid.*
119 See, Note of the Belgian representative to the President of the Security Council dated 24th November, 1964. UN Doc. S/6063; SCOR, Supp. Oct.-Dec. 1964, At 189-192.
120 Lillich, "Self-Help", *supra*, note 3 at 340.

This intervention, however, is not free from criticism. Some broad political and economic objectives have been proffered as motivating factors. Some African states, Czechoslovakia, Ecuador, Poland and the Soviet Union considered the mission as a pretextual humanitarian intervention aimed at consolidating the central government of Tshombe's power.[121] References were made to 'colonialism' and the fact that the Stanleyville operation was a dangerous precedent which might threaten the independence of African states.[122] Perhaps these criticisms were levelled due to the fact that by the time the foreign troops withdrew, Tshombe's position *vis-à-vis* the rebels had been strengthened. One writer thus concludes that "the combined military operation was enough to destroy the rebel stronghold. It is clear that this had been the prime objective of US and Belgian policy from the beginning".[123] It is suggested that if the central government gained any advantages from the mission, that would possibly be pure coincidence. Of course, the rescue operations would necessarily have involved some kind of conflict with the rebels in the process of extricating the hostages.

Apart from these condemnations, however, other states praised the Belgian action at the United Nations. The United Kingdom asserted that the intervention was only humanitarian and that the international community should be thankful for it.[124] Similarly, France declared that Belgium could not be held to be an aggressor since the purpose of the action was that of saving human lives. The French delegate noted that

> [the Belgian] mission of protecting lives and property is the direct result
> of the failure of the Congolese authorities and is in accord with a
> recognized principle of international law, namely, intervention on
> humanitarian grounds.[125]

1960!

---

121 See, *Yearbook of the United Nations, 1964* (New York: United Nations, 1966) at 96-98.
122 *Ibid.* at 96.
123 Verwey, *supra*, note 2 at 401.
124 15 UN SCOR, 873rd Meeting, 13 July 1960, para.130. Cited in Ronzitti, *supra*, note 2 at 31.
125 15 UN SCOR, 873rd Meeting, 13 July 1960, para.144. Quoted in *ibid.*

Italy held that Belgian troops had intervened to keep law and order and to prevent more serious incidents from occurring. Argentina supported the Belgian action, calling it legally justifiable, and finally the Ecuadorian position was not one of outright condemnation of the action.[126]

A possible legal justification for this operation is that the intervention took place at the invitation of the Congo government and from the fact that the aim of the operation was to rescue nationals. With regard to the consent factor, some writers like Brownlie, have suggested the legality of the operation was grounded in the fact that it was undertaken at the request of the Congo government and thus was not based on the principle of humanitarian intervention. Apart from doubts as to whether the central government of the Congo was in effective control of the country at the time, Sornarajah for one has argued "[i]f a customary principle of international law that intervention is permissble if requested or authorized by the legitimate government survives the Charter" then "there is little reason humanitarian intervention, which is also a principle of customary international law , cannot be regarded as having survived the Charter. If the total context of the mission is taken into account, the argument can be put forth that "the United States treated the Congolese invitation as just another factor permitting it to participate in an humanitarian intervention, rather than as the *sine qua non* of such intervention's legitimacy."[127] Additionally, the Congo action was not only undertaken to protect its nationals since the United States justified its action, in part, as an intervention to protect lives of citizens of the Congo, its own nationals, and those of other foreign countries. Majority of scholars who have examined this case have deemed it to be lawful.

The Stanleyville operation was undertaken in circumstances in which both the UN and the Organization of African Unity (OAU) were unable to act with the necessary dispatch given the urgency of the situation in the Congo. It is quite clear that circumstances justifying humanitarian intervention were present. The justification for the operation emphasised

---

126 *Ibid.*

127 Sornarajah, "Internal Colonialism and Humanitarian Intervention" (1981) 11: 1 *Georgia Journal of International and Comparative Law* 45 at 65; Lillich, "Self-Help", *supra*, note 3 at 340.

its humanitarian character in addition to the fact that humanitarian outcomes were achieved. Significantly, this intervention was not condemned
by the Security Council, which could be interpreted as an implicit approval of the legitimacy of humanitarian intervention in this case.[128]
Lillich, for instance, "reaches the inescapable conclusion that if ever
there was a case for the use of forcible self-help to protect lives, the
Congo rescue operation was it".[129]

b.   The Dominican Republic Intervention of 1965

The events preceding and following the Dominican Republic intervention
seem to be much more complicated than the Congo situation.[130] Briefly, an interim military government which ousted the Constitutional government of President Bosch in a putsch in 1963 was subsequently challenged by a revolt on 24 April 1965. As a result, civil strife erupted
which left the Republic without an effective government, followed by
the breakdown of law and order. On April 28, 1965, US Marines landed
in Santo Domingo in order to protect US nationals and those of other
countries in the wake of the unfolding events.[131]

---

128 See 19 UN SCOR Supp. (Oct.-Dec.1964) at 328 UN Doc. S/Res 129 (1964);
    De Schutter, "Humanitarian Intervention: A United Nations Task" (1972)
    3 *California Western International Law Journal* 21 at 23.
129 *Supra*, note 127.
130 For a more detailed account of the facts see for example, Thomas &
    Thomas, *supra*, note 11; Slater, *Intervention and Negotiation: The United
    States and the Dominican Crisis* (New York, 1970); Nanda, "The United
    States' Action in the 1965 Dominican Crisis: Impact on World Order-Part
    I" (1966) 43 *Denver Law Journal* 439;(Part II) (1967) 44 *Denver Law
    Journal* 225.
131 Prior to sending its forces into Santo Domingo, a note had been sent to
    the US Embassy signed by Colonel Benoit, President of the Military Junta
    to the effect: "[r]egarding my earlier request I wish to add that American
    lives are in danger and conditions of public disorder made it impossible
    to provide adequate protection, I therefore ask you for temporary interven-
    tion and assurance, in restoring order in this country". (1965) 4 *International
    Legal Materials* at 565. It is, however, doubtful to rely on this note as a

In stating reasons for the US intervention after the first five hundred marines were sent in, President Johnson said: "[f]or two days American Forces have been in Santo Domingo...in an effort to protect the lives of Americans and nationals of other countries in the face of increasing violence and disorder".[132] He later on indicated in greater detail:

> We didn't intervene. We didn't kill anyone. We didn't violate any embassies. We were not perpetrators. But as ...we had to go into the Congo to preserve the lives of American citizens and haul them out when they were being shot at, we went into the Dominican Republic to preserve the lives of American citizens and citizens of a good many other nations – 46 to be exact, 46 nations. While some of the nations were denouncing us for going in there, their people were begging us to protect them.[133]

Given the situation in the Dominican Republic at the time, the reasons advanced so far for the intervention, and the fact that thousands of foreigners were indeed evacuated, [134]it is not difficult to point out the humanitarian rationale involved here. Action by the United Nations or the Organization of American States (OAS) in terms of consultations and negotiations would have proved costly in terms of lost lives given the time span within which some immediate action was needed.

---

request for intervention since it appears that at the time there was no effective government in control of affairs in the country. However, Lillich notes that the US, torn between inaction or going in to help one of the contending factions, "...chose instead a more complicated and, ...more constructive course. [It] landed troops in the Dominican Republic in order to preserve the lives of foreign nationals – nationals of the United States and many other countries". Meeker, "The Dominican Situation in the Perspective of International Law" *United States Department of State Bulletin* (1965) at 62. Quoted in Lillich, "Self-Help", *supra*, note 3 at 340.

132 *New York Times*, May 1, 1965, at 6, col.4.
133 United States Department of State Bulletin (1965) at 20. Quoted in Lillich, "Self-Help", *supra*, note 3 at 342.
134 See Security Council Debate, 3-4 May, 1965, *United Nations Yearbook 1965*, at 141.

The Dominican situation, however, runs into problems when, inconsistent with their earlier objectives, the US declared later that its aim was to prevent a communist take-over.[135] It did not leave the Dominican Republic, but maintained its presence for over a year, with a troop build-up of over 20, 000 military personnel. The reasons offered for this presence was that the breakdown of law and order necessitated the preservation of a situation for a period of time which would enable the OAS to act collectively.[136] The troops subsequently formed the core of an Inter-American Peace Force which was established with the purpose of cooperating in restoring conditions to normal. This drew criticisms from some states that the establishment of this Force was a prohibited intervention in a situation of domestic conflict.[137]

Support for the Dominican action on humanitarian grounds came from states such as the United Kingdom, France, the Netherlands, and Nationalist China.[138] The OAS, apart from approving the American action in the Dominican Republic, actually replaced the American forces with its own peacekeeping troops.[139] Cabranes, for instance, argues that the norm of non-intervention in the Inter-American system has undergone a "profound metamorphosis" as a result of OAS approval of

---

135 See, Nanda, Part II, *supra*, note 130 at 225 and accompanying notes 6-16. President Johnson had declared in connection with the crisis that "...the American nations cannot, must not and will not permit the establishment of another communist government in the Western Hemisphere. This was the unanimous view of All American nations when, in January, 1962 they all declared, and I quote: 'The principles of communism are incompatible with the principles of the American system". *Documents on American Foreign Relations, 1965*, at 245.

136 New York Times, May 9, 1965, at E3, col.4. Quoted in Lillich, "Self-Help", *supra*, note 3 at 343.

137 See, Thomas & Thomas, *supra*, note 11 at 49-52.

138 20 UN SCOR (1198th mtg.) at 37 (1965) (United Kingdom);20 UN SCOR (1198th mtg.) at 111-112 (1965) (France); 20 UN SCOR (1203rd mtg.) at 4 (1965) (Netherlands);20 UN SCOR (1202nd mtg.) at 19 (1965) (Nationalist China).

139 See Cabranes, "Human Rights and Non-Intervention in the Inter-American System" (1967) 65 *Michigan Law Review* 1147 at 1174-1175.

the Dominican action.[140] This action, however, came under criticism from communist countries.[141]

A purported or possible basis for justification of the Dominican action has been on the more narrow ground of intervention to protect nationals abroad.[142] A requirement of the right of self-defence to protect nationals abroad is the removal of troops once one's nationals have been evacuated. As noted earlier, however, the United States not only

---

140 See *ibid.*, at 1171-1175.
141 See Nanda, "Part I", *supra*, note 130 at 464.
142 See for example Fenwick, "The Dominican Republic: Intervention or Collective Self-Defense" (1966) 60 *American Journal of International Law* 64; Meeker, *supra* note 131, at 60-63.The principle of self-defence to protect nationals abroad was also subsequently used as basis for US involvement in the Mayaguez incident of 1975, and the Israeli raid on Entebbe in 1976. In the Mayaguez incident, Cambodian forces, on 12th May, 1975, seized an American vessel – the "Mayaguez" – and its crew in what Cambodia claims to be her territorial waters. Diplomatic efforts to secure the release of the ship and its crew having proved futile, President Ford authorized US forces to board the illegally seized ship and land on a Cambodian island, with the object of rescuing the crew and the ship, and also to conduct strikes against nearby Cambodian military installations. For factual details and comments on this incident see for example, *Digest of United States Practice in International Law* (US Government Printer's Office: Washington, 1975) at 777-783; Rowan, *The Four Days of the Mayaguez* (1975); Paust, "Comment: The Seizure and Recovery of the Mayaguez" (1976) 85 *Yale Law Journal* 774;Note, "Pueblo and Mayaguez: A Legal Analysis" (1977) 9 *Case Western Reserve Journal of International Law* 79. In the Entebbe rescue operation, an Air France plane with over 250 passengers aboard en route from Tel Aviv to Paris via Athens was hijacked on June 27, 1976 after leaving Athens. The hijackers, claiming to be members of the Popular Front for the Liberation of Palestine, forced the plane to Entebbe Airport in Uganda where it was given permission to land. The hijacking ended on 4th July, 1976 with an Israeli commando raid on Entebbe Airport freeing 105 hostages held by the hijackers. For comments on this incident see Green, *supra*, note 3; "Rescue at Entebbe-Legal Aspects" (1976) 6 *Israel Yearbook on Human Rights* 312; Note, "Entebbe: Use of Force for the Protection of Nationals Abroad" (1977) 9 *Case Western Journal of International Law* 117.

remained in the Dominican Republic despite the completion of the evacuation of her nationals and the nationals of other countries, but engaged in a further troop build-up in the Dominican capital, justifying its action on the basis of helping to maintain and restore law and order. This state of affairs suggested the presence of other motives on the part of the United States.

Nevertheless, it can be said of the Dominican situation that the initial United States response showed a commitment to intervene based on humanitarianism. Explaining further the circumstances under which the United States took coercive action, Ambassador Stevenson stated in the Security Council:

> [W]e could have decided not to do anything – at least for the time being. But the lives of thousands of people from nearly 40 countries hung in the balance...The United States initially landed troops under these emergency conditions to preserve the lives of foreign nationals – nationals of the United States and of many other countries. Such action is justified both on humanitarian and legal grounds.[143]

Ultimately, the Security Council did not condemn the Dominican Republic intervention. Although one can argue that this example confirms the legality of the principle of humanitarian intervention, the subsequent presence of the United States, however, cannot be justified for the same reason. This example, perhaps, shows the limits within which the doctrine can be applied. The initial aim of saving lives having been accomplished, the United States should have withdrawn its troops. However, maintaining its presence beyond that limited objective lends credence to the view that motives other than purely humanitarian considerations were involved.

---

143 (1965) 52 Department of State Bulletin 877, quoted in Nanda, "Part I", *supra*, note 130 at 462. Several other statements by United States officials stressed the humanitarian aim of the operation. See *ibid.*, at 472-473.

c.   *The East Pakistan (Bangladesh) Intervention of 1971*

The Indian intervention in East Pakistan which resulted in creation of the independent state of Bangladesh provides an instance of humanitarian intervention. The origins of this intervention could be traced back to the partition of India in 1947 as a result of which Pakistan came into being, composed of two different parts geographically separated by a distance of over 1, 000 miles. It was also divided by ethnic, cultural and linguistic differences. The two common factors, namely Islam and alienation from India, which held these parts together, were, however, not sufficient to ensure stability.[144] By the late 1960s political and economic domination of East Pakistan by West Pakistan had resulted in increasing political discontent.

The Pakistani general elections of December 1970 resulted in an overwhelming victory for Sheikh Mujibur Rahman's East Pakistani Awami League party, which campaigned for political and economic autonomy.[145] Following results of the elections, there were simmering fears in West Pakistan, given the demand for autonomy and the possibility of being ruled by the Awami League Party. The National Assembly having been postponed indefinitely, [146]the situation degenerated into mass demonstrations with the East Bengalis clamouring for total independence. With no possibility of peaceful settlement of the political impasse in sight, the Pakistani army moved into Dacca on March 25, 1971, unleashing a reign of terror. There were reported cases of mass murders and other human rights atrocities committed by the Pakistani army.[147] The Report of the International Commission of Jurists observed:

---

144 For details of events leading to the breakup of Pakistan and comments on the Indian intervention in East Pakistan see for example, International Commission of Jurists, *The Events in East Pakistan, 1971* (Geneva, 1972); Nanda, "A Critique of the United Nations Inaction in the Bangladesh Crisis" (1972) 49 *Denver Law Journal* 53; Tesón, *supra*, note 3 at 179-188.

145 International Commission of Jurists, *ibid.*, at 12.

146 *Ibid.* at 13-14.

147 *Ibid.* 24-27.

> The principal features of this ruthless oppression were the indiscriminate killing of civilians, including women and children and the poorest and weakest members of the community; the attempt to exterminate or drive out of the country a large part of the Hindu population; the arrest, torture and killing of Awami League activists, students, professional and business men and other potential leaders ...; the raping of women; the destruction of villages and towns; and the looting of property. All this was done in a scale which is difficult to comprehend.[148]

The result of these atrocities saw the death of at least one million people and the influx of over ten million people seeking refuge in India.[149] These flow of refugees put severe strains on India's economy. The refugee situation thus made it impossible for India to remain indifferent to the conflict. Prior to the intervention, the Indian Prime Minister had appealed to other states and, in vain, to the UN to do something about the situation in which "the general and systematic nature of inhuman treatment inflicted on the Bangladesh population was evidence of a crime against humanity".[150] But no international action was taken. Relations between India and Pakistan deteriorated, erupting into a full-scale war on December 3, 1971 – a war that lasted 12 days and ended with the surrender of the Pakistani Army.[151] In the aftermath of the intervention, political prisoners were released, refugees returned to East Pakistan and finally, Bangladesh was established as a new independent state.

Adducing reasons for its intervention, India claimed it had reacted to the aggression committed by Pakistan, in effect, that it was the lawful exercise of the right of self-defence. It also claimed the action was necessary for the protection of Bengalis from gross and persistent violations of human rights by the Pakistani army, whilst at the same time addressing the problem of over 10 million Bengali refugees that crossed

---

148 *Ibid.*, at 26-27.
149 The precise number of refugees is in dispute. Whilst the Pakistani government claimed there were no more than 2 million people, the Indian government claimed otherwise. What is certain is that this influx of people put a severe strain on India's economy. See, Tesón, *supra*, note 3 at 182.
150 Quoted in Verwey, *supra*, note 2 at 401.
151 International Commission of Jurists, *supra*, note 143 at 43-44.

into its territory. India's representative at the Security Council stated that

> [r]efugees were a reality. Genocide and oppression were a reality. The extinction of all civil rights was a reality. Provocation and aggression of various kinds by Pakistan from 25 March onwards were a reality. Bangladesh itself was a reality, as was its recognition by India. The [Security] Council was nowhere near reality.[152]

Elsewhere, the Indian representative again notes "that we have on this particular occasion absolutely nothing but the purest of intentions: to rescue the people of East Bengal from what they are suffering".[153] Thus, in India's opinion, its presence was necessary to put a stop to the atrocities and to prevent further massacres.

India's point of view was supported by the Soviet Union. It pointed to Pakistan's attack on India as an invasion of India's territorial integrity. It also drew attention to the refugee situation as having created security problems for India, but emphasized the fact that the main causes of the conflict were the "inhuman acts of oppression and terrorism" perpetrated in East Bengal by Pakistan, and that a ceasefire was only possible after Pakistani atrocities had come to an end.[154] Other states belonging to the Eastern bloc – i.e Czechoslovakia, Poland, Hungary, Bulgaria, Mongolia, and also Bhutan, sided with India's point of view emphasizing

---

152 See, UN *Monthly Chronicle*, January 1972, at 25.
153 Statement of Ambassador Sen to the UN Security Council, UN Doc.S/PV. 1606, 86(1971). Cited in Franck & Rodley, "The Law, The United Nations and Bangla Desh" (1972) 2 *Israel Yearbook on Human Rights* 142 at 164. Some writers claim India did not invoke humanitarian considerations as a reason for intervention. Others note that it did not claim the doctrine as her main line of defence. See for example, Hassan, *supra*, note 2 at 884 footnote 167; Akehurst in Bull ed., *supra*, note 26 at 96; Ronzitti, *supra*, note 2 at 96. But as Tesón correctly observes, whether India invoked it or not is not important. The significant thing to note is the totality of the circumstances which called for intervention on grounds of humanity. Tesón, *supra*, note 3 at 186.
154 26 UN SCOR, 1606th meeting, 4 December 1971, paras 253, 267, 268, 270, 271. Cited in Ronzitti, *supra*, note 2 at 97.

the severe breaches of human rights and the atrocities committed by Pakistan.[155]

Some states reacted negatively to the intervention. Pakistan, China, and the United States accused India of aggression and argued that India had no right to intervene in Pakistan's treatment of the East Pakistani population.[156] In the Security Council, Saudi Arabia, Argentina, and Tunisia variously opposed the intervention by condemning "aid given by one state to secessionist movements in another", "secession, subversion and interference in the internal affairs of a State", and "intervention by a third party in the internal affairs of a State".[157] In the General Assembly, most delegates referred to the situation in East Pakistan as an internal one, asserting that India had to respect Pakistan's sovereignty and territorial integrity.[158]

The validity of India's intervention has been the subject of considerable debate. First, the purported justification for the Indian action, in part, was on the basis of self-defence. This was a direct response to the earlier preemptive air strike launched by Pakistan. India's action therefore can be explained by her being a victim of a full scale war initiated by Pakistan and used proportionate force in reacting to the aggression. Thus, in principle, the right of self-defence was involved and claimed.

Secondly, the Indian action can be justified on the basis of humanitarian intervention. Tesón for instance characterizes it partly, as one of rendering foreign assistance to a people struggling for their right to self determination – a collective human right, and secondly, as intervention with the objective of ending acts of genocide, that is, humanitarian intervention proper. For him, the strength of India's claim to legality is that these two aspects of humanitarian intervention are present in the

---

155 26 UN GAOR, Plen. meetings, 2003rd meeting, 7 December 1971, paras 38-39, 43, 145, 206, 326, 377, 416. Cited in *ibid.*
156 *Supra*, note 151 at 5, 7-8, 10-11.
157 *Ibid.*, at 32, 37.
158 *Ibid.*, at 90. The delegate from Ghana, for example, declared that once one permitted oneself the higher wisdom of telling another Member State what it should do with regard to arranging its own political affairs, one opened a Pandora's box. *Ibid.*

Indian example.[159] Majority of writers have echoed a viewpoint somewhat similar to the conclusions of the East Pakistan Staff Study which stated:

> In our view the circumstances were wholly exceptional; it was becoming more and more urgent to find a solution, both for humanitarian reasons and because the refugee burden which India was bearing had become intolerable with no solution in sight. Events having been allowed to reach this point, it is difficult to see what other choice India could have made.
>
> It must be emphasized that humanitarian intervention is not the ground of justification which India has herself put forward. As we have seen, India claimed to have acted first in self-defense, and secondly, in giving support to the new government of Bangladesh which she recognized when hostilities began. We have given our reasons for not accepting the validity of these claims. If India had wished to justify her action on the principle of humanitarian intervention she should have first made a preemptory demand to Pakistan insisting that positive action be taken to rectify the violations of human rights. As far as we are aware no such demand was made.
>
> In conclusion, therefore, we consider that India's armed intervention would have been justified if she had acted under the doctrine of humanitarian intervention, and further that India would have been entitled to act unilaterally under this doctrine in view of the growing and intolerable burden which the refugees were casting upon India and in view of the inability of international organizations to take any effective action to bring to an end the massive violations of human rights in East Pakistan which were causing the flow of refugees. We also consider that the degree of force used was no greater than was necessary in order to bring to an end these violations of human rights.[160]

---

159 See Tesón, 2nd ed., *supra*, note 3 at 206-207. But see Clark and Beck, *International Law and the Use of Force: Beyond the UN Charter Paradigm* (London: Routledge, 1993) at 119 (rejecting Tesón's argument and making a case for taking into account India's motives in a legal assessment of this intervention).

160 East Pakistan Staff Study, The Review, International Committee of Jurists, No. 8, 1972, at 62. Quoted in Behuniak, *supra*, note 3 at 176-177.

Contrary to the East Pakistan Staff Study and comments to a similar
effect by some writers however, India did invoke humanitarian reasons
for her action in East Pakistan. India's representative in the General Assembly had stated that

> the reaction of the people of India to the massive killing of unarmed
> people by military force has been intense and sustained ... There is
> intense sorrow and shock and horror at the reign of terror that has been
> let loose. The common bonds of race, religion, culture, history and
> geography of the people of East Pakistan with the neighbouring Indian
> state of West Bengal contribute powerfully to the feelings of the Indian
> people.[161]

Indeed, many commentators, citing the widespread slaughter of East
Bengalis by the West Pakistani army, have considered this intervention
to be a leading case of humanitarian intervention.[162] Others, however,
have taken a sceptical view of the Indian action and considered it to
be unlawful.[163] Comments have been made to the effect that more importantly, the operation was a strategic one undertaken by a partisan
actor. India was interested politically in the secession of East Pakistan.
It thus seized the opportunity to curtail Pakistan's power and to diminish

---

161 See, 26 UN GAOR 2002th, UN Doc. A/PV 2002 (1971), at 14. Quoted in
    Tesón, 2nd. ed., *supra*, note 3 at 207, footnote 187. See also footnote 153.
162 See for instance, Ronzitti, *supra*, note 2 at 95. Fonteyne holds the opinion
    that "...the Bangladesh situation probably constitutes the clearest case of
    forceful individual humanitarian intervention in this century". Fonteyne,
    supra, note 3 at 204. Walzer supports this intervention as humanitarian by
    arguing "it was a rescue, strictly and narrowly defined". Walzer, *supra*,
    note 34 at 105.
163 See for example, *supra*, note 18; Brownlie, "Thoughts on Kind-Hearted
    Gunmen" in Lillich ed. *supra*, note 2 at 139. Frank and Rodley have com-
    mented: "[T]he Bangladesh case ... does not constitute the basis for a
    definable, workable, or desirable new rule of law which, in the future,
    would make certain kinds of unilateral military interventions permissible".
    Frank and Rodley, "After Bangladesh: The Law of Humanitarian Interven-
    tion by Military Force" (1973) 67 *American Journal of International Law*
    275 at 276.

the territory of its political and military rival.[164] It is probable that taking into consideration the overall political dynamics for control of the region, it was in India's interest to take some form of action to cause the break-up of Pakistan and thus reduce the threat posed by its neighbour. If that happened, then predictably India would have emerged as a dominant power in the region.

However, if one brings into focus the entirety of the crisis, there was no doubt that given the massive scale on which human rights were being violated, India's action could be looked upon as intervention to stop the human rights atrocities that were being perpetrated.[165] India's "various motives converged on a single course of action that was also the course of action called for by the Bengalis".[166] As Sornarajah argues, "the existence of self-interest should not affect the legality of humanitarian intervention. Therefore, at least on occasions where political expediency coincides with the existence of humanitarian grounds for intervention, human rights may be protected".[167] The Bengali people welcomed the intervention which not only freed them from the massive scale of repression but also enabled them to obtain their independence – the creation of Bangladesh, which was quickly recognized by the UN and subsequently admitted to that body.

Another possible basis for justification of India's action relates to the UN's inability to deal with the situation over the period in which these massacres were going on.[168] There was no doubt that the mas-

---

164 See, Verwey, *supra*, note 2 at 402; Bazyler, *supra*, note 3 at 589.

165 Tesón points out this action could also be viewed as rendering foreign assistance to a people engaged in a struggle for their right to self-determination, which is a collective human right. However, he notes that it is not necessary to draw those distinctions since claims of self-determination and human rights violations both converge in this example. Tesón, *supra*, note 3 at 185.

166 Walzer, *supra*, note 34 at 105.

167 *Supra*, note 127 at 70.

168 According to Nanda "there was no doubt regarding the nature or extent of the Pakistani military's atrocities...[T]he United Nation's inaction...is equally well documented". Nanda, *supra*, note 92 at 319.

sacres were a matter of international interest, yet no action was taken.[169] India interested itself in the situation and went to the rescue, withdrawing its forces promptly. The fact that the UN did not condemn the intervention could also be interpreted as an implied recognition of the doctrine. Given the extraordinary circumstances in East Pakistan, which some writers view as being of genocidal proportions, this case fits into the category of acts 'shocking the conscience of mankind' for which intervention to redress the situation was necessary.[170] Despite the self-interested nature of the Indian action, this intervention nevertheless, ultimately achieved the task of protecting human rights and was not condemned by the Security Council.[171]

d.   The Tanzanian Intervention in Uganda of 1979

The brutal dictatorship of President Idi Amin came to an end in April 1979, with his overthrow by Ugandan rebels aided by Tanzanian army

---

169 The International Commission of Jurists suggested that the Security Council, inter alia, could have investigated the allegations of atrocities being committed prior to the Indian attack under the authority of Article 34 of the Charter. Further, it found that had the Security Council investigated, it would have discovered a "threat to the peace" in accordance with Article 39. In conclusion, it pointed out that the Council had an array of measures it could have taken to stop the carnage, from recommending dispute resolution methods under Article 36 to using force under Article 42. International Commission of Jurists, *supra*, note 144 at 488-489.

170 Tesón, after studying this case, states the action "...directed toward rescuing the Bengalis from the genocide attempted by Pakistan, is an almost perfect example of humanitarian intervention". Tesón, *supra*, note 3 at 185. See also Reisman, comment in "Conference Proceedings" Lillich ed., *supra*, note 2 at 17-18;Farer, "Humanitarian Intervention: The View from Charlottesville" in *ibid.*, at 149-157; Nawaz, "Bangla-Desh and International Law" (1971) 11 *Indian Journal of International Law* 459

171 Sornarajah maintains that "the absence of condemnation of the Indian intervention by the international community amounts to a condonation of intervention" to prevent mass atrocities against the Bengalis. *Supra*, note 127 at 73.

units. Amin's reign, from 1971 until his ouster from power in 1979, had been consistently notorious for its gross violations of human rights.[172] Prior to the Tanzanian invasion, relations between the two countries had been far from cordial.[173] There had been a series of border clashes between them. However, the immediate cause precipitating Tanzania's invasion stemmed from Uganda's incursion into the former's territory in October 1978. Ugandan troops, crossing into Tanzanian territory, occupied a 710 square mile strip of that country known as the Kagera salient.[174] Amin thereafter declared annexation of that territory and the creation of a new boundary between the two countries.[175] In light of this aggression, the Organization of African Unity (OAU) did nothing to condemn it but urged Uganda to withdraw its forces.[176] Amin's troops withdrew after 15 days of plunder but continued in their harassment of the Tanzanians along the border.[177] By February 1979,

---

172 There had been widespread reports of executions, rape, torture, and arbitrary arrests. See, for example, Amnesty International, *Human Rights in Uganda Report*, June 1978, Doc.AFR 59/05/78. One international human rights expert testifying in 1978 of the situation in Uganda at the time said: "Since the present regime came to power in 1971 there has been a complete breakdown in the rule of law. Today, every Ugandan citizen is in daily fear of his or her own safety. Government security forces virtually control the country and have assumed practically unlimited powers to kill, torture, and harass innocent civilians. In fact, all of these practices have become routine occurrences". *Uganda: The Human Rights Situation: Hearings Before the Subcommittee on Foreign Economic Policy of the Senate Committee on Foreign Relations*, 95th Cong., 2d Sess. 11 (1978) (Statement of Michael H. Posner). Quoted in Hassan, *supra*, note 2 at 892. Putting in perspective the extent of human rights atrocities committed by the regime, Hassan observes that "Amin's Uganda...has been classified with Hitler's Germany and Stalin's Russia as, historically, the world's three most brutal regimes". Hassan, *ibid.*, at 893.

173 For an account of prior relations between the two countries and details of the conflict see, Umozurike, "Tanzania's Intervention in Uganda" (1982) 20 *Archiv Des Volkerrechts* 301; Hassan, *ibid.*

174 *New York Times*, November 1, 1978, at 15.

175 *New York Times*, November 2, 1978, at 2.

176 *Supra*, note 173 at 303.

177 *Ibid.*, at 304.

the Tanzanian army, along with Ugandan exiles and refugees, had launched a full scale invasion into Uganda. In April 1979, these combined
forces toppled Amin's regime. A new provisional government of the
Ugandan National Liberation Front under Yusuf Lule was formed.[178]

At the commencement of the conflict Tanzania grounded its intervention as a reaction to the aggression against it at the end of October 1978,
pointing specifically to the occupation of the Kagera salient.[179] Given
the fact that Ugandan forces had already withdrawn from the territory
in question and also, that the nature of the response far exceeded the
bounds of proportionality, it is difficult to sustain this claim of self-
defence.[180] In referring to the intentions of President Nyerere of Tanzania[181] as well as the length and scope of the invasion, Hassan observes that "Tanzania did not contemplate a singular objective. From the
beginning, [it] seemed determined to pursue a military solution and overthrow [of] Amin's government".[182] Taking into consideration the lack
of goodwill between these two countries it is not difficult to imagine
that other objectives were on the Tanzanian agenda during the conflict.

After the capture of Kampala, Tanzania declared on April 12 its
limited objective.[183] It invoked humanitarian considerations as one
of its objectives.[184] Its Foreign Minister stated that the fall of Amin
was "a tremendous victory for the people of Uganda and a singular
triumph for freedom, justice and human dignity".[185] Some writers note

---

178 Hassan, *supra*, note 2 at 880-881.
179 Ronzitti, *supra*, note 2 at 102.
180 See *supra*, note 11.
181 Nyerere metaphorically referred to "driving this snake from our house".
    Quoted in Hassan, *supra*, note 2 at 893.
182 *Ibid.*
183 It should be pointed out that Nyerere declared from the outset Tanzania's
    aim was not to punish Amin. "The aim of uprooting Amin was not our
    task [he said]; it was the task of the people of Uganda..." (1979) 16 *Africa
    Research Bulletin* (Political, Social and Cultural Series) at 5223. Quoted
    in Ronzitti, *supra*, note 2 at 103.
184 See Ronzitti, *ibid.* However, Hassan is of the view that once the war started
    Tanzania never even invoked humanitarian reasons for its intervention.
185 *Ibid.*

that Tanzania did not invoke humanitarian considerations in this conflict.[186] Whilst it may be moot whether it did or not, it is important to realize that Tanzania did not seek any territorial aggrandizement. Even if its objective was to remove Amin from power, that aim by itself is not inconsistent with the doctrine of humanitarian intervention. If we recall the classical statement by Vattel, [187]this case would seem to fit the situation he envisaged. The brutality of the Amin regime against his own citizens is a well known fact which does not need recounting here. One writer describes this as "the efficiency of the state's repressive machinery" which had become "destructive of human rights".[188] The Ugandan people were left with no possible alternative but to seek foreign assistance in getting rid of this tyrant.

The international community expressed relief regarding the overthrow of the Amin regime. The United States supported Tanzania from the beginning, although on grounds of self-defence.[189] Strong support for Tanzania was received from the United Kingdom, Zambia, Ethiopia, Angola, Botswana, Gambia, and Mozambique. The Soviet Union announced the withdrawal of its military presence in Uganda and the suspension of arms supplies after Amin's initial invasion of Tanzania.[190] Rwanda, Guinea, Malawi, Canada and Australia also quickly recognized the new government.[191] Kenya remained neutral initially but later offered its cooperation to the new Ugandan government.[192]

At the summit meeting of the Organization of African Unity (OAU) in July 1979, most African states remained silent on the Tanzanian action. Only a few states – notably Sudan and Nigeria, condemned the action. Sudan criticized Tanzania for its invasion of Uganda and interfering in its internal affairs in violation of the principles of the OAU. This position was supported by Nigeria which also expressed concern

---

186 See for example, Hassan, *supra*, note 2 at 894.
187 See Chapter 1.
188 *Supra*, note 173 at 313.
189 Tesón, *supra*, note 3 at 165.
190 *Ibid.*
191 Ronzitti, *supra*, note 2 at 105.
192 Tesón, *supra*, note 3 at 165.

about the danger of the precedent set by the Tanzanian action.[193] In response to this criticism, President Binaisa of Uganda stated that member states of the OAU should not "hide behind the formula of non-intervention when human rights are blatantly violated".[194] This statement lent support for the principle of humanitarian intervention. In essence, the silence of most African states indicated an implicit approval of the Tanzanian intervention. Thomas, for instance, writes: "[t]he general African consensus...seemed to settle at the level of tacit approval of Tanzanian action, with open praise witheld due to the knowledge that such actions could be abused".[195] Putting aside considerations that such actions are susceptible to abuse, however, it would seem at the time that most African states refrained from explicitly endorsing the Tanzanian action during the OAU meeting, for fear of becoming targets of intervention given the appalling human rights record of some of the governments.

A purported justification for the Tanzanian intervention is self-defense. Scholars, however, have had different views as to whether the exercise of this right was lawful in this instance. Some have claimed Tanzania's action was a continuation of self-defense in reaction to the initial Ugandan aggression. Hassan has argued that it was lawful for Tanzania to carry out an extensive counteroffensive to repel the Ugandan army from within her territory, and even continued in "hot pursuit" to ensure a peaceful cessation of the conflict, but maintains, the ultimate overthrow of the Amin regime cannot be legitimate regardless of Uganda's initial provocation. For him, the self defense justification ceased when Ugandan troops retreated.[196] Murphy, on the other hand, has indicated that there is widespread acceptance that a state exercising the right of self-defence may not only expel the aggressor but may pursue them into their own territory and, in some situations, overthrow their

---

193 Nigeria's negative reaction might be attributed to the fact that it still bore Tanzania a grudge over the latter's support of Biafra during the Nigerian civil war. See Thomas, *New States, Sovereignty and Intervention* (Aldershot: Gower Publishing Co., 1985) at 111.

194 *Keesing's Contemporary Archives*, 1979 at 29669-29674, 29840-29841.

195 Thomas, *supra*, note 5 at 112.

196 See Hassan, *supra*, note 2 at 902-903.

government if necessary to prevent recurrence of the initial attack. Thus, according to him, "Tanzania's claim that it was acting in self-defense is not clearly erroneous, unless it is shown that Tanzania's security would not have been further threatened if Idi Amin remained in power".[197] However, the fact that Tanzania stayed for months following the capture of Kampala makes the argument about self-defense doubtful. As Nanda point outs, the Tanzanian invasion was not "necessary and proportional" since the Tanzanian army stayed in Uganda for several months following Amin's overthrow.[198]

Humanitarian considerations offer a more cogent explanation for the Tanzanian action. Most commentators who have examined this case, like the Indian intervention in East Pakistan, have concluded that it was justified on humanitarian grounds.[199] There is no question that the egregious violation of human rights in Amin's Uganda "especially the casual killings of a large number of people, provided the justification for humanitarian intervention: Amin's treatment of subjects was revolting to the human conscience and the efficiency of the state's repressive

---

197 See Murphy, *Humanitarian Intervention: The United Nations in an Evolving World Order* (Philadelphia: University of Pennsylvania Press, 1996) at 106-107.

198 Nanda, "Tragedies in Northern Iraq, Liberia, Yugoslavia, and Haiti – Revisiting the Validity of Humanitarian Intervention under International Law - Part I (1992) 20 *Denver Journal of International Law and Policy* at 321. Umozurike also supports this view maintaining: "Tanzania's military intervention in Uganda cannot be justified as an act of self-defence" and that "[i]t might have been so justified if Tanzania merely cleared the Ugandans from the Kagera salient". *Supra*, note 173, at 312.

199 See Wolf, "Humanitarian Intervention" *Michigan Yearbook on International Legal Studies Annual*, 1988, 333 at 350; *Supra*, note 172 at 59; Suzuki, "A State's Provisional Competence to Protect Human Rights in a Foreign State" (1980) 15 *Texas International Law Journal* 231 at 239-240; Tesón 2nd. ed., *supra*, note 3 at 195 (concluding "the Tanzanian intervention in Uganda was a legitimate use of force to stop ongoing serious deprivations of the most fundamental human rights"). See also, *supra*, note 197 at 107 (maintaining "the reason for Tanzania's intervention is best characterized as one involving mixed reasons of self-defense and protection of human rights).

machinery made action by the people ineffective".[200] In that regard, one writer has argued

> if Tanzania was courageous enough to do what several other states would have wished to do and if it was acting as the "international conscience" in replacing a regime which most governments believed to be abhorrent and whose domestic policies violated all the international legal standards relating to human rights and fundamental freedoms, then its actions should be supported explicitly by that international community and by its law.[201]

Bazyler, while recognizing that Tanzania's motive may not have been pure, nevertheless, concludes it was guided partly by humanitarian concerns. He writes:

> The sheer brutality of Idi Amin's regime, the unwillingness of the United Nations and the Organization of African Unity to do anything about Amin despite knowledge of his brutalities, and the limited intervention by Tanzanian forces, indicate that, on balance, the Tanzanian intervention in Uganda can be justified on humanitarian grounds.[202]

In sum, although one could argue that there were other motives involved in the Tanzanian intervention, nevertheless, if one takes into consideration the inability of the OAU and the UN to act given the massive scale of human rights violations in Amin's Uganda, Tanzania had no option but to intervene in the cause of humanity. President Nyerere had stated that "It is a good precedent ... If Africa as such, is unable to take up its responsibilities, it is incumbent upon each State to do so..., it is a lesson to Amin and people of his kind".[203] Thus, Tanzania was obliged to intervene given the lack of collective action on the part of the OAU.

The Tanzanian action in effect ended the egregious human rights violations that characterized the brutal regime of Idi Amin and did result

---

200 *Supra*, note 173 at 312.
201 Quoted in *supra*, note 172 at 74-75.
202 Bazyler, *supra*, note 3 at 591.
203 Quoted in Ronzitti, *supra*, note 2 at 103.

in an improvement of the human rights situation in Uganda. It did not exert any political influence over Uganda, install a puppet government nor did it seek to annex any Ugandan territory after the intervention. As Tesón comments, "...the widespread feeling that the human rights cause had been served caused the international community to refrain from criticizing the Tanzanian intervention".[204]

e.   *Vietnam's intervention in Cambodia (Kampuchea), 1978*

The Vietnamese intervention in Cambodia offers another illustration of the use of force for the protection of human rights. In April 1975, the Khmer Rouge forces of Pol Pot took over power from the Republican government.[205] Soon thereafter it embarked upon a programme of total reorganization of the country. In the process of this reorganization, massive violations of human rights by the regime against its own citizens took place.[206] There were reported cases of starvation, torture, mass killings and deportations. In a three year period, an estimated number of over 2 million (out of a total population of 7 million) were reported dead through starvation, disease and slaughter.[207] The enormity of the human rights violations in Kampuchea at the time has been described as of genocidal proportions.[208]

---

204 Tesón, *supra*, note 3 at 167.
205 The genesis of the Cambodian calamity was a result of the Vietnam -Indo-chinese conflict. Cambodia escaped the conflict in the 1960s but became involved in it in the 1970s. In early 1970, Lon Nol forces deposed Norodom Sihanouk's regime, which had attempted to keep its neutrality in the In-dochinese conflict. Consequently, a civil war began between the American-backed Khmer republican forces and the Khmer Rouge communists sup-ported by North Vietnam and China. Bazyler, *supra*, note 3 at 551.
206 See, Ronzitti, *supra*, note 2 at 98.
207 See, Bazyler, *supra*, note 3 at 551.
208 The Chairman of the UN Human Rights Subcommission described it as "the most serious to have occurred anywhere since Nazism". Quoted in *ibid.* at 552.

Despite the international community's expression of outrage at the human rights atrocities, no effective measures were taken to stop what was happening in Kampuchea.[209] In December 1978, Vietnamese troops and the Kampuchean United Front for National Salvation (made up of Cambodian refugees in Vietnam) invaded Kampuchea and overthrew the Pol Pot regime, installing a Vietnamese-supported government.[210]

In the UN Security Council debate following the intervention, Vietnam set out its rationale for undertaking military action against Cambodia. Its official position was that the Kampuchean affair comprised two distinct conflicts: first, the conflict between Vietnam and Kampuchea; and second, the civil war in Kampuchea. Vietnam had become involved in the former conflict only after prior Kampuchean aggression. Thus, its use of force had been undertaken only in self-defence. Regarding the latter, its cause originated from the inhuman conditions which the citizens of Kampuchea were being subjected to by their government. The civil war was fought by the Kampuchean people themselves who eventually overthrew the inhumane Pol Pot regime.[211]

In the Security Council, the Soviet Union, Cuba, Czechoslovakia, the German Democratic Republic, Hungary, Mongolia, Poland, and Bulgaria supported the Vietnamese position. These states pointed to the inhumane conditions in which the Cambodian people were being held and

---

209 Ronzitti remarks that the UN failed to do anything but pass resolutions. In 1978, the US Senate hearings on the Cambodian situation condemned the government for committing human rights atrocities against its own citizens. During the Senate hearings, Senator George McGovern called for the use of force to restore human rights in that country. He said: "I am wondering under those circumstances if any thought is being given, either by our Government or at the United Nations or anywhere in the international community of sending in a force to knock this Government out of power, just on humanitarian grounds". See Indochina: Hearings before the Subcommittee on East-Asian and Pacific Affairs of the Senate Committee on Foreign Relations, 95th Congress, 2d Sess. (1978). Quoted in Ronzitti, *supra*, note 2 at 98.

210 Ronzitti, *ibid.*, at 98-99.

211 *Ibid.*

stated that the Pol Pot regime had been overthrown solely by the United Front for National Salvation.[212]

Other members of the Security Council challenged these representations. China did not comment on the inhumane conditions in which the Kampuchean population were being held. Given the perennial tensions between China and Vietnam, China declared Vietnam had committed aggression against Kampuchea, thus violating that country's political and territorial sovereignty. The United Front, it contended, was nothing but a puppet organization created and run by Vietnam.[213] China, of course, had been a supporter of the Khmer Rouge. However, it is also worth mentioning that those states that supported Vietnam's action were opposed to the Khmer Rouge regime. The Non-Aligned countries held Vietnam responsible for violating Kampuchea's territorial integrity. They did not explicitly condemn Vietnam but asked for its withdrawal from Kampuchea. Most of these states did not raise the issue of human rights violations, except Bolivia, Nigeria and Singapore which mentioned the issue. They were, however, of the view that such human rights violations did not justify intervention by a third state.[214] Some Western States also condemned the Vietnamese action. The United States, however, did not declare it is prohibited to use force against a government that committed grave breaches of human rights within its territory. The Security Council, however, was unable to adopt any resolution.[215] At its 34th session, the General Assembly adopted a number of resolutions censuring "foreign intervention" in Kampuchea and called for the withdrawal of foreign forces from that country.[216] On the whole, it seems to be the case that international reaction to this case was shaped by the bitter Cold War rivalries rather than any concern for human rights atrocities prevalent before the Vietnamese intervention.

It has been observed that Vietnam had other motives. It harboured territorial ambitions over Kampuchea and seized the opportunity, given

---

212 See *ibid.*, at 99-101 and the footnotes cited therein.
213 *Ibid.*
214 *Ibid.*
215 *Ibid.*
216 See, *ibid.*, at 101.

the situation, to invade Kampuchea and install a puppet government.[217]
Added to this is the fact that over a decade after the invasion Vietnamese
troops and advisors were still present on Kampuchean soil.[218] Although
it is worth mentioning that in February 1979, Vietnam had signed a
Treaty of Friendship with the government of the new People's Republic
of Kampuchea, formed in early January. That treaty of Friendship provided the legal basis for the acknowledged presence of Vietnamese
troops inside Kampuchea until their declared withdrawal.[219] The danger
here, as Thomas comments, is that while interventions may relieve the
immediate reign of terror or the persecution of a particular group, they
can also end up in the substitution of one oppressor by another. Alternatively, they may create new uncertainties and dangers springing from
a different geopolitical configuration.[220] Kampucheans freed from the
terror of the Pol Pot regime, for example, found themselves dependent
on Vietnam on the one hand, with the added threat of the Khmer Rouge,
supported by the West, on the Thai border on the other.[221]

The purported basis for the Vietnamese intervention was self-defense.
Cambodian aggression against Vietnam supported a proportionate response aimed at neutralizing Cambodian forces along Vietnam's border.
What is less clear, according to one analyst, is whether Vietnam's response justified seizure of the capital, installation of a puppet regime,
and the presence of Vietnamese troops in Cambodia, although it could
be argued that despite the superiority of its forces, Vietnam believed
the overthrow of the Pol Pot regime was the only option left in elimin-
ating the Cambodian threat.[222]

A possible basis for justifying this intervention on humanitarian
grounds was the existence of large scale atrocities. The Pol Pot regime
had killed between one-quarter to one-third of the Cambodian population,

---

217 Bazyler, *supra*, note 3 at 608.
218 *Ibid.* at 609. It has been claimed that the troops departed in early 1993.
219 Leifer, "Vietnam's Intervention in Kampuchea: The Right of State v. The
    Right of People" in Forbes & Hoffman eds., *supra*, note 6 at 145.
220 Thomas, "The Pragmatic Case Against Intervention" in Forbes & Hoffman
    eds., *supra*, note 6 at 94.
221 *Ibid.*
222 *Supra*, note 197 at 104.

and by so doing had lost the legal right to govern the Cambodian people. The justification for a humanitarian intervention thus existed, at least initially, when Vietnam undertook its military action against Cambodia.[223] As Wolf suggests, the international community's negative reaction to this case "does not constitute a negation of the doctrine of humanitarian intervention" since cold war rivalries shaped opinion either in favour or against the Vietnamese intervention. Viewed in this light, strict issues of legality thus played only a minor role in international reaction to the intervention.[224]

On the basis of the facts noted, it is difficult to discern whether in fact, the objective of the Vietnamese was merely humanitarian.[225] There is no doubt, however, that the Kampuchean case was "a perfect candidate for humanitarian intervention"[226] given the massive scale of human rights violations. The failure of the international community, including the UN, to find a diplomatic solution or to take any concrete measures of response, left the Vietnamese course of action as the viable option and the immediate solution to end the atrocities that were being committed.

5   CONCLUSION

In sum, at least in principle, the whole basis for humanitarian intervention is grounded in prior agreement about the internationalization of human rights as embodied in Articles 55 and 56 of the UN Charter,

---

223 Bazyler, *supra*, note 3 at 608. See however, 610 (arguing even though the invasion did result in the ouster of one of the most ruthless regimes in the post-World War II period, it cannot be justified on humanitarian grounds since Vietnam harboured other motives).

224 Wolf, *supra*, note 199 at 352.

225 Leifer, in his analysis of the Kampuchean situation concludes that the motivation for intervention should ideally have been humanitarian. But in this particular case, intervention "was governed by strategic priorities and the international responses to that intervention by the corresponding priorities of interested parties". See Leifer, *supra*, note 219 at 155.

226 *Ibid.*

as well as the International Bill of Human Rights. This impressive international human rights regime is gradually having the effect of altering
treatment by a state of its own citizens from an issue of domestic concern to matters within the domain of the international. Thus action to
support them is not impermissible intervention contrary to Article
2(7).[227] The advent of the UN Charter suggests that the customary institution of humanitarian intervention still exists, and is not inconsistent
with the purposes of the UN. Thus, in the event of failure of collective
action under the Charter, there is a revival of forcible self-help measures
to protect human rights. This is buttressed by the doctrinal writing. As
Reisman and McDougal argue, the UN Charter not only confirmed the
legitimacy of humanitarian intervention but also strengthened it. They
state that

> "...the Charter strengthened and extended humanitarian intervention,
> in that it confirmed the homocentric character of international law and

---

227 For critics who make the argument that even if customary international
law recognized humanitarian intervention prior to 1945, the Charter's
general prohibition in Article 2(4) has had such an impact on customary
international law that the doctrine can no longer be valid, Tesón responds
by arguing thus: "First, one has to prove that subsequent state practice is
consistent with the absolute prohibition". This, he demonstrates, is not the
case. Furthermore, he argues "those who take that view – that the Charter
radically changed the law in 1945 – must also deal with the equally
revolutionary impact of the law of human rights upon traditional international law". He concludes: "...anyone who in the face of the impressive
rise of human rights concerns simply asserts that post 1945 international
law must be seen as containing a rigid prohibion of war, *even* to remedy
serious human rights deprivations carries a considerable burden of
proof...There was a customary principle prohibiting the use of force at the
time the Charter was adopted. In contrast, the human rights articles of the
Charter opened the door to a much more innovative development: a concept
of the law of nations as centered on the individual, not the nation-state".
Tesón, 2nd ed., *supra*, note 3 at 157.

set in motion a continuous authoritative process of articulating international human rights..."[228]

Analysis of state practice in the period under consideration showed the
existence of the principle of humanitarian intervention in situations of
egregious violations of human rights.[229] The examples of state practice
discussed here demonstrate that states believe the right of unilateral
humanitarian intervention is available to them as an option grounded
in either the Charter or customary international law.[230] Opinio juris
follows from the articulation of the rule that human rights are a matter

---

228 Reisman and McDougal, *supra*, note 3 at 171. Even though Wolf in this
regard favours the survival of the right of humanitarian intervention under
the UN Charter, he arrives at that conclusion via a different route. Although
he admits that the prohibition on the use of force was intended to be absolute, and that the original intent of the framers of the UN Charter was
not to strengthen humanitarian intervention, nevertheless, he demonstrates
that state practice can modify the Charter, and such modification for him,
is legitimate because it is not inconsistent with the general purposes of the
Charter. See Wolf, *supra*, note 199 at 363, footnote 168.

229 Similarly, Reisman's assessment of the period under consideration
concludes: "[t]he post-UN practice of humanitarian intervention affirms the
continuing validity of the institution and the conditions under which it will
be deemed lawful...Assuming compliance with these conditions,
humanitarian intervention will be lawful under the Charter as well as under
general international law". Reisman, "Humanitarian Intervention to Protect
the Ibos" in Lillich ed., *supra*, note 2 at 187.

230 See Simon, "The Contemporary Legality of Unilateral Humanitarian Intervention" (1993) 24 *California Western International Law Journal* 117 at
150. Writing in 1981, Sornarajah asserts that "[i]n view of the many post-
Charter interventions justified on the basis of humanitarian grounds, it is
a bit late to argue that such interventions are illegal uner the Charter".
Supra, note 127 at 75. See also Chatterjee, "Some Legal Problems of the
Support Role in International Law: Tanzania and Uganda" (1981) 30 *International and Comparative Law Quarterly* 755 at 765 (indicating "[s]hould
[s]tate practice be considered to be a constituent factor of international law
then one might say that the UN period has, in fact, established intervention
as a lawful act whether under the pretext of 'essential self-defence' or
humanitarian intervention".).

of international concern and that use of force to remedy the most serious human rights violations is not prohibited in international law. Even though there is no consensus on the validity of such actions, as Wolf remarks:

> [a]bstract declarations from...the General Assembly condemning inter-
> vention in the broadest terms should not be taken as persuasive evidence
> of *opinio juris*...The inconsistency between nations' theoretical state-
> ments on the prohibition on the use of force and their actual, real world
> responses to such use of force is manifest...In the final analysis, the
> conviction of most states and scholars who oppose humanitarian inter-
> vention is of questionable strength. When states are confronted with
> real-world instances of intervention to prevent mass slaughter which
> do not implicate intense global rivalries, ...they will not condemn them.
> And when scholars who support an absolute interpretation of the pro-
> hibition on the use of force are challenged with the moral imperative
> of terminating genocide, they will go no further than to label armed
> intervention as a meaningless 'technical' breach of law. In light of such
> *de facto* approval by scholars and states of every ideological tendency,
> an argument rejecting the legality of humanitarian intervention based
> on *opinio juris* is unpersuasive".[231]

The scale of human rights atrocities committed in the Ugandan, Pakistani and Cambodian cases, and the reasons put forth in these and other ex-amples discussed, indicated the articulation of non-humanitarian and humanitarian concerns. The choice of not proferring humanitarian reasons in some of the examples as some scholars contend, it seems, was based on tactical considerations rather than legal constraints.[232] In any case, the fact that the intervenors invariably had mixed motives

---

231 Wolf, *supra*, note 199 at 358-359. But see Ronzitti, *supra*, note 2 at 108-109.

232 See for example, *supra*, note 197 at 143 (noting the doubtful validity of an acceptance of the doctrine of humanitarian intervention by the inter-national community since in virtually all instances (e.g the Indian and Vietnamese situations) the interventions were justified on a basis other than a doctrine of humanitarian intervention.

should not be a basis for condemnation of the whole humanitarian enterprise.

It seems to be the case that the context of the Cold War dictated, by and large, support or condemnation in state practice for humanitarian intervention. The extent of approval or censure varied in each case depending on its impact on the wider geopolitical relationship between the superpowers, even though these interventions were into states where the respective governments were engaging in gross abuse of the human rights of their citizens, and the interventions had the effect of putting a stop to those violations. Thus, it would appear the principle did not enjoy much support as some writers contend, mainly because humanitarian values during the Cold War were subservient to geopolitical considerations. Even if the doctrine did not enjoy wide support in state practice, these cases would appear not to invalidate the doctrine. None of these cases where extreme conditions warranted intervention to protect human rights drew explicit condemnation from the General Assembly or the Security Council, Kampuchea notwithstanding. Perhaps this was as much for political reasons as for support of the principle of humanitarian intervention. The silent acquiescence on the part of the vast majority of states, however, arguably may be interpreted as a tacit acknowledgement of international principles concerning the doctrine and its practice in the period under consideration.

3

THE PRACTICE OF HUMANITARIAN INTERVENTION IN THE POST-COLD WAR ERA

1 INTRODUCTION

The 1990s have witnessed changes in the international system so profound that they would have been unimaginable several decades ago. The demise of the Cold War, the disintegration of the Soviet Union, and the events that surrounded the Persian Gulf War changed perceptions of the behaviour of states and international institutions in the global arena. As Lillich remarks with regard to restructuring of the international legal order, "[t]he conclusion of the Cold War likewise presented a once-in-a lifetime opportunity for the nations of the world, acting individually, collectively, and through the UN, ... to help achieve the two principal purposes of the UN: the maintenance of international peace and security and the promotion and encouragement of human rights and fundamental freedoms". However, the euphoria generated in the aftermath of the Gulf War and the promise of a new world order[1] based on the rule of law – a system in which the world would become a safer and more peaceful place – gave way to the stark reality of the phenomenon of intra-state conflicts, and the consequent violence and transborder refugee flows

---

[1] Lillich, "The Role of the UN Security Council in Protecting Human Rights in Crisis Situations: UN Humanitarian Intervention in the Post-Cold War World" (1994) 3 *Tulane Journal of International and Comparative Law* 1 at 2. For a detailed discussion of the concept of a new world order see Kegley Jr., "The New Global Order: The Power of Principle in a Pluralistic World" (1992) 6 *Ethics and International Affairs* 21; Carpenter, "The New World Disorder" (1991) *Foreign Policy* 24: Henrikson, "How Can the Vision of a 'New World Order be Realized" (1992) 16 *Fletcher Forum of World Affairs* 63.

they engender, which jeopardize the nation-state system and global stability. The international community is thus presented with opportunities
and formidable challenges in dealing with this state of affairs.

One of the mechanisms or instruments employed by the international
community in dealing with these crises has been the use of multilateral
intervention. In the wake of recent humanitarian crises, the requirements
of multilateral cooperation in dealing with international peace and
security have led to a growing recognition among states of the obsoles-
cence of traditional notions of absolute sovereignty. The taboo that
customarily rules out of order even the discussion of civil wars, tyrannies
and disasters, unless they clearly impact on other states, has begun to
weaken.[2] It is also significant that there seem to be changing attitudes
among certain third world states who have been, traditionally, the
staunchest guardians of the principle of sovereignty. Childers and Urquhart, for example, see a growing readiness among these states to find
"genuinely disinterested and UN-directed humanitarian intervention without formal government request or sanction".[3] While an unprecedented
level of cooperation has taken place within the UN in sanctioning post-
Cold War humanitarian operations, it is also instructive to note that disagreements and hesitancy have nonetheless been evident, thereby
weakening multilateral action to redress humanitarian crises.

Having made these remarks, it is instructive to note that there is an
emerging body of practice on humanitarian intervention in the post-Cold
War era. Recent UN operations in Northern Iraq, Somalia, Bosnia, Rwanda, Haiti, and regional efforts in Liberia all reveal a humanitarian dimension, whether this be creation of humanitarian corridors, delivery of
humanitarian assistance, or establishment of safe havens. These various
actions have, by virtue of their UN mandates, been formally collective

---

2   Righter, *Utopia Lost: The United Nations and World Order* (New York:
    The Twentieth Century Fund Press, 1995) at 77.

3   They support this assertion by citing intimations of readiness from India
    and Zimbabwe to develop "general principles and guidelines" for interven-
    tion to create "corridors of peace and tranquillity" during the Security
    Council Summit in January 1992. See Childers and Urquhart, *Renewing
    the United Nations System* (Uppsala: Dag Hammerskjold Foundation, 1994)
    at 18.

in nature, adding to their legitimacy and marking them out from earlier unilateral humanitarian interventions discussed in the previous chapter. These actions have ushered in a more vigorous approach to UN conflict management efforts, be it in situations of massive violations of human rights resulting from state collapse or civil wars.

This chapter will examine the scope of humanitarian action and the challenges and debates surrounding such intervention in their legal, moral, and practical dimensions in Northern Iraq, Somalia, Bosnia, Rwanda, Liberia, and Haiti in order to determine issues of legitimacy and whether a conclusion can be reached on increasing support in international practice. However, before examining these case studies, a few preliminary remarks placing them in context will be in order.

The international community is increasingly recognizing the interdependence of the preservation of international peace and security and the protection of fundamental human rights. This is because the many threats to, and the breaches of international peace and security revolve around issues of human rights. The post-Cold War era has witnessed situations in which egregious violations of human rights have posed a threat to international peace and security. The demise of the Cold War removed the saliency of the ideological factor (ie the struggle between East and West, Capitalism and Socialism) in international relations, but has witnessed the proliferation of intra-state conflicts in such places as the former Yugoslavia, Somalia, Liberia, Rwanda, and Afghanistan, to mention just a few. These conflicts have often caused widespread human suffering and their repercussions affect international peace and security. In this regard the former UN Secretary General, Javier Perez de Cuellar noted:

> Today in a growing number of cases, threats to national and international security are no longer as neatly separable as they were before ... civil strife takes a heavy toll on human life and has repercussions beyond national borders.[4]

---

4   *Report of the Secretary-General on the Work of the Organization*, September 1990, UN Doc. A/45/1, section IV.

The post-Cold War era has provided a major test for the UN regarding its potential and limits. In order to come to grips with these challenges, the UN has shown an ability to innovate by taking steps toward the development of collective mechanisms for authorizing intervention in support of human rights.

In December 1991, the UN General Assembly to this end adopted an extraordinary resolution aimed at effectively strengthening the coordination of the UN's humanitarian assistance in emergencies, as well as pressuring non-consensual governments to permit aid to people in need during civil wars and other internal conflicts.[5] The favourable climate under which the UN has begun to perform its role paved the way for a Security Council meeting on 31 January 1992, at the level of Heads of State and Government. Most leaders at that meeting referred to human rights as an issue of concern for the international community.[6] While

---

5   G.A. Res.A/RES/46/182 (1991).
6   In stressing the fact that a new era has begun in which governments can no longer hide behind state sovereignty and violate the human rights of their citizens, the UN Secretary General Boutros Boutros-Ghali stated: "[s]tate sovereignty takes a new meaning in this context. Added to its dimension of rights is the dimension of responsibility, both internal and external. Violations of state sovereignty is and will remain an offense against the global order, but its misuse also may undermine human rights and jeopardize a peaceful global life. Civil Wars are no longer civil, and the carnage they inflict will not let the world remain indifferent. The narrow nationalism that would oppose or disregard the norms of a stable international order and the micronationalism that resists healthy economic or political integration can destruct a peaceful global existence. Nations are too interdependent, national frontiers are too porous, and transnational realities in the spheres of technology and investment on one side and poverty and misery on the other are too dangerous to permit egocentric isolationism ... Now that the Cold War has come to an end, we must work to avoid the outbreak or resurgence of new conflicts. The upsurge of nationalities, which induces countries with multiple ethnic groups to divide, constitutes a new challenge to peace and security ... Nationalist fever will increase ad infinitum the number of communities that lay claim to sovereignty, for there will always be dissatisfied minorities within those minorities that achieve independence. Peace, first threatened by ethnic

conflict and tribal warfare, could then frequently be troubled by border disputes.A new strategy will have to be adopted by the United Nations in order to respond to the irredentist or pro-autonomy claims of ethnic and cultural communities. It will have to take into account the abundant supply of arms, the aggravation of economic inequalities among different communities, the flow of refugees". "United Nations Security Council Summit Opening Addresses by Members" US Federal News Service, January 31, 1992, at VM-5-2, 3-4, VM-5-3, 1. Quoted in Scheffer, "Toward a Modern Doctrine of Humanitarian Intervention" (1992) 23 *University of Toledo Law Review* 253 at 283, footnote 128.

7   Here are excerpts from what some of the leaders had to say. The British Prime Minister John Major stated that "[t]he opening line of our charter, the Charter of the United Nations, doesn't talk about states or governments, it talks about people ... I hope, like the founders of the United Nations themselves, that we can today renew the resolve enshrined in the charter, the resolve to combine our efforts to accomplish the aims of the charter in the interests of all the people that we are privileged to represent. That is our role ... ". Russian President Boris Yeltsin stated: "[n]ow we must accomplish the most difficult task. That is the creation of legal, political, and socio-economic guarantees to make democratic changes irreversible ... Our principles are clear and simple: primacy of democracy, human rights and freedoms, legal and moral standards ... I think that we need a special rapid response mechanism ... to ensure peace and stability. Upon the decision of the Security Council it could be expeditiously activated in areas of crisis ... My country firmly supports steps to consolidate the rule of law throughout the world". US President George Bush declared that "we must advance the momentous movement toward democracy and freedom ... and expand the circle of nations committed to human rights and the rule of law ... The will of the majority must never degenerate into the whim of the majority. This fundamental principle transcends all borders. Human dignity, the inalienable rights of man, these are not the possessions of the state. They are universal. In Asia, in Africa, in Europe, in the Americas, the United Nations must stand with those who seek greater freedom and democracy. And that is my deep belief. That is the belief of the American people. And it's the belief that breathes life into the great principle of the Universal Declaration of Human Rights". Prime Minister Wilfried Martens of Belgium stated: "for Belgium it is essential that the Security Council and the Secretary General take full account of the importance of human rights being universally respected in international peacekeeping and security issues. They should act accordingly with the full weight of their authority

some were in favour of a more definite role for the Security Council in human rights issues,[7] others cautioned against intervention in the internal affairs of states.[8] They, however, declared that

---

... This new solidarity now entails the collective respect for international law, and now it should also include human rights. Last October in the General Assembly, Belgium declared that states are internationally responsible for their national policy on human rights. Every state present here will agree that the fate of civilian populations which are the victims of internal repression fully justifies the compassion and concern of our organization. Indeed, all members of the organization concur in their determination to defend human rights. As it is stated in the Charter of the United Nations, they have committed themselves to acting jointly to this end. My country is of the view that the raison d'etre of the principle of non-interference is to allow states to foster, in freedom, the well-being of their populations. However, no government should use this principle as a legal argument to condone abuses of human rights. The state – the right of any state should be at the service of human rights ... Belgium suggests ... that the Security Council deal with these cases at a rather early stage and that it support any action taken elsewhere to put an end to unacceptable situations which might become a direct threat to international peace and security". Quoted in Scheffer, *ibid.*

8   The Chinese Prime Minister Li Peng stated: "[i]n our view, such basic principles as sovereign equality of member-states and non-interference in their internal affairs as enshrined in the charter of the United Nations should be observed by all its members, without exception ... In essence, the issue of human rights falls within the sovereignty of each country. A country's human rights situation should not be judged in total disregard of its history and national conditions. It is neither appropriate nor workable to demand that all countries measure up to the human rights criteria or models of one or more number of countries ... [China] is opposed to interference in the internal affairs of other countries using human rights as an excuse". India's Prime Minister Narasimha Rao cautioned that: "the Charter is only as legitimate and secure as its underpinning by the collective will of the international community. At every step, the interpretation of the Charter as well as the actions of the Security Council must flow from that collective will and not from the views or predilections of a few. A general consensus must always prevail. What is right and just must become transparent ... Members of the Security Council ... should insist on this consensus. Scrupulously [sic] avoiding the temptation to dictate for quick results ... It is also important to note that the – [inaudible] – of human rights are

[t]he absence of war and military conflicts amongst states does not in itself insure international peace and security. The non-military sources of instability in the economic, social, humanitarian and ecological fields have become threats to peace and security. The United Nations membership as a whole needs to give the highest priority to the solution of these matters.

The members of the Council pledge their commitment to international law and to the United Nations Charter. All disputes between states

---

conditioned by the social, traditional and cultural forces that [inform?] different societies. While the endeavour of the UN, as being intimated in this meeting, is to gradually move towards creating uniform international norms for human rights. Such [sic] norms should not be unilaterally defined and set up as absolute preconditions for interaction between states and societies in the political or economic spheres". Quoted in *ibid.*, at footnote 127. The Zimbabwean foreign minister, N.M. Shmuyarira, on behalf of President Mugabe observed: "[i]n the era we are entering, the Council will be called upon to deal more and more with conflict and humanitarian situations of a domestic nature that could pose threats to international peace and security. However, great care has to be taken to see that these domestic conflicts are not used as a pretext for the intervention of the big powers in the legitimate affairs of small states, or that human rights issues are not used for totally different purposes of destabilizing other governments. There is, therefore, the need to strike a delicate balance between the rights of states, as enshrined in the Charter, and the rights of individuals, as enshrined in the Universal Declaration of Human Rights. Zimbabwe supports very strongly both the Universal Declaration and the Charter on these issues. Zimbabwe is a firm subscriber to the principles in the United Nations Declaration on Human Rights. However, we cannot but express our apprehension about who will decide when to get the Security Council involved in an internal matter and in what manner. In other words, who will judge when a threshold is passed that calls for international action? Who will decide what should be done, how it should be done and by whom? This clearly calls for a careful drawing up and drafting of general principles and guidelines that would guide decisions on when a domestic situation warrants international action, either by the Security Council or by regional organizations. This could be one of the tasks this Council could entrust to the Secretary General". Quoted in van Boven, "The Security Council: The New Frontier" (1992) 48 *The Review* (International Commission of Jurists) at 12-13.

should be peacefully resolved in accordance with the provisions of the
Charter.
The members of the Council reaffirm their commitment to the collective
security system of the Charter to deal with threats to peace and to
reverse acts of aggression.[9]

The summit thus sought to strengthen the authority of the UN to negotiate
peaceful resolution of conflicts and to intervene in circumstances that
endanger humanity. It directed the UN Secretary General to report "on
ways of strengthening and making more efficient within the framework
and provisions of the Charter the capacity of the United Nations for preventive diplomacy, for peacemaking and for peacekeeping".[10]

In his report to the Security Council subsequent to the summit, the
UN Secretary General Boutros Boutros Ghali encouraged the idea of
greater institutionalization of the conflict management role of the Council. The report argued for conclusion of the military agreements envisaged in Article 43, re-establishment of the Military Staff Committee,
institutionalization of peacekeeping forces, creation of "peace enforcement" units, and an increased role for the international Court of Justice. Furthermore, the report pointed out that one of the UN's security
roles in the post-Cold War period was to "address the deepest causes
of conflict: economic despair, social injustice and political oppression".[11]

In sum, it seems clear that the UN has begun to take seriously, and
to address issues relating to egregious human rights violations or suffering which constitute threats to international peace and security. The
case for humanitarian intervention by the UN is grounded in the duty
and responsibility of the Security Council to take whatever measures
are necessary to maintain international peace and security. The basis
for this assertion can be found in Chapter VII, and the responsibility of

---

9   "Security Council Summit Declaration: 'New Risks for Stability and
     Security'" *New York Times*, (Feb.1 1992) A4.
10   *ibid.*
11   See, *An Agenda for Peace; Preventive Diplomacy, Peacemaking and Peace-
     keeping; Report of the Secretary-General*, UNDoc.A/47/277 (1992), at
     Para.42-54.

member states under article 25 of the UN Charter. However, the notion that human rights violations within a state are a threat to international peace and security is a somewhat contentious one.[12] The international response and the practical measures taken in that direction will now be analysed through the case studies.

2   NORTHERN IRAQ

The repression of the Kurdish people of Iraq predates the 1991 Gulf War and its aftermath.[13] It has been part of years-long policy of Arab colonial domination and the denial of their right to self-determination.[14] Following the dissolution of the Ottoman Empire at the end of World War 1, the Treaty of Sevres (1920) provided the Kurds with the prospect of an independent Kurdish state. The provision of the Treaty giving the Kurds "an absolute unmolested opportunity to autonomous development" was never implemented.[15] The Treaty of Lausanne (July 1923), ignored completely the claims of the Kurds and divided the Kurdish territory between Iraq and Iran. Thus, Kurdish aspirations of self-determination

---

12 See Ofuatey-Kodjoe, "Human Rights and Humanitarian Intervention" in Legault, Murphy & Ofuatey-Kodjoe, *The State of the United Nations: 1992* (Academic Council on the United Nations System Reports and Papers No.3, 1992) 33 at 42.

13 The Kurdish people are estimated to be about 20 million. They are divided among four states in the Middle East region. They make up 19-24% of the Turkish population, 23-27% of the Iraqi population, 10-16% of the Iranian population and 8-9% of the Syrian population. They speak two major dialects and are predominantly sunni. Adelman, "Humanitarian Intervention: The Case of the Kurds" (1992) 4: 1 *International Journal of Refugee Law* 4 at 5.

14 Akhavan, "Lessons from Iraqi Kurdistan: Self-Determination and Human-itarian Intervention against Genocide" (1993) 1 *Netherlands Quarterly of Human Rights* 41 at 42

15 *Supra*, note 13 at 6.

with the goal of forming a separate Kurdish state never materialized due to geopolitical considerations on the part of the European powers.[16]

The Kurds have continuously revolted against rule from Baghdad, and from 1961 to 1971 were engaged in armed rebellion.[17] Even though agreement was reached with Baghdad which provided some measure of autonomy, [18]the reality of the situation, however, was that the Iraqi government marginalized and excluded the Kurds and began a colonial "Arabization" program consisting of large-scale Kurdish deportations and forced Arab settlement in the region.[19] Again in the 1980s, the Kurdish population started a rebellion that was ruthlessly crushed. From 1985, Saddam Hussein's regime engaged in a systematic program of destruction of Kurdish towns and villages, and the use of poison gas against the Kurdish population.[20] The failure of humanitarian intervention on behalf of the Kurds by the international community was partly due to the fact that despite his atrocities against the Kurdish population, Saddam Hussein was an effective bulwark against Iran in the Persian

---

16 *Ibid.*
17 Following this decade-long conflict which claimed about 60, 000 casualties and a displacement of 300, 000 people, an agreement was reached which provided for Kurdish autonomy, with the seizure of power by the Arab Ba'th Socialist Party.*Ibid.*
18 The agreement guaranteed official recognition of the Kurdish language in Kurdish areas, non-discrimination, affirmative action, administrative autonomy, equal economic development, repatriation, and significantly, official recognition that Iraq was comprised of two main nationalities – Arabs and Kurds recognized as having national and minority rights. These rights included guaranteed rights to self-rule, proportionate representation in the Iraqi legislature and the Vice-Presidency of the Republic. This agreement broke down after four years concerning disputes of the control of oil revenues and the territorial boundaries of the autonomous region. *Ibid.*
19 *Supra*, note 14 at 42.
20 Beres, "Iraqi Crimes and International Law: The Imperative to Punish" (1993) 21 *Denver Journal of International Law* 335 at 345. For a detailed study of this systematic repression see Middle East Watch, *Human Rights in Iraq* (New Haven: Yale University Press, 1992).

Gulf, and thus enjoyed a friendly though uneasy relationship with the West.[21]

In the aftermath of the Gulf War in February 1991, the Iraqi Kurds were again targets of atrocities perpetrated by the regime of Saddam Hussein. The defeat of Iraq by the Allied powers in "Operation Desert Storm" and the consequent signals of support to overthrow the regime of Saddam Hussein[22] presented the Kurdish rebels an opportunity to consolidate their position in the region. Iraqi military presence in Kurdistan was further reduced due to additional demands of containing the Shi'te rebellion in the south. Kurdish rebels taking advantage of the state of affairs infiltrated the region and made significant military advances. This situation was reversed with Saddam's forces attacking Kurdish cities, levelling entire neighbourhoods and engaging in wholesale massacres of civilian populations. News reports recounted this devastation thus: "they've [the Kurds] been driven from their villages, intentionally starved, fired on from the air and the ground, even massacred with poison gas".[23] The Allied powers issued stern warnings against the use of chemical weapons but vacillated on the use of helicopter gunships and other military action against civilians. According to Akhavan, there were many indications that the Allied powers were apprehensive of the 'fragmentation' and territorial 'dismemberment' of Iraq and that they were willing to countenance massive human rights violations as the price to be paid for maintaining a 'stable' government in Iraq.[24]

---

21 *Supra*, note 14 at 43.
22 President Bush, at the height of the war, had made remarks to the American Academy for the Advancement of Science thus: "[b]ut there's another way for the bloodshed to stop and that is for the Iraqi military and the Iraqi people to take matters into their own hands to force Saddam Hussein, the dictator to step aside and to comply with the UN and then rejoin the family of peace-loving states". *Financial Times*, London, 16 Feb.1991, quoted in Koshy, "Morality and International Law: An Ethic of Intervention?" in Conference Report, *The Challenge to Intervene: A New Role for the United Nations* (Uppsala: Life & Peace Institute, 1992) 93 at 108.
23 *Supra*, note 14 at 43. See, "Double Trouble for the Kurds" *New York Times*, April 1, 1992, at A24, col. 1.
24 Akhavan, *Ibid.*

Added to this, some members of the Security Council were not particularly receptive to the idea of renewed military strikes against Iraq.
This development imposed severe strains on the issue of nonintervention
in the internal affairs of states. However, the situation was exacerbated
by a mass exodus of refugees into Turkey and Iran, giving rise to tensions between those countries and Iraq. The magnitude of the repression
and the refugee problem were borne out of the fact that out of a total
Kurdish population of approximately 3-4 million in Iraq, over 1.5 million
refugees were generated in a short period of time.[25] The regional security factor led to a reconsideration of the Allied powers hitherto policy
of non-intervention. The Iraqi mistreatment of its Kurdish population
became a matter that threatened international peace and security in the
region, and subsequently provided the legal basis for Security Council
action.

In taking account of these developments, the Security Council adopted Resolution 688[26] which condemned Iraq's repression of the Kurds
and other groups as a threat to international peace and security. It
demanded that "Iraq immediately end this repression" and insisted that
it "allow immediate access by international humanitarian organizations
to all those in need of assistance in all parts of Iraq and to make

---

25 *Ibid.* A report issued by the United States Senate Committee on Foreign
    Relations stated that more than two million Iraqi Kurds had sought refuge
    on the Iraq-Iran borders and that they were dying at a rate of up to 2, 000
    a day at the time. The author of the Report, Peter Galbraith observed that
    "[m]y visit to liberated Kurdistan, over the weekend of March 30-31 [1991],
    coincided with the collapse of the Kurdish rebellion and the beginning of
    the humanitarian catastrophe now overwhelming the Kurdish people. I was
    an eyewitness to many of the atrocities being committed by the Iraqi army,
    including the heavy shelling of cities, the use of phosphorous artillery shells,
    and the creation of tens of thousands of refugees. From Kurdish leaders
    and refugees I heard firsthand accounts of other horrors including mass
    executions and the levelling of large sections of Kurdish cities". Staff of
    Senate Committee on Foreign Relations, 102d Cong., 1st Sess., Civil War
    in Iraq 2 (Comm.Print 1991). Quoted in Beres, *supra*, note 20 at 347.
26 U.N. Doc.S/RES/688 (1991). Reprinted in (1991) 30 *International Legal
    Materials* 858. This resolution was passed by ten votes to three (Cuba,
    Yemen, Zimbabwe) with two abstentions (China and India).

available all necessary facilities for their operation". It requested the UN Secretary-General to use all the resources at his disposal to address "urgently the critical needs of the refugees and displaced Iraqi population". Finally, it appealed to member states and to humanitarian organizations "to contribute to these humanitarian relief efforts".

The legitimacy of this resolution by the Security Council was vigorously debated, since the participants understood the resolution would establish a precedent shaping perceptions of the proper role of the Security Council in future situations arising out of internal conflict. On the one hand, France argued that massive human rights violations, whether or not they constituted a threat to international peace and security, warranted intervention by the Security Council, which "would have been remiss in its task had it stood idly by, without reacting to the massacre of entire populations, the extermination of civilians, including women and children".[27] Other states supporting the resolution stressed the international repercussions of Iraq's repression of its civilian population in the flows of refugees to neighbouring States.[28] On the other hand, China and other states opposing the resolution made reference to Article 2 (7), noting the Security Council should not consider or take action on questions concerning the internal affairs of any State.[29] The Iraqi response as would be expected was antagonistic. For Iraq, it was paradoxical that the Security Council should interest itself in letters from Iran and Turkey concerning the Kurds when those states did not have a good record of treatment of the Kurds in their own jurisdictions.[30]

Actual intervention in Iraq to protect the Kurds, "Operation Provide Comfort", was undertaken by troops from the United States, Britain, France, and armed forces from other countries. The United States, Britain

---

27 French Representative to the UN Security Council, quoted in *supra*, note 14 at 44.
28 See UN Doc. S/PV 2982.
29 *Ibid.*
30 UN Doc.S/22460. Cited in Gray, "After the Ceasefire: Iraq, the Security Council and the Use of Force" (1994) 65 *The British Yearbook of International Law* 159 at 160.

and France declared first a "no-fly zone" in the North, and "Operation Southern Watch" in Southern Iraq where the Shi'ite population was threatened. Armed forces were also used to create humanitarian enclaves protected from the Iraqi military. Iraq protested these measures, for they were undertaken when it (Iraq) was negotiating with the UN over access for humanitarian organizations. These countries, however, relied on resolution 688 to legitimize their actions. Apart from military forces used in the operation, thirty other countries contributed relief supplies and some fifty non-governmental organizations (NGOs) either offered assistance or participated in the operation.[31]

Overall, the UN aid effort in Iraq relied on allied military intervention in northern Iraq in its early stages to establish a security zone; allied threats to respond to any Iraqi air operations in northern Iraq; the deployment of a UN force to provide limited protection to UN humanitarian workers; and, an agreement negotiated with the Iraqi government to establish the logistics of the humanitarian effort throughout Iraq.[32]

An analysis of this action uncovers the ever-present tension between sovereignty and non-intervention on the one hand, and the protection of human rights on the other. Issues relating to the legitimacy of the humanitarian action in Iraq and the value of the operation as a precedent are debatable.

The moral case for the humanitarian initiative in Northern Iraq is compelling. The justification for humanitarian action to redress gross and systematic abuse of human rights is imperative. The Iraqi violations of the rights of its Kurdish people within its own jurisdiction was directly related to the rights of other states to intervene, and to use such force as was necessary to remedy the situation where regional peace and security was threatened. In this case, the repression was so great as to cause a mass exodus of people into the neighbouring states, threatening the peace and security of those states. The Security Council, responsible

---

31 Tesón, "Collective Humanitarian Intervention" (1996) 17: 2 *Michigan Journal of International Law* 323 at 365-346.

32 Scheffer, Gardner, & Helman, *Post-Gulf War Challenges to the UN Collective Security System: Three Views on the Issue of Humanitarian Intervention* (Washington, DC: United States Institute of Peace, 1992) at 8-9.

for maintaining international peace and security, would be justified in demanding intervention for humanitarian purposes, and in fact, did just that.[33]

To buttress the dimension of moral legitimacy in this case, where the state is guilty of gross and persistent human rights violations, the consent of the governed can no longer be presumed. Similarly, the innocent victims of humanitarian crises cannot have chosen or consented to their fate. Legitimacy in this respect will mean that a government should respect the human rights of its citizens. Where the opposite happens, non-intervention will no longer be morally required, and the government would have lost its moral authority to demand that external actors remain uninvolved in its internal matters.[34] From an ethical point of view governments are domestically and internationally mere agents of the people. Consequently, their international rights derive from the rights of the citizens who inhabit and constitute the state.

The ethical aspect of the UN action in Iraq, however, would have been strengthened if it had clearly mentioned the rights of the Kurdish people. Resolution 688 did not refer to the Kurds as a people, nationality, group or minority, but instead made reference to "the Iraqi population in many parts of Iraq, including most recently in Kurdish-populated areas". The observation has been made that in doing this, "[t]he Security Council thus failed to highlight the measures of the Iraqi government aimed against the Kurds as people, measures which many considered were tantamount to genocidal actions".[35] By drawing a link between action on the Kurdish-populated areas with Security Council Resolution 687 (the resolution on the ceasefire) and thus making it part of a package of punitive actions against Iraq, the UN further devalued the moral dimensions of this case.[36] Mayall, for instance, has argued that the obligation to "do something" about the Kurds did not spring

---

33 *Supra*, note 13 at 24.
34 See Walzer, *Just and Unjust Wars* (New York: Basic Books, 1977) at 101-108; Donnelly, "Human Rights, Humanitarian Crisis, and Humanitarian Intervention" (1993) XLVIII *International Journal* 607 at 615-616.
35 *Supra*, note 22 at 108.
36 *Ibid.*

from generalised duties to protect human rights wherever they are threatened, but from specific responsibilities incurred by the Western powers from the Gulf War. Undoubtedly, had the repression occurred in any other circumstances than as a result of the Gulf War, it is inconceivable that western governments would have responded to pressures from public opinion to intervene for purposes of humanity.[37] Although one could fault the UN-sanctioned action on this score, account should also be taken of the fact that the immediate and urgent humanitarian concerns were met, demonstrating at least some moral concern for the plight of the Kurds even though the broader political question of Kurdish self-determination was not addressed.

Another arena of debate regarding UN action in Northern Iraq concerns the scope of Resolution 688. Apart from the debates preceding its passage discussed earlier, some commentators have argued, first, that the Resolution does not validate strictly internal human rights violations, without transboundary effects, as threats to international peace and security.[38] They claim that it explicitly provides that it is the external effects of the Iraqi repression that are threats to international peace and security. Moreover, the Resolution did not authorize the Security Council to use force to protect human rights in these circumstances, since it contained no reference to Chapter VII. Chapter VII is the only chapter in the Charter that authorizes or permits the Security Council to use or approve the use of force.[39] Although the Security Council ordered Iraq to permit humanitarian assistance, the Resolution fails to mention collec-

---

37 Mayall, "Non-intervention, Self-Determination and the 'New World Order'" (1991) 67: 3 *International Affairs* at 426-428. See also, Roberts, "Humanitarian War: Military Intervention and Human Rights" (1993) 69: 3 *International Affairs* 429 at 437 (noting "Operation Provide Comfort" occurred in the immediate aftermath of the Gulf war, and that in those circumstances the allied powers had reason to take responsibility for the plight of the Kurdish refugees).

38 See, for example, Gordon, "Humanitarian Intervention by the United Nations: Iraq, Somalia, and Haiti" (1996) 31: 1 *Texas International Law Journal* 43 at 49; Malanczuk, *Humanitarian Intervention and the Legitimacy of the Use of Force* (1993) at 18.

39 *Ibid.*

tive enforcement measures, and thus given its narrow scope, it should not be viewed as approving intervention for humanitarian purposes, because humanitarian interventions by definition involve the use of force.[40] Resolution 688 did not specifically authorize the use of force, and the Secretary-General did not request it, although he did in the end acquiesce in the intervention.[41]

Added to this is the issue of state sovereignty. Unlike Somalia, where there was no functioning government, and Haiti, where there were competing governments, Iraq had a single, sovereign functioning government. In this regard, some states questioned the authority of the UN to intervene against a sovereign government to redress human rights violations. In this context, the allied action of protecting the Kurds in Northern Iraq posed a direct challenge to Iraq, and was a violation of Iraqi sovereignty. In effect, since Resolution 688 was relied upon to legitimize the actions in Northern Iraq, as mentioned earlier, the legality of these acts becomes questionable according to this viewpoint.[42]

It would seem that claims relating to Security Council action under Resolution 688 as legally binding only because it was in response to a "threat to the peace" is an exercise in excessive formalism. Resolution 688 was sufficiently open-ended to provide a legal basis for the allied action. According to Tesón, the relevant issue here is not whether the Security Council can do anything it wants so long as it is styled a "threat to international peace and security". As Tesón argues, setting aside word games, this situation was a human rights issue about Iraq's treatment of its own citizens. A reasonable reading of Resolution 688 is that the Security Council was essentially concerned about the human rights abuses themselves. The reference "to the threat to peace and security was added for good measure".[43]

The element in the UN action in Northern Iraq is the resuscitation of the sovereignty debate. Was UN action in Iraq a violation of Iraqi sovereignty, as argued above, or does the response to the plight of the

---

40 *Ibid.*
41 *Supra*, note 13 at 19-21.
42 *Supra*, note 38 at 49.
43 *Supra*, note 31 at 344.

Kurds suggest a shift in international opinion toward reconstructing state sovereignty to take account of massive human rights violations? A case can be made for the assertion that there is a movement towards reconstructing sovereignty to take into consideration human rights violations.

First, although the UN Secretary-General may have had initial reservations about the scope of the humanitarian mission in Northern Iraq, he argued for a change in the traditional understanding of state sovereignty in light of the international community's interest in taking action where massive human rights violations are involved. In his September 1991 final Report to the General Assembly, Perez de Cuellar noted:

> [Protection of human rights] now involves a more concerted exertion of international influence and pressure ... and, in the last resort, an appropriate United Nations presence, than what was regarded permissible under traditional international law.
>
> It is now increasingly felt that the principle of non-interference with the essential domestic jurisdiction of States cannot be regarded as a protective barrier behind which human rights could be massively or systematically violated with impunity ...
>
> We need not impale ourselves on the horns of a dilemma between respect for sovereignty and the protection of human rights ... What is involved is not the right of intervention but the collective obligation of States to bring relief and redress in human rights emergencies.[44]

The Secretary General thus argued that international boundaries have been erased in certain domains of concern. Chopra comments there is already a shift in jurisdiction from the territorial 'place' of the domestic arena to the 'space' of issues deemed matters of international concern, such as international crimes, which are committed against the international community as a whole, which are not distinguished by their *locus delicti*.[45] In effect, it becomes quite obvious that the official UN

---

44 Report of the Secretary-General on the Work of the Organization, UN GAOR, 46th Sess., Supp. No.1, at 5, UN Doc. A/46/1 (1991).

45 Chopra, "The Space of Peace-Maintenance" (1996) 15 *Political Geography* 335 at 342.

view of state sovereignty underwent significant reevaluation in light of the Gulf War and Operation Provide Comfort.[46]

Western leaders have also used Operation Provide Comfort to change the traditional understandings of sovereignty and nonintervention in internal affairs of states. The British Foreign Secretary Douglas Hurd, in this regard, remarked that the demarcation between internal and external policies of a nation is 'not absolute'.[47] French Foreign Minister Roland Dumas argued that the French concept of the 'duty to intervene'[48] emerged from the Iraqi oppression in a similar way that the concept of 'crimes against humanity' emerged from the Holocaust. In France, he noted, it is a crime not to help someone who is in danger.[49] Similarly, the US Ambassador to the UN, Thomas Pickering observed that

> The response to the plight of the Kurds suggests a shift in world opinion towards re-balancing of the claims of sovereignty and those of extreme humanitarian need. This is good news since it means we are moving closer to deterring genocide and aiding its victims. However, it also means we have much careful thinking to do about the

---

46 *Supra*, note 31 at 347.
47 Helm et al., *The Independent*, 11 April 1991., quoted in Freedman & Boren, "Safe havens for Kurds in Post-War Iraq" in Rodley eds., *To Loose the Bands of Wickedness-International Intervention in Defence of Human Rights* (London: Brassey's 1992) 43 at 81-82.
48 Following the lead of Bernard Kouchner, founder of Medecins sans Frontiers and French Secretary of State for Humanitarian Affairs, some French legal experts and humanitarian non-governmental organizations have formulated a theory of an international right of victims to assistance, and of an international duty to assist them, culminating in a right of international humanitarian intervention. See for example, Beigbeder, *The Role and Status of International Humanitarian Volunteers and Organizations: The Right and Duty to Humanitarian Assistance* (Dordrecht: Martinus Nijhoff Publishers, 1991) at 353-384; Garigue, "Intervention-Sanction and 'Droit d'ingerence' in International Humanitarian Law" (1993) XLVIII *International Journal* 668.
49 Fitchett, International Herald Tribune, 13-14 April 1991; "That Slippery Slope", Economist, 13 April 1991; Mortimer, Financial Times, 20-21 April 1991. Cited in *supra*, note 47 at 82.

nature of, and the limitations upon, intervention to carry out humanitarian assistance programs where States refuse, in pursuit of 'policies
of repression', to give permission to such assistance.[50]

Echoing similar viewpoints at the London Summit in July 1991, the
Group of Seven issued a political declaration noting

> ... the urgent and overwhelming nature of the humanitarian problem
> in Iraq caused by violent oppression by the government required excep-
> tional action by the international community, following UNSCR 688.
> We urge the UN and its affiliated agencies to be ready to consider
> similar action in the future if circumstances require it.[51]

These developments effectively encourage intervention to protect human
rights since the rights of individuals are often violated by their own
governments. The steady erosion of traditional understandings of state
sovereignty is making it easier for international organizations, governments, and non-governmental organizations (NGOs) to intervene when
governments refuse to meet the needs of their citizens and substantial
numbers of people are at risk.[52] As one commentator suggests "[i]t
may be that the international community has begun to accept the proposition that the interests of people come before the interests of
states".[53] In short, Iraq's treatment of the Kurds shows the international
community's commitment to the view that sovereignty and nonintervention could no longer shield genocidal and other repressive acts which
are themselves forbidden by international law and treaties.

Having noted these developments, what then is the value of the
Security Council action in terms of its status as a precedent? Some
writers have noted the improbability of the birth of a new order, or
caution against arriving at the conclusion that the case of the Iraqi Kurds

---

50 Speech to US Council on Foreign Relations, 8 May 1991, quoted in *ibid.*
51 *Ibid.*
52 Deng, *Protecting the Dispossessed: A Challenge for the International Com-
    munity* (Washington, DC: The Brookings Institution, 1993) at 15.
53 Stedman, "The New Interventionists" (1993) 72: 1 *Foreign Affairs* 1 at 16.

sets a clear precedent for humanitarian intervention.[54] Fine, for instance argues "neither the United States nor the United Nations is inclined to pay any price, bear any burden, meet any hardship, support any friend, or oppose any foe under a human rights banner". "The world will come to view the Kurdish enclaves", according to him, "as a curio of international law, like Guantanamo Bay or Gibralta".[55] He gives a number of reasons, [56]the coalescence of which explain the break with international law customs in Kurdish Iraq, and concludes the absence of one or more of these factors explains the lack of international militancy toward massive human rights violations in other regions of the world.[57]

Thus, the allied action in Northern Iraq, for some, is neither reassuring as humanitarian intervention, nor does it signify the emergence of a new legal norm. It reinforces increasing fears that the global order that is being structured is maintained by a self-appointed cop whose actions are post-facto legitimized by the UN.[58]

Contrary to the above assertions, the intervention in support of the Iraqi Kurds has broader significance, for the following reasons. First, this case demonstrated the Security Council's willingness to act in response to internal repression, when the consequences of that repression

---

54 See for example *supra*, note 37.
55 Fine, *Legal Times*, 13 May 1991, Vol.13 at 20. Quoted in *supra*, note 22 at 110.
56 The reasons he gives why Northern Iraq is an exceptional action are: 1. The universal revulsion against Saddam Hussein and the consequent rejection of his invocation of international law. 2. The partial responsibility of the coalition forces, especially the United States for the plight of the Kurds. 3. The strong support of Turkey for Kurdish enclaves. 4. The fact that Russia or China did not use the veto because of urgently needed financial and trade benefits. 5. The impact of the mass media, especially of television, on public opinion. 6. Genocidal action by Iraq against the Kurds providing a foundation in international law for the enclaves. 7. The military impotence of Iraq to oppose the Kurdish enclaves. 8. The expectation that the enclaves need be there only for a short period. *Ibid.*
57 *Ibid.*
58 See Koshy, *ibid.*, at 111; Wheeler, "Pluralist or Solidarist Conceptions of International Society: Bull and Vincent on Humanitarian Intervention" (1992) *Millennium: Journal of International Studies* 463 at 483.

resulted in transboundary refugee flows, even though the limits of the precedent are also apparent. As shown earlier, five members of the Security Council expressed doubts about a greater role for the Council in conflicts that they saw as essentially internal affairs.

Second, this case addressed the humanitarian crisis in Iraq as just that, avoiding the more contentious political issue of the self-determination of the Iraqi Kurds. Allied leaders did not take sides on the issue of Kurdish self-determination, but saw in the creation of humanitarian enclaves the prospect or possibility of an open dialogue that would ensure that the human and political rights of all Iraqi citizens are respected. In this regard, former UN Secretary General Perez de Cuellar argued in favour of a "collective obligation of States to bring relief and redress in human rights emergencies" rather than a more open-ended right of intervention.[59]

Finally, the UN action in Iraq resulted in a motivation for institutional reforms mapping out UN humanitarian responses, such as through the creation of corridors of peace or zones of tranquillity.[60] To this end, the General Assembly adopted in December 1991 by consensus Resolution 46/182 to strengthen UN coordination of humanitarian emergency assistance. This resolution, among other things, lays down guiding principles for humanitarian assistance that take account of both state sovereignty and the needs of "victims of natural disasters and other emergencies".[61] These principles indicate a movement from the traditional focus on the primacy of state sovereignty and on state-initiated requests for assistance. The resolution also resulted in the establishment of the Department of Humanitarian Affairs which should enable the UN and other humanitarian agencies working with the UN to respond in a timely manner and effectively in future humanitarian emergencies.[62]

---

59 Quoted in Stromseth, "Iraq's Repression of its Civilian Population: Collective Responses and Continuing Challenges" in Damrosch ed., *Enforcing Restraint: Collective Intervention in Internal Conflicts* (New York: Council on Foreign Relations Press, 1993) 77 at 99.

60 *Ibid.*, at 101.

61 Resolution 46/182, annex, para.1. Quoted in *ibid.*

62 *Ibid.*, at 101-102.

3   SOMALIA

The international response to the tragedy in Somalia was a more complex undertaking than the intervention in Northern Iraq since Somalia had no functioning government. The degeneration of Somali society into civil strife and anarchy was puzzling for some observers since Somalia is one of the few homogenous states in Africa with a common language, a common culture and a single religion, Islam.

The roots of the tragedy can be traced to both internal and external factors. Internally, after its independence in 1960, [63]"the Somali government was a mere political superstructure resting on the tectonic plates of the main organising units of Somali society, the clans", according to Farer.[64] Successful government depended on a delicate balancing act because of a system of client and patron built upon traditional clan relationships. When Barre took over power in a coup in 1969, the principle of Somali politics remained the same but gradually lost its balance.[65]

The calamity that befell Somalia began partly with the policies pursued by Siad Barre in the 1970s and 1980s. The Barre government's lack of legitimacy and imposition of centralized rule worsened the negative results of his policies. The relative stability of Somali society

---

63 It should be noted that although Somali society is culturally cohesive, colonization fragmented the people, dividing them among British Somaliland, Italian Somaliland, Ethiopian Somaliland (the Ogaden region) and the Northern Frontier District of British Kenya. The present state of Somalia was a result of decolonization of the former British Somaliland Protectorate and Italian Somaliland in 1960, which united to establish the Somali Republic. See, Samatar, *Somalia: A Nation in Turmoil* (London: Minority Rights Group, 1991) at 17, cited in Crawford, "UN Humanitarian Intervention in Somalia" (1993) 3 *Transnational Law and Contemporary Problems* 273 at 274

64 Quoted in Slim & Visman, "Evacuation, Intervention and Retaliation: United Nations Humanitarian Operations in Somalia, 1991-1993" in Harriss ed., *The Politics of Humanitarian Intervention* (London: Pinter, 1995) 145 at 146.

65 Slim & Visman, *ibid.*, at 147.

in the 1970s and 1980s was dependent on the skilful manipulation of domestic politics. Barre's hold on power was sustained by the suppression of critics, detention and military reprisals against his opponents, manipulation of clan interests and rivalries, and the occasional buying out of opposition groups with cash. By the 1980s, however, the increase in interclan rivalries had weakened his military base. It increasingly became obvious that he neither possessed the skill to bring together the various sectional interests nor the leadership necessary to pull the country out of its political quagmire, with the worsening economic situation.[66]

Externally, geopolitical considerations such as Somalia's strategic proximity to the oil-rich Middle East, was of great value to the superpowers during the Cold War. Both superpowers sought a military presence in Somalia and generally in the Horn of Africa. The paramount interest of both the United States and the Soviet Union was not to help Somalia but to pursue their own global and regional agendas by carving out spheres of influence. Superpower rivalry in the 1970s and 1980s thus gave Somalia a leverage through which it got considerable economic and military aid. With the demise of the Cold War, the United States and the former Soviet Union lost interest in the competition in the Horn of Africa and subsequently withdrew their presence.[67] One consequence of Superpower competition was the acquisition and stockpiling of enormous military arsenal by states in the region.[68] These arms acquisitions – a legacy of the Superpower rivalry – thus played a prominent role in changing the magnitude, direction and extent of the anarchic conditions prevalent in Somalia in the early 1990s.[69]

The end of the Cold War diminished superpower influence in Somalia. The result of this was that previously suppressed long-standing

---

66 Makinda, *Seeking Peace from Chaos: Humanitarian Intervention in Somalia* (Boulder: Lynne Rienner Publishers, 1993) at 17.

67 *Ibid.*, at 51.

68 At the height of the Soviet-Somali relations in the mid- 1970s for example, Somalia had the best equipped army in sub-Saharan Africa. By 1976, it was estimated to have more than 250 tanks, 300 armoured personnel carriers, and over 52 fighter jets. Its army during this period increased from 12, 000 in 1970 to 30, 000 in 1977. *Ibid.*, at 57.

69 *Ibid.*

grievances were unleashed in the form of ethnic conflicts, destabilizing the Horn of Africa. Bitter clan fighting became the norm in central and southern Somalia as the twenty-one year dictatorship of Siad Barre came to an end in January 1991 and created a power vacuum.[70] Intense fighting in and around Mogadishu quickly spread throughout the rest of the country. Heavily armed bandits, many of whom were members of the various major factions, others with seemingly no real allegiance, took advantage of the anarchy caused by civil war to seize control of parts of the country, looting, pillaging, controlling the distribution of food and raping women.[71] In effect the civil war left Somalia in ruins with no functioning government.[72]

By the summer of 1992 it was estimated that the situation had reached crisis proportions with over 1.2 million Somalis displaced either

---

70 The various political movements that had long opposed the Barre regime could not agree on a way of power-sharing after Barre's ouster. Ten or more clan-based factions that succeeded him thus exercised varying degrees of control. Civil strife began with militia moving from the north to fight what was left of Barre's army in the more affluent south with its trading cities of Kismayu and Mogadishu. As family members of the militia groups subsequently followed them, coupled with a lingering drought, there was a general population movement. The situation in the south degenerated into a state of chaos as traditional methods of conflict resolution failed to yield any peaceful settlement of running the affairs of the country. Violent clashes between two of the political movements vying for control of Mogadishu, the capital, took place in September 1991, and again between November 1991 to February 1992. The political situation was further worsened when pro-Barre forces attempted to recapture power through invasion of the southern part of the country from their base of operation on the border with Kenya in April 1991, and subsequently, in April 1992. See Augelli & Murphy, "Lessons of Somalia for Future Multilateral Humanitarian Assistance Operations" (1995) 1: 3 Global Governance: A Review of Multilateralism and International Organizations 339 at 340.

71 Knight & Gebremariam, "United Nations Intervention and State-Building in Somalia: Constraints and Possibilities" Paper presented at 8th Annual Meeting of the Academic Council on the United Nations System, 19-21 June 1995, New York City, at 2.

72 Clark, "Debacle in Somalia: Failure of Collective Response" in Damrosch ed., supra, note 59 at 212.

internally or externally in Ethiopia, Yemen and Kenya.[73] About 4.5 million people, roughly half of the population, were threatened with severe malnutrition and malnutrition-related diseases, and suffered more than 300, 000 deaths.[74] It was against this background of humanitarian catastrophe that the events precipitating international intervention should be located.

After the overthrow of Barre, various humanitarian relief efforts were frustrated by the actions of the warring factions to prevent relief supplies from reaching their enemies. There was a general atmosphere of insecurity in the country which led to the delivery of relief supplies in all parts of the country being stopped. The most important issue at the time was how to secure conditions under which various UN agencies and NGOs could distribute relief assistance to people that needed it the most.[75] Meanwhile, several attempts to mediate the conflict had failed.[76] Mediation efforts had failed because the various clans and subclans hated each other intensely; the faction leaders had virtually no legitimacy, since their supporters could switch their loyalties anytime; and, the number of factions and political movements kept increasing.[77]

Given this grim situation, the Security Council adopted Resolution 733 on January 23, 1992. It directed the Secretary General to immediately "undertake the necessary action to increase humanitarian assistance" to the people of Somalia, and called upon all parties to

---

73 Prunier, "Somalia: Civil War, Intervention and Withdrawal (1990-1995)" (1996) 15: 1 *Refugee Survey Quarterly* 35 at 54.

74 (1993) 30: 1 UN *Chronicle* at 1.

75 Jonah, "Humanitarian Intervention" in Weiss & Minear eds., *Humanitarianism Across Borders: Sustaining Civilians in Times of War* (Boulder: Lynne Rienner Publishers, 1993) at 72.

76 See *supra*, note 66 at 32-36.

77 *Ibid.*, at 32. It was for these reasons that the UN Secretary-General Boutros-Ghali's report to the Security Council in March 1993 argued that: "[n]ational reconciliation is a difficult process in the best of circumstances; it is particularly difficult in Somalia because of the multiplicity of parties, factions and other leaders, and the total absence of law and order in all parts of the country". See, Security Council Document S/25354 of 3 March 1993.

cooperate with the Secretary General and to facilitate the delivery of aid.[78]

In March 1992, the major factions in the civil conflict agreed to a UN mediated ceasefire,[79] which led to the establishment in April of the United Nations Operations in Somalia (UNOSOM I) with a mandate to restore peace and protect humanitarian relief operations. The truce was largely ignored among the factions, and the delivery of humanitarian aid by the UN and other humanitarian NGOs was greatly hampered by armed gangs not only in Mogadishu, but throughout the country.[80] The deteriorating situation was followed by the unanimous adoption of Security Council Resolution 794 on December 3, 1992.[81] This Resolution went beyond a mere insistence on providing access to humanitarian relief agencies. The Council recognized the "unique" situation in Somalia and declared that it fell under Chapter VII.[82] It determined that "the magnitude of the human tragedy" caused by the conflict and the obstacles being created to "the distribution of humanitarian assistance constituted a threat to international peace and security". Furthermore, the Council authorized member states "to use all necessary means" to "create a secure environment" for the delivery of humanitarian assistance. It stated that "impediments to humanitarian relief violated international humanitarian law" and that individuals in Somalia had a right to that

---

78 UN Doc.S/RES/733 (1992).
79 This ceasefire involved General Mohammed Farah Aideed of the United Somali Congress and interim President Ali Mahdi Mohammed.
80 Attacks were carried out on relief consignments and vehicles, medical and relief facilities impeding delivery of food and medicine essential for survival of the civilian population. The situation was such that the aid agencies employed members of these armed gangs to protect cargoes from theft. These guards, however, turned round to steal the relief supplies.
81 UN Doc. S/RES/794 (1992).
82 Article 39 of the Charter states that the Security Council can "determine the existence of any threat to the peace, breach of the peace, or act of aggression and shall make recommendations, or decide what [legally biding] measures shall be taken ... .to maintain or restore international peace and security". Under Article 25 of the Charter, member states agree "to accept and carry out" decisions made by the Council with regard to Chapter VII.

assistance. Finally, it stated that anyone interfering with humanitarian assistance "will be held individually responsible in respect of such acts".

Unlike Resolution 688, it is instructive to point out that China voted in favour of Resolution 794 although it is not entirely clear how far humanitarian considerations played a role in its decision. Wheeler and Morris observe that the most positive explanation for China's position might be its willingness to cooperate with the international community as it explores a limited conception of multilateral intervention for the protection of human rights. However, they caution that it is easy to overstate the extent to which experiments with norms of humanitarian intervention are finding collective support in the society of states. For them, China is at best only just becoming receptive to the notion that sovereignty and non-intervention can be overridden in the protection of human rights. This stems, in part, from China's attempt at maintaining friendly relations with the West, but the extent to which it reflects the gradual evolution of consensual moral principles in the international community is debatable.[83]

Following the adoption of Resolution 794, the United States deployed a humanitarian military-relief force to create a secure environment for the delivery of food and medicine to the people of Somalia. The US-led Unified Task Force (UNITAF) marked the beginning of "Operation Restore Hope" which enabled the UN and humanitarian NGOs to undertake their extensive operations. This was the most successful phase of the multilateral action. By the end of April 1993, the multilateral forces had helped in improving conditions significantly in Somalia. In May, the US-led action was concluded, and responsibility passed over to the UN under Resolution 814, which established UNOSOM II, allowing the use of force as envisaged under Chapter VII. The responsibility of UNOSOM II, in broad terms, was to complete, through disarmament and reconciliation, the task begun by UNITAF for the restoration of peace, stability, law and order in Somalia.

---

83 Wheeler & Morris, "Humanitarian Intervention and State Practice at the End of the Cold War" in Fawn & Larkins eds., *International Society after the Cold War: Anarchy and Order Reconsidered* (London: Macmillan Press Ltd., 1996) at 135 at 150.

The operation took a turn for the worse with the UN mandate expanding to include "nation-building" which involved disarming the factions and arresting uncooperative faction leaders. Acting under this mandate 24 members of the Pakistani UN peacekeeping force were killed on June 5, 1993. This incident seriously undermined the role of the UN peacekeeping force and its ability to control an increasingly volatile situation. In a unanimous vote the Security Council passed Resolution 837 that called for the total disarmament and the arrest and prosecution of those responsible for the killings. In an unprecedented turn of events, US forces under UN command on June 12, 1993, carried out retaliatory attacks in the Somali capital in an effort to bring the anarchic situation to an end, and to restore conditions of normalcy. In the months that followed, the search for General Aidid, who had been blamed for the killings, led to the deaths of many Somalis, UN peacekeeping forces and foreign journalists. The violence intensified until early October when US forces suffered heavy casualties with twelve soldiers killed, seventy-five wounded and six missing in action.[84]

American policy began to shift when President Clinton announced intentions of reinforcing US military presence in Somalia and proceeding with the political dialogue that had already began among the Somali factions. Secretary of State Warren Christopher subsequently announced that the US had made mistakes regarding the Somali operation and that the search for Aidid was no longer the main focus of the operation. The US began disengaging from Somalia with France, Italy and other Western nations following suit.[85]

UN efforts at encouraging negotiations were without success. Given the situation, Security Council Resolution 897 was passed which sought to limit UN involvement by restricting UN forces to tasks such as keeping the roads open to allow humanitarian aid channelled to the interior. When UNOSOM's mandate expired by the end of March 1995, neither the Somali factions nor the humanitarian NGOs requested an extension.

---

84 *Supra*, note 73 at 342.
85 *Ibid.*

It was very clear that UN peace management efforts had failed.[86] In sum, the Somalia experience evolved through four phases: conventional ceasefire observation between July and November 1992; forcible delivery of humanitarian assistance between December 1992 and March 1993; combat operations between June and October 1993; and nation-building after October 1993.[87]

Since the withdrawal of UN forces in March 1995, the political situation in Somalia has remained at a stalemate. The various Somali faction leaders have failed to honour their commitments towards an all-inclusive national reconciliation conference and forming a government. Nevertheless, while there had been no progress towards that end, the worst scenario of an all out civil war had been averted.[88]

The Somalia experience embodies the debate involving making a moral case for non-intervention versus intervention. Was there a moral obligation for the international community to respond to the humanitarian crises that was Somalia? In making a case for non-intervention, some would argue that even if in practice the state, as in Somalia, is one that lacks a 'general will' or is experiencing a crisis of authority, because of fighting involving different factions the ultimate consequences of which will be to tear the society apart, foreign intervention is still seen as a greater evil. It is best to leave resolution of the crisis to the local people. Cynics contend that efforts aimed at promoting peace through outside intervention merely prolong conflict or result in a stalemate.

Alternatively, for others Somalia required a response, including the military means necessary to render humanitarian aid effective, and thus morally justifiable. As Walzer argues, non-intervention is not an absolute moral rule. If what is going on locally becomes intolerable, humanitarian intervention is morally necessary whenever cruelty and suffering are extreme and local forces seem incapable of putting an end to them.[89]

---

86 Mutharika, "The Role of the United Nations Security Council in African Peace Management: Some Proposals" (1996) 17: 2 *Michigan Journal of International Law* 537 at 548.

87 *Supra*, note 45 at 349.

88 See Somalia, "Security Council calls on Somali Political Leaders to Return to Inclusive Negotiation" in *UN Chronicle*, 33: 2 October 1996, at 52-53.

89 Walzer, "The Politics of Rescue" (1995) 62: 1 *Social Research* 53 at 55.

For him, the agent of last resort to put an end to suffering is anyone near enough and strong enough to stop what needs stopping, but he realizes this is not always easy.[90] In this case, the Organization of African Unity (OAU) would have been the appropriate body capable of stopping the conflict in its early stages before it took a turn for the worse, since that regional organization would have understood better what was going on, and would have been able to grapple with the dynamics of the local politics.

The OAU, however, for various reasons, and most particularly its reluctance to intervene in internal conflicts on the continent, was ineffective in dealing with the Somali conflict. One might add, however, that there is some indication towards change in the OAU approach in dealing with situations such as Somalia or Liberia. At its summit in July 1992, African states were prepared to sanction intervention in internal conflicts aimed at the delivery of humanitarian relief. The report presented by the OAU Secretary-General to the Council of Ministers in Dakar in June 1992 is perhaps indicative of an awareness about changing attitudes in so far as the OAU is concerned. The report stated: [91]

---

90 *Ibid.*

91 The report stated in part: "The conspicuous lack of clarity regarding norms in international law which regulate the conduct of third parties is even more acute with respect to internal conflicts, whether with respect to the prevention or resolution of the latter. When, for instance, can the Secretary-General or the Bureau of the Assembly of Heads of State and Government 'intervene'in a situation of escalating tensions in a Member State, to prevent the development of a full-scale conflict? In other words, what is the 'entry point'? The basis for 'intervention' may be clearer when there is a total breakdown of law and order, as in the case of Liberia, and where, with the attendant human suffering, a spill-over effect is experienced within the neighbouring countries. In such a situation 'intervention' may be justified on humanitarian grounds as well as on the need to restore law and order. However, pre-emptive involvement should also be permitted even in situations where tensions evolve to such a pitch that it becomes apparent that a conflict is in the making. This would transform into real terms the OAU's expressed commitment to conflict prevention". Report of the Secretary-General on Conflicts in Africa: Proposals for a Mechanism for Conflict Prevention and Resolution, Addis Ababa, Organization of African

It is arguable ... that within the context of general international law as well as humanitarian law, Africa should take the lead in developing the notion that sovereignty can be legally transcended, by the 'intervention' of 'outside forces', by their will to facilitate prevention and/or resolution, particularly on humanitarian grounds. In other words, given that every African is his brother's keeper, and that our borders are at best artificial, we in Africa need to use our own cultural and social relationships to interpret the principle of noninterference in such a way that we are enabled to apply it to our advantage in conflict prevention and resolution. In developing the law, in this context, account should also be taken of the need to create and maintain an enabling environment for economic development and progress.

The tragedy of Somalia represented a real test of the ability of the international community to intervene for humanitarian reasons. As the international community was confronted with media images of starving men, women and children which had replaced pictures of wicked gunmen fighting each other, public opinion was swayed in favour of taking some kind of action. Western leaders clearly understood that the deplorable situation in Somalia could not be allowed to continue and that humanitarian intervention was an option.

Thus, the moral legitimacy of the Somali operation was not in doubt. There certainly was a moral obligation for the UN to act, and by acting the Organization alleviated the human suffering that was a consequence of the civil conflict. It is encouraging that member states have at least accepted this obligation. This is reflected in the resolution that established the UN Department of Humanitarian Affairs (DHA).[92] There is under the Resolution a recognition by member states of the necessity to provide the international community with access to people in humanitarian need, and also to provide for their welfare in humanitarian crisis.

Unity, document CM/1710 (LVI), presented to the Fifty-sixth Ordinary Session of the Council of Ministers in Dakar (Senegal), June 22-27, 1992, 12. Quoted in Veuthey, "Assessing Humanitarian Law" in *supra*, note 78 at 134-135. It should also be noted that the Security Council acted in Somalia at the request of African member states. See also, *ibid.*, at 74.

92 See GA Res. 46/182 of 1991.

According to Jan Eliasson, UN Under Secretary-General for Humanitarian Affairs, this resolution has been used "as a diplomatic, formal basis for various negotiations" in creating humanitarian corridors for the provision of assistance to people in need.[93] In Somalia, the Security Council should have acted earlier than it did, as it took significant media pressure, public opinion, and some prodding from the UN Secretary-General[94] to convince the western political establishment of the necessity for initiating "Operation Restore Hope".

What are the legal implications of the Somali action? Some commentators have expressed scepticism regarding its value as a precedent. For them Resolution 794 contains caveats. They argue that although that Resolution was innovative in its acceptance that human suffering can constitute a threat to international peace and security, its significance was undermined by the use of terms such as 'unique', 'extraordinary' and 'exceptional'. This has to be seen, therefore, as an attempt to differentiate Somalia from other cases of internal disorder or instability.[95]

---

93 Eliasson, "The UN and Humanitarian Assistance" (1995) 48: 2 *Journal of International Affairs* 491 at 493. The experience of the UN in the delivery of humanitarian relief to vulnerable groups in conflict, however, has had mixed results. In the case of the Sudan, UNICEF succeeded in negotiating "corridors of tranquillity" to allow for the delivery of humanitarian aid. There was the widespread belief then that an appropriate solution had been found. It was applied in Angola and Mozambique, and attempted in Iraq. Practically, however, the corridors of tranquillity have not worked as anticipated. Warring parties can still prevent the delivery of relief supplies. One option that the UN has used is to conduct negotiations on the ground with the parties to the conflict who are preventing delivery. See *supra*, note 75 at 70.

94 The UN Secretary General had observed from Bosnia how the enormous tragedy in Somalia was being eclipsed by the overwhelming international attention being paid to the 'rich man's war' in the former Yugoslavia. This prompted the media and the international community to reframe the crisis in Somalia in terms more accessible to western public opinion. *Supra*, note 64 at 148.

95 Wheeler and Morris observe that these terms were inserted specifically to assuage the fears of states such as China which may have otherwise blocked a Chapter VII enforcement action. See *supra*, note 83 at 151.

It is argued that while the case is unique because there was no functioning government, the Security Council set a precedent by placing overwhelming humanitarian needs above the traditional restraints against intervention in the internal affairs of sovereign states.[96] Resolution 794 marked a significant inroad into the principle of humanitarian intervention. Unlike Resolution 688 which, as some contend, did not explicitly authorize the use of force to assist the Iraqi Kurds, Resolution 794 recognized that massive human rights violations amounted to a threat to peace and security, and called for the use of "all necessary means" to secure the delivery of humanitarian aid in chaotic situations such as was in Somalia. Although the Resolution was couched in the language of the civil war posing a "threat to the peace" as a result of the massive refugee flows fleeing the fighting, the Council's action is unprecedented to the extent that it clearly specifies the use of collective intervention for humanitarian purposes.[97] Tesón forcefully encapsulates the case for the Security Council action thus:

---

96 Tesón goes even further to argue that "international law properly interpreted did authorize collective humanitarian intervention at the time the Security Council was called upon to act on the Somalian situation. That right was not created by Resolution 794". He maintains that the language in that Resolution, "to the effect that the situation in Somalia had a 'unique character' of a 'deteriorating, complex, and extraordinary nature' does not bar this conclusion. It is obviously true that the situation was unique and extraordinary, in the sense that only this kind of extreme situation warrants the collective use of force. This is perfectly consistent with the doctrine of humanitarian intervention. The doctrine does not recommend the use of force to remedy every human rights problem, ... [o]nly serious human rights violations that cannot be remedied by any other means warrant proportionate collective forcible intervention for the purpose of restoring human rights, provided that the victims themselves welcome the intervention, as they did in Somalia". *Supra*, note 31 at 354.

97 This resolution stemmed from the Secretary General's assessment that UNOSOM was not "an adequate response to the tragedy" whose "unique character" was of a "deteriorating, complex and extraordinary nature, requiring an immediate and exceptional response". See, UN *Chronicle* 30: 1 March 1993 at 13.

[t]he main concern prompting enforcement action by the Security Council was the extreme situation created by a combination of famine, death,
and disease caused by the civil war; the breach of *humanitarian* [em-
phasis in original] law by the warring factions; and the general situation
of anarchy.[98]

Not only did the Resolution specify collective intervention for human
rights purposes, but it goes further by enunciating individual responsibility in situations of interference with humanitarian assistance.[99] The
resolution sent a strong signal that the UN will no longer be prevented
from interfering on humanitarian grounds in the internal affairs of member states. Even so, it probably should not be construed as giving the
Security Council a broad right of intervention in less outrageous
cases.[100]

Somalia provides support for the legitimacy of humanitarian intervention. The overwhelming support that the intervention received[101] provides evidence of new attitudes and readiness to intervene on grounds
of humanitarian concerns. However, observers have also commented
on Somalia as the turning point in the trajectory – when optimistic ideas
about humanitarian intervention were replaced by realism concerning
the limits of such actions. The failures of US and UN military efforts
in Somalia have led to the so-called 'Somalia syndrome' where collective
interventions to prevent mass starvation, genocide, massive exodus of

---

98 *Supra,* note 31 at 351.
99 In late November 1992 for example, the UN Secretary General had reported
    violations of humanitarian law against UN relief workers, including attacks
    on Pakistani peacekeeping forces and the shelling of a World Food Pro-
    gramme ship as it attempted to enter the Mogadishu harbour. See Letter
    Dated 24 November 1992 From the Secretary-General Addressed to the
    President of the Security Council, UN SCOR, 47th Sess., UN Doc. S/24859
    (1992). Cited in *ibid.,* at 350. See also, Jean ed., *Life, Death and Aid: The
    Médecins Sans Frontières Report on World Crisis Intervention* (London:
    Routledge, 1993) at 102.
100 Tesón, *Ibid.,* at 355.
101 See Lewis, "Key UN Members Agree to US Force in Somalia Mission" *New
    York Times*, Dec. 3 1992, at A1.

refugees, and egregious violations of human rights are no longer deemed either politically or operationally feasible.[102] There are obviously lessons to be learnt, as Weiss succinctly puts it, in "overcoming the Somalia syndrome".[103]

Although the successful phase of "Operation Restore Hope" provided a secure environment for relief distribution, the experience took a turn for the worse with the expansion of the UN mandate to include "nation-building" involving disarming the warring factions and arresting uncooperative leaders, as noted earlier. Briefly put, it seems to be the case that unclear and shifting objectives spelled failure and probably compounded the problem. This unfortunately added to neo-isolationist sentiments among politicians who in principle were disposed to support humanitarian missions.[104] However, in cases where preventive and peaceful measures have failed, the international community should muster the moral fortitude to act forcefully, argues Harff.[105]

Furthermore, Weiss has commented that Somalia illustrates a situation in which the US and its Western allies "have not systematically prepared UN operations, with the result that symbols dwarf effective action".[106] In such situations, governments are "particularly prone to crisis induced reactions chosen for their symbolic value and ease of execution rather than their decisive effect".[107] "Visceral reactions are to seek either magical 'quick fixes' or else adhocery, hoping that warring factions will come to their senses". For him, Somalia provided evidence

---

102 See for example, Weiss, "Military – Civilian Humanitarianism: The 'Age of Innocence' is Over" (1995) 2: 2 *International Peacekeeping* 158-174.

103 See Weiss, "Overcoming the Somalia Syndrome – 'Operation Rekindle Hope'?" (1995) 1 *Global Governance: A Review of Multilateralism and International Organizations* 171.

104 As Harff observes, ideally, the development of clear policy guidelines, engagement in a systematization of information about past experience in preventive diplomacy, and anticipation of crises before they evolve are needed. Harff, "Rescuing Endangered Peoples: Missed Opportunities" (1995) 62: 1 *Social Research* 23 at 25.

105 *Ibid.*

106 Weiss, "The United Nations and Civil Wars" (1994) 17: 4 *The Washington Quarterly* 139 at 143.

107 *Ibid.*

that neither approach or reaction is the basis for a military policy that is workable and are both potentially counterproductive.[108]

The lessons of Somalia may be important for future management of what has been characterised as "failed states". In examining the Somalia operation, one notes the various Security Council resolutions remained unclear in prescribing the methods of political settlement and for 're-establishment of national and regional institutions and civil administration'. The result, as Hoffmann comments, is that the operation was plagued by a rift between those who (like the US – some of the time) wanted to rebuild political life 'from the bottom up' (according to the model of 'encouraging institutions') and those (particularly in the UN bureaucracy) who opted for a model 'accommodating existing forces', and of working with the factional leaders, from the top down.[109] This rift specifically did much to reduce the UN's capacity to reach a political solution. Added to this is the fact that expansive mandates can also bog down the UN so much as to limit its capabilities or desire to carry out even the simple task of delivering humanitarian assistance or traditional peacekeeping when it ought to be done.[110] This problem can only be resolved at the political level.[111]

---

108 *Ibid.*

109 Hoffmann, "The Politics and Ethics of Military Intervention" (1995/6) 37: 4 *Survival* 29 at 47.

110 See Dallmeyer, "National Perspectives on International Intervention: From the Outside Looking In" in Daniel & Hayes eds., *Beyond Traditional Peacekeeping* (London: Macmillan Press, 1995), 20 at 33.

111 As the Report of the Independent Working Group on the future of the UN aptly suggests: "[w]hen conditions change in a country after an initial UN force deployment, and proposals are made to augment the action originally mandated by the Security Council, Member States and their publics have a right to know what new operations they are being asked to support and what additional risks are entailed. Keeping the mandates distinct is also essential to protect UN personnel and the integrity of the mission ... . When the Security Council adopts a resolution authorizing the use of military force of any kind, the resolution should clearly state whether that force will be used for peacekeeping, peace-enforcement under Article 40 of the Charter, or collective security under Article 42. It should be clearly provided that forces acting on behalf of the Council will not exceed the Council's man-

The significance of "Operation Restore Hope" for future humanitarian
operations is that the UN succeeded in assuring the delivery of humanitarian relief to Somalis, and perhaps, saving millions of lives. It also
partially succeeded in bringing the warring factions together and averting
a worst case scenario of an all out civil war. In defining the scope of
its humanitarian mandate, the UN will necessarily confront the problems
of political institution building. Caution must, however, be exercised
in terms of the unchecked use of Chapter VII powers to carry out "peace
building" operations.[112] Chapter VII should be used to authorize "peace-
building" missions only as a last resort.[113]

In sum, Somalia provides an example of Security Council authorization for collective humanitarian intervention, at least in situations
where there is no functioning central government leading to civil war
in which massive human rights violations occur. Resolution 794 was

---

date. In addition, any change in the original mandate must be approved
by the Security Council and explained to the participating Member States".
See Report of the Independent Working Group on the Future of the United
Nations, *The United Nations in its Second Half-Century* (New York: Ford
Foundation, 1995) at 20-21.

112 It should only be used in exceptional circumstances where the Security
Council finds the situation so deteriorated that it cannot wait for a peace
agreement to be in place before taking action, or where the warring parties
oppose an international presence but the Security Council decides that such
action would constitute a threat to the peace. Han, "Building A Peace that
Lasts: The United Nations and Post-Civil War Peace-Building" (1994) 26
New York University Journal of International Law and Politics 837 at 868.

113 Donnelly, for one, observes that international agencies have no special
competence in state-building, let alone nation-building. Such tasks, he
argues, by their very nature must be left to local actors. International
agencies may be able to engage in subsidizing start-up costs and the
provision of limited sorts of technical assistance. A functioning system of
government, for him, must be established and maintained by the people
who will operate and live under it. This is the case if the international
community wants that government to respect the human rights of its
citizens, otherwise the new government may become a potential cause of
another humanitarian intervention. Donnelly, "Human Rights, Humanitarian
Crisis, and Humanitarian Intervention" (1993) XLVIII *International Journal*
607 at 639.

an explicit statement of the right of intervention in response to a humanitarian crisis. Setting aside the ultimate outcome of the Somalia operation, it represents the clearest articulation of the principle of humanitarian intervention.

4   THE FORMER YUGOSLAVIA

The intricate and complicated conflict in the former Yugoslavia[114] created one of the most difficult dilemmas and a critical test case for the Western alliance and the UN in terms of international intervention and conflict resolution in the post-Cold War period.

Yugoslavia was created around a Serbian nucleus during a series of wars in the nineteenth and twentieth centuries as the Ottoman Empire gradually lost its grip on the Balkan territories.[115] The strong leadership of Marshal Tito from the end of World War II held the state together and successfully contained ethnic tension during the Cold War. Upon Tito's death in 1980, cracks within the Yugoslav Republic began to emerge. The post-Tito period led to the rearrangement of the governmental structure which was designed to balance competing ethnic groups and interests. This was done by rotating the Presidency among the six republics. One writer remarks that this arrangement in effect contained the seeds of its own destruction.[116]

Partly in response to increasing Serb nationalism and growing anticommunism, independence movements in Croatia and Slovenia gained

---

114 The former federal Republic of Yugoslavia consisted of six republics, namely Slovenia, Croatia, Serbia, Bosnia-Herzegovina, Montenegro, Macedonia and two autonomous regions – Kosovo and Vojvodina. See Weller, "The International Response to the Dissolution of the Socialist Federal Republic of Yugoslavia" (1992) 86 *American Journal of International Law* 569.

115 *Supra*, note 31 at 366. For an exposition of Yugoslavia's troubled history see Steinberg, "International Involvement in the Yugoslavia Conflict" in Damrosch ed., *supra*, note 59, 27.

116 See Steinberg, *ibid.*, at 31-32.

momentum in the late 1980s.[117] After the fall of the communist government, the republics making up Yugoslavia followed the route towards
secession. The Slovenian parliament declared it would no longer follow
Federal legislation,[118] and Croatia took similar steps toward greater
political autonomy. Despite attempts at renegotiating the Federal constitution along loose confederal lines, the political, economic and ethnic
cracks between the various republics widened. On June 25, 1991, Slovenia and Croatia proclaimed their independence. They rejected what
in their estimation was a situation of "economically stifling, politically
outdated, and nationalistically divisive policies of Belgrade".[119] The
result was the outbreak of warfare.[120] Initial international response
to the Yugoslav crisis came from the Conference on Security and Cooperation in Europe (CSCE), the European Union (EU) and the UN. In
spite of opposition from the US, members of the EU granted recognition
to both Slovenia and Croatia on January 15, 1992, under pressure from
Germany.

The outbreak of civil strife in Bosnia-Herzegovina was almost predic-
table and inevitable. Bosnia is ethnically mixed.[121] As Alija Izetbegovic
remarks, the national groups were thoroughly mixed, "almost like the

---

117 *Ibid.*

118 *Supra*, note 114 at 569.

119 Economides & Taylor, "Former Yugoslavia" in Mayall ed., *The New Interventionism 1991-1994: United Nations Experience in Cambodia, Former
Yugoslavia and Somalia* (Cambridge: Cambridge University Press, 1996)
59 at 62.

120 On June 27, 1991, the predominantly Serbian Yugoslav National Army
(JNA) attempted to seize control of Slovenia's international borders. This
attempt was resisted by the Slovenes, with a consequent withdrawal of the
JNA. By July, warfare had erupted between the Croatian armed forces and
the JNA. This fighting arose because the 12% Serbian minority in Croatia
was determined not to relinquish its links with Serbia. Thus, it appeared
the JNA was an instrument of Serbian policy. *Ibid.*

121 In 1991, Bosnia's population was estimated at 4, 364, 00 – of which 43.7%
were Muslims, 31.3% Serb, and 17.2% Croat. See Rubenstein, "Silent
Partners in Ethnic Cleansing: The UN, The EC, and NATO" (1993) 3: 2 *In
Depth – A Journal for Values and Public Policy* 35 at 37.

colors in a Jackson Pollack painting".[122] The rights and interests of Bosnia's mixed population had been protected under Tito's rule, which maintained their equality under the multi-national Yugoslav state. As the federation was disintegrating, this unstable ethnic mix within Bosnia's borders could no longer be held together. A referendum was held on February 29 and March 1, 1992, in which an overwhelming majority of voters favoured independence. The Serbian population boycotted and rejected the result of this referendum. Nevertheless, the government of Bosnia declared independence on March 3, 1992. The signs of violence were clearly written on the wall in the aftermath of this declaration. The chances of violence were amplified by the EC's recognition of Bosnia-Herzegovina, a situation which the Serbs were not prepared to tolerate.[123] Rebel Bosnian Serb forces began engaging in violent activity aimed at toppling the government. The chaos and ethnic strife that followed resulted in widespread and massive human rights violations in which all sides to the conflict were involved. In an effort to preserve their hegemony and capture more territory for a greater Serbian state, the Serbs engaged in the practice of "ethnic cleansing" involving a program of genocide and forced evacuations.[124] Hundreds of thousands of people were killed and close to two million people were displaced from their homes and became refugees as a result of this practice. The atrocities that were reportedly committed were compared by some to the severity and extent of those committed by the Nazis during World War II.[125]

As noted earlier, this intricate conflict meant the international community had to deal with more interlocutors. These not only included the authorities in Serbia but also the Serb Republic of Krajina; Croatian authorities in Croatia, the Croatian military and militias in Bosnia and Herzegovina; the Bosnian government and Bosnian Serb authorities in

---

122 Quoted in *ibid.*, at 56, footnote 3.
123 *Supra*, note 123.
124 See Kinzer, "Serbian Forces Surround a City in a Muslim Enclave in Bosnia" *New York Times*, August 10, 1992, at A1.
125 See *supra*, note 31 at 366, and the sources cited in footnote 180.

the self-declared Republic of Serbska, and the splinter Muslim faction in the autonomous zone of Western Bosnia (Bihac).[126]

Given the complexity of the Yugoslav crisis it was no surprise that the international community was cautious in its reaction and showed a reluctance to intervene. It was in this context that the international community became involved initially through the CSCE, then the EC, and the UN. The EC, seized with the situation, tried to mediate the conflict which member governments saw as a European issue.[127] After attempts to arrange a series of ceasefires and bring about a peaceful resolution of the conflict had failed, [128]Austria, Canada, Hungary, and

---

126 Minear, Clark, Cohen et al., *Humanitarian Action in the Former Yugoslavia: The UN's Role 1991-1993*, Occasional Paper #18 (Providence: Watson Institute for International Studies, 1994) at 3.

127 Lord Owen for example informed a British Parliamentary committee thus: "[a]t the start of all this the United States did not want to be involved in Yugoslavia and the Europeans did not want them to be involved if truth be told. The European Community were very happy this should be a European event to the extent of us developing our peacekeeping operation and we were not too keen to involve the UN". Lord Owen, Testimony before the Foreign Affairs Committee of the House of Commons of the United Kingdom, 10 December 1992, 108. Quoted in Keating & Gammer, "The 'New Look' in Canada's Foreign Policy" (1993) XLVIII *International Journal* 720 at 729-730.

128 The Vance-Owen plan, for example, did not meet the minimum conditions for the achievement of a stable peace because it aimed at preservation of a multi-ethnic state, not ethnic separation. Each of the ten Cantons under the plan would have contained large minorities. Some of the Cantons would have included enclaves totally surrounded by an opposing ethnic group. The later 1994 Contact Group proposal to divide Bosnia 51% -49% between a Muslim-Croat federation and the Bosnian Serbs would have been better, but incorporated serious instabilities such as the isolated Muslim enclaves of Zepa, Sreberenica, and Gorazde, two of which were later overrun with great loss of life. See Kaufmann, "Possible and Impossible Solutions to Ethnic Civil Wars" (1996) 20: 4 *International Security* 136 at 164.For a more detailed analysis of the CSCE and EC response in negotiating a political settlement to the Yugoslav conflict see for example Gow & Freedman, "Intervention in a Fragmenting State: The Case of Yugoslavia" in Rodley ed., *supra*, note 47 at 93-131; *supra*, note 114 at 570-575.

particularly Yugoslavia[129] and other countries requested the Security Council to become involved by sending peacekeeping forces and imposing a mandatory oil embargo on Yugoslavia.

The Security Council finally considered taking some form of action. In its initial meeting on September 25, 1991, the Yugoslav delegate pointed out that "Yugoslavia can no longer be simply repaired. It should be re-defined".[130] India argued that consent manifested in a formal request by Yugoslavia would be needed for the Council to consider intervention. China and Zimbabwe reminded members of the significance of nonintervention in the internal affairs of other states.[131] Yemen cautioned that in future the Security Council would encounter similar situations requiring creative approaches.[132] Zaire viewed the conflict as a "civil war".[133] Russia stressed the "significance of a political settlement, not only for inter-governmental conflicts, but also for intra-State conflicts ... show[ing] how dangerous the growth of separatism and national extremism [is], not only for each individual country but for entire regions".[134] Britain affirmed "the strong international dimension" of the conflict, while the US referred to the danger of escalation and the "dangerous impact on Yugoslavia's neighbours, who face refugee flows, energy shortfalls and the threat of a spillover of fighting" as a matter of primary concern.[135]

In response to these concerns, Resolution 713 was unanimously passed. The initial mandate of the UN expressed concern that the continuation of the war constituted a threat to international peace and security. Acting under Chapter VII of the Charter, it decided that all states implement a general and complete embargo on all deliveries of

---

129 The Yugoslav request stated the federal presidency's backing for a meeting especially when it seemed some members of the Security Council were going to raise objections under Article 2 (7) of the Charter. *Supra*, note 114 at 577-578.
130 Quoted in *ibid.*, at 578.
131 *Ibid.*
132 *Ibid.*
133 *Ibid.*, at 579.
134 *Ibid.*
135 *Ibid.*

weapons and military equipment. Following from that the Council also adopted Resolution 743 on February 21, 1992 which established the United Nations Protection Force (UNPROFOR). This force was created following the Secretary-General's recommendation that in the context of the ceasefire then in effect, such a force could become successful in consolidating the ceasefire and facilitating negotiation of a comprehensive settlement.[136] As noted earlier, recognition of Bosnia-Herzegovina by the EC intensified the violence in that republic in the spring of 1992. As large portions of territory came under the control of the JNA and Serbian militias, reports of atrocities being committed began surfacing. Security Council Resolution 752 was adopted calling for, among other things, both parties to stop fighting and to respect the territorial integrity of each republic. Resolution 757 came after that, calling for economic sanctions against Serbia for its continued and egregious human rights violations.

The Security Council's contemplation of employing coercive measures came in the summer of 1992. On August 13, 1992, the Security Council passed Resolution 770. Acting under Chapter VII, the Council called upon states "to take nationally or through regional agencies or arrangements *all measures necessary* to facilitate in coordination with the United Nations the delivery ... of humanitarian assistance ... in ... Bosnia and Herzegovina". While it recognized that the situation in Bosnia constituted a "threat to international peace and security", it was also "deeply concerned" by the "reports of abuses against civilians imprisoned in camps, prisons and detention centres" which had so shocked the international community that it referred to the use of all necessary measures to have them closed. This resolution further expanded the mandate of UNPROFOR to deliver humanitarian assistance, and in performing this task to use "all measures necessary".[137] To this

---

136 *Supra*, note 119 at 66.
137 UNPROFOR II's mandate according to the UN Secretary-General was to "support UNHCR's efforts to deliver humanitarian relief throughout Bosnia and Herzegovina, and in particular to provide protection, at the UNHCR's request, where and when UNHCR considered such protection necessary". Quoted in *ibid.*, at 68.

end, several thousand UN peacekeepers were put on the ground to protect humanitarian convoys with totally inadequate military back-up. These forces relied almost entirely on negotiations to get humanitarian assistance to where it was needed the most, which frequently resulted in delays and disruptions. Added to this was the fact the UN and NGO officials were not immune from attack.

Faced with the failure of several attempts at protecting the Bosnian muslims, the Security Council passed Resolution 781 which directed the imposition of a "no-fly" zone over Bosnia to prevent Serbian attacks from hindering the delivery of humanitarian relief supplies. Not only were the Bosnian Muslims vulnerable to Serb attacks in the UN declared safe zones; even UN peacekeepers and humanitarian aid workers became hostages to the whims of local combatants. One commentator remarks that the Bosnian Serbs in those circumstances viewed the UN Resolutions as attempts by the US and EC to give the appearance of protecting the Muslims while doing nothing.[138] As it became clear that the so-called UN designated "safe zones" were anything but safe and enforcement action proved difficult, the Security Council, under Resolution 816, authorized member states to "take all necessary measures in the airspace of the Republic of Bosnia and Herzegovina in the event of further violations to ensure compliance with the ban on flights". Unlike disagreements regarding the interpretation of resolutions concerning Iraq, the Security Council this time specifically approved the enforcement by NATO fighter planes. Acting under authority of these Resolutions, NATO fighter planes embarked on a series of bombing campaigns against Bosnian Serb positions that violated the "safe havens" designated by the UN to deter further attacks. NATO's use of force may have ended the commission of further atrocities in Bosnia and facilitated more realistic proposals towards ending the war. In December 1995, the warring parties started negotiations designed to bring the war in Bosnia to an end. The initialling of the agreements known as the Dayton Peace

---

138 Darnton, "Serbs Feel Invincible" New York Times, June 5 1993, cited in *supra*, note 121 at 41.

Accord in November 1995 culminated in a peace settlement signed in
Paris on December 14, 1995.[139]

The Dayton Agreement, despite paying lip service to a unitary Bosnia, ratifies and seeks to strengthen existing territorial divisions. It gives
grounds for qualified hope for a stable, relatively peaceful Bosnia. It
requires the withdrawal of all Bosnian Serb forces from the Sarajevo
suburbs as well as from a corridor stretching from Sarajevo to Gorazde,
and assigns these areas to the Bosnian government. It also establishes
a NATO-led implementation Force for Bosnia (IFOR) to oversee the implementation of the military part of the Peace Plan.[140] Recently, the US
Special Envoy Richard Holbrooke has returned to Bosnia in a bid to

---

139 The Dayton Accord consists of a set of international treaties, viz: the
    General Framework Agreement for Peace in Bosnia and Herzegovina, twel-
    ve Annexes (each constituting an international treaty) and the Agreement
    on Initialling, which deals with the modalities of conclusion and entry into
    force of the other agreements. Most of the General Framework Agreement,
    concluded by the Republic of Bosnia and Herzegovina, the Republic of
    Croatia and the Federal Republic of Yugoslavia, obliges the parties to
    "respect and promote fulfilment" of each annexed agreement. This annexed
    Agreements set forth conditions for peace in Bosnia and Herzegovina and
    are concluded mainly by Bosnia and Herzegovina and the two entities
    directly involved in the conflict (which are not parties to the General Frame-
    work Agreement) i.e. the Republika Srpska and the Federation of Bosnia
    and Herzegovina. The General Framework Agreement thus guarantees the
    implementation of the annexed agreements from both political and juridical
    viewpoints. See Gaeta, "The Dayton Peace Agreements and International
    Law" (1996) 7: 2 *European Journal of International Law* 147. See also,
    "The General Framework Agreement for Peace in Bosnia and Herzegovina"
    reproduced in (1996) XLVII *Review of International Affairs* 1-36. For a
    detailed analysis of the human rights guarantees under the Dayton Peace
    Accord and their implementation see for example, Sloan, "The Dayton
    Peace Agreement: Human Rights Guarantees and their Implementation"
    (1996) 7: 2 *European Journal of International Law* 207.
140 For a brief review of NATO's role under the Peace Plan see for example,
    Solana, "NATO's Role in Bosnia" (1996) April 15, *Review of International
    Affairs* 1-3. See also, Talamanca, "The Role of NATO in the Peace
    Agreement for Bosnia and Herzegovina" (1996) 7: 2 *European Journal
    of International Law* 164.

break the stalemate in the accord's implementation, and issued a warning to the effect that if the regional leaders fail to deliver on their commitments, penalties will be imposed. The Croatian President and the Bosnian Muslim leader have jointly issued statements promising to halt recent ethnic violence, to acknowledge the right of refugees to return to their homes, and to see to it that Croatian war crimes suspects are surrendered for trial by the international war crimes tribunal in the Hague. The US wants to see the Dayton accord in force and working before the NATO-led implementation force pulls out next year, and is frustrated with the lack of progress so far.[141]

The war in the former Yugoslavia raised particularly difficult questions and dilemmas for the international community on the issue of intervention in its moral, legal and practical dimensions. Morally, there was a sense of revulsion occasioned by atrocities committed in the course of the conflict as images of emaciated prisoners held in Serb-controlled concentration camps, the shelling of cities with women and children dying or wounded with no food or medical supplies, and accounts of murders and rape filled television screens around the world. In those circumstances, international public opinion certainly favoured taking action to redress this abhorrent state of affairs. Some critics argue that foreign policy or international response should not be driven by emotional reactions fostered by the media. In line with this mode of thinking, hesitation characterised involvement in the Yugoslavian civil war in its early stages as Western governments believed military intervention in Bosnia would pose unacceptable risks to the lives of soldiers committed to such an endeavour, and that intervention would not end the fighting. Indeed, some policymakers in the US, for example, argued against the commission of ground troops in Bosnia for fear of becoming bogged down in a quagmire, and of sustaining casualties of major proportions[142] – an enterprise that would have in the end been difficult

---

141 *New York Times*, August 7, 1997 at A3.

142 There is a view current in American military circles termed the "Powell Doctrine" which suggests US intervention should only be undertaken if, and only if, success can be achieved decisively and with minimal losses through the employment of overwhelming force. This thinking poses

to justify to their domestic constituents. The Somalia syndrome reinforced this view, and led to a cautionary approach. Yet the unwillingness
and inability to act in the early stages of the conflict had a crippling
effect on the UN and put its credibility at stake. Resolution 770, for
example, promised more than member governments were willing to do.
"All measures necessary" were never taken to ensure that humanitarian
aid was delivered. In the words of Higgins: "we have chosen to respond
to major unlawful violence not by stopping that violence, but by trying
to provide relief to the suffering. But our choice of policy allows the
suffering to continue".[143]

The provision of humanitarian assistance surely alleviated human
suffering and saved lives. Under the protection of UNPROFOR much
needed relief supplies were brought to alleviate the hardships endured
by besieged communities. But this provision of humanitarian relief also
had serious military and political consequences. Some Bosnian Muslims,
for instance, considered the delivery of inadequate relief as merely
sustaining them until they could be killed by the Serbs. UNPROFOR was
powerless in protecting the inhabitants of Sarajevo who constantly came
under shelling and sniper fire; the declaration of "safe havens" meant
nothing as Serb gunners pounded those enclaves; agencies like the

---

problems for American military intervention, even if it is solely for
humanitarian purposes. See Krauthammer, "Drawing the Line at Genocide"
The Washington Post, December 11, 1992. Quoted in Lewy, "The Case
for Humanitarian Intervention" (1993) Fall *Orbis* 621 at 623. In 1992, for
instance, Lieutenant-General Barry McCaffrey, representing the Joint Chiefs
of Staff, told the U.S Congress that between 60, 000 and 120, 000 soldiers
would be needed just to ensure the delivery of relief supplies, and pointed
out that as many as 400, 000 troops would be needed to implement a
ceasefire. Similarly, General Lewis Mackenzie of Canada cautioned the
US Senate that "if [y]ou get involved with the delivery of humanitarian aid,
you'll have Americans killed" Gordon, "Conflict in the Balkans: 60, 000
Needed for Bosnia, A US General Estimates" *New York Times*, August 12,
1992, at A8. Cited in Eisner, "Humanitarian Intervention in the Post-Cold
War Era" (1993) 11 *Boston University International Law Journal* 195 at
219.

143 Higgins, "The New United Nations and Former Yugoslavia" (1993) 69
International Affairs at 469.

UNHCR were compelled to escort refugees from Serb-held areas. The UN was seen by many of the war victims as accomplices to the atrocities that had been committed.

The Security Council, as noted earlier, gave UNPROFOR a humanitarian mandate without the necessary military backup given the situation on the ground. Although Resolution 776 authorised UNPROFOR to support UNHCR efforts in the delivery of humanitarian aid, UNPROFOR's use of force was deemed politically undesirable, due to the increased risk of troop casualties. Moreover, the unwillingness to use force in delivering humanitarian assistance may be partly viewed as the desire to remain neutral or impartial. Indeed the very deployment of a UN force on the ground gave Western governments a justification for not undertaking air strikes for fear of hitting their own troops or turning them into Serb hostages. As the former UN under-secretary general for peacekeeping operations, Kofi Annan, admits, "[t]he reality is there are situations when you cannot assist people unless you are prepared to take certain [military] measures".[144] The UN humanitarian assistance program was used as an excuse for the lack of military intervention. Weiss argues that humanitarian assistance combined with inadequate military force was a "powerful diversion" substituting for more creative military strategies to end the war.[145] Taking action in providing inadequate military support for the delivery of humanitarian assistance to people in need, while neglecting responsibility for protecting those same people against murder, ethnic cleansing and rape, led to a deep moral crisis in the UN's humanitarian action.[146]

---

144 Quoted in Weiss, "UN Responses in the Former Yugoslavia: Moral and Operational Choices" (1994) 8 *Ethics and International Affairs* 1 at 6.

145 *Supra*, note 105 at 166. See also, Roberts, *supra*, note 37 at 443.

146 Robert Jackson observes with regard to interpreting the international response that "[t]he ... involvement in Bosnia did not indicate moral indifference or a lack of humanitarian concern on the part of those leaders of states who were in a position to do something. Nor did it indicate the easiest choice in the circumstances – that would have been to wash their hands of Bosnia and do nothing at all. It indicated anguish and frustration concerning what, if anything, could be done about the human suffering the conflict was causing". He goes on to maintain that "[i]t also reflected an absence

The Security Council Resolutions discussed earlier provided legal justification for humanitarian intervention in the former Yugoslavia. Resolution 770, among others, authorized the use of force by states to ensure the delivery of humanitarian assistance. While the Council recognized that the situation in Bosnia constituted a threat to international peace and security, it also made references to the egregious human rights violations that were going on, in which civilians were subjected to murders, ethnic cleansing, and rapes. In the debates preceding the passage of Resolution 770, even delegates who were skeptical about authorizing individual states to act as opposed to a collective UN intervention conceded that the situation in the former Yugoslavia called for the use of force. India for example referred to the desperate plight of the civilian population which demanded urgent response not excluding the use of force. The Indian representative stated that India was

> not opposed to the concept of the use of force in the present situation ... We have no doubt whatever that the critical and desperate plight of the population demands urgent and effective reponse on the part of the international community and that such a response cannot and must not exclude the use of force.[147]

The delegate from Zimbabwe noted the "pain and agony of fratricidal carnage that has accompanied the disintegration of what used to be the Socialist Federal Republic of Yugoslavia". He continued: "Zimbabwe has consistently supported efforts within the Security Council that we believed had a chance of assisting to bring about peace and stability

---

of confidence that armed intervention could successfully deal with the problem; indeed, the main Western military powers feared that it would cause an even greater loss of life to the civilian population of Bosnia and to their own forces. Concerned about the humanitarian problem but worried about the safety of their own people, those leaders followed what they evidently believed was the only responsible course of action open to them at the time". Jackson, "Armed Humanitarianism" (1993) XLVIII *International Journal* 579 at 603.

147 See *Provisional Verbatim Record of the Three Thousand One Hundred and Sixth Meeting*, UN SCOR, 47th Sess., plen.mtg., at 9-17. UNDoc. S/PV.3106 (1992).

... ". Thus, "Zimbabwe is of the view that any necessary measures taken or arrangements made to deal with this crisis have to be undertaken as a collective enforcement measure ... ". The representative from Ecuador maintained "the international community cannot be insensitive to the suffering of defenceless human beings ... [a]ccordingly the states that answer the Council's call will be authorized to use every means necessary to achieve the specific aim in question because of the exceptionally urgent circumstances that prevail in Bosnia and Herzegovina".[148] The debates show a strong endorsement for the doctrine of humanitarian intervention.

The intervention by NATO forces is partly explicable in the sense of it having a humanitarian dimension. It was an action undertaken pursuant to authorization from the UN with the aim of ending the abhorrent human rights situation as a result of the conflict.[149] Although initial UN authorization was limited to the use of air power to securing delivery of humanitarian assistance and enforcement of the "no-fly" zones, those limited purposes were exceeded in some instances. NATO, for example, responded by taking strong action against the Bosnian Serb bombing of a Sarajevo market in which 37 people were killed.[150] Situations of this kind, though, depict the difficulties involved in the insistence upon the neutrality of humanitarian interventions. Two kinds of problems are encountered here.[151] One is the territorial issue involving the merits of the dispute, claims put forward by the various parties,

---

148 See, *ibid.*, at 9-10, 14-16.
149 See for example, *Provisional Verbatim Record of the Three Thousand One Hundred and Ninety-First Meeting*, UN SCOR 48th Sess., plen.mtg. at 19-21, UN Doc.S/PV.3191 (1993) referring to statements by delegates such as the US (pointing to the international community resolve to enforce Security Council resolutions against those who commit unspeakable violations of human rights), France (commenting on the use of force to enforce the no-fly zones), Cape Verde (maintaining that the Security Council must use its authority to put a stop to the tragedy of the Bosnian people) and Pakistan (citing the abhorrent campaign of "ethnic cleansing"). Cited in *supra*, note 31 at 368.
150 *Ibid.*
151 *Ibid.*

questions relating to who has the right to which part of the territory, and whether secession is justified, etc. These are hard cases about which any intervenor must strive to be impartial. The second situation involves human rights abuses, and violations of international humanitarian law generally. Neutrality or impartiality will not be the issue here as intervention must target the perpetrators, and compel them to put a stop to those practices. If both sides to the conflict are guilty, then it is incumbent to stop them.[152] The traditional UN peacekeeping approach and its insistence upon neutrality and impartiality between the perpetrators and their victims has come under a lot of criticism. In Bosnia, the circumstances of the war were such that the intervenors had to ignore directives on impartiality and take sides in support of the victims. Such an action, however, need not prejudge the merits of the dispute.[153]

UN involvement in the Former Yugoslavian conflict could be justified on three grounds. First, there was the refugee situation. The impact of massive exodus of refugees across borders was evident. More than 500,000 Yugoslav refugees fled into other European countries. Bosnian Serbs and Croats were resettled in Serbia while temporary sanctuary was found for hundreds of thousands of Bosnian Muslims and Croats who were displaced as a result of the conflict.[154]

Second, the humanitarian situation resulting from the war was equally severe. The Bosnian Serb military strategy which centred on attacking Muslim communities consequently left large segments of the civilian population bereft of essential supplies of food, medicine, power, and water. These disruptions carried with them starvation, exposure to the natural elements of the weather and disease. Humanitarian concerns were thus significant and fell within the mandate of the UN Security Council.

Third, human rights violations perpetrated especially by the Bosnian Serbs for instance, mistreatment of Muslims held in concentration camps and widespread rape of Muslim women shocked the international community. The human rights situation by itself provided the necessary

---

152 *Ibid.*

153 *Ibid.*

154 Steinberg, "International Involvement in the Yugoslavian Conflict" in Damrosch ed., *supra*, note 59, at 53.

justification for involvement by the CSCE as evidenced in the Moscow Declaration of October 1991.[155] In the Moscow Declaration, leaders of the CSCE suggested their preparedness regarding intervention to enforce a member-state's obligation to respect human rights. The least that can be done in that regard will be to send rapporteurs without the target state's consent. The CSCE proceeded cautiously regarding the former Yugoslavia, following the EC's and the UN's lead, though by mid 1992 it had sent human rights monitors into Serbian areas.[156]

In sum, the situation in the former Yugoslavia showed the Security Council's preparedness, at least in principle, to authorize the use of force for humanitarian reasons. Humanitarian concerns certainly played a prominent role in the international response to the conflict.

5   RWANDA

The civil war and the consequent series of massacres that followed in the wake of the death of Rwanda's President, Juvenal Habyarimana, on April 6, 1994, have been described by most commentators as constituting genocide.[157] Rwanda is not a simple case of tribal or ethnic conflict as has been presented by some observers. The root causes of

---

155 Conference on Security and Cooperation in Europe, "Document of the Moscow Meeting on the Human Dimension", October 3, 1991. (1991) 30 *International Legal Materials* 1670.

156 *Supra*, note 154 at 53-54.

157 The conventional sense of the word genocide indicates a human community based on ethnic, national, or religious ties is singled out for extermination. The Convention on the Prevention and Punishment of the Crime of Genocide, 1948, defines genocide as "acts committed with intent to destroy, in whole or in part, a national, ethnical, racial or religious group, such as:
   a) Killing members of the group;
   b) Causing serious bodily or mental harm to members of the group;
   c) Deliberately inflicting on the group conditions of life calculated to bring about its physical destruction in whole or in part;
   d) Imposing measures intended to prevent births within the group;
   e) Forcibly transferring children of the group to another group".

the civil war are traceable to the impact of Belgian colonisation on Hutu-Tutsi relations in Rwanda, and to political manipulation of that cleavage by Belgian and Rwandan elites in competition in the period preceding Belgian decolonisation.[158] As the Report by African Rights notes,

> Hutus and Tutsis existed a century ago, but the two categories were defined in very different terms in those days. They were far less mutually hostile. Colonial rule and its attendant racial ideology, followed by independent governments committed to Hutu supremacy and intermittent inter-communal violence, have dramatically altered the nature of the Hutu-Tutsi problem, and made the divide between the two far sharper and more violent. In short, the political manipulation of ethnicity is the main culprit for today's ethnic problem.[159]

Hutus and Tutsis did not have a mutual ancestral hatred for each other. The ethnic divide is attributable to the political and social reorganisation that was largely the influence of colonialism.[160] Throughout the period of colonial rule, support vacillated between the two groups. The intention of the colonial powers was to "divide and rule" – a strategy that basically changed the nature of the relationships between the two groups. Colonial Rwanda thus contributed to the character of Rwandan society.[161]

Upon attainment of independence from Belgium in 1962, violent political competition and clashes resulted in the deaths of thousands of

---

158 See Jones, "Intervention Without Borders: Humanitarian Intervention in Rwanda, 1990-1994" (1995) 24: 2 *Millennium: Journal of International Studies* 225 at 226; Destexhe, "The Third Genocide" (1994-95) 97 *Foreign Policy* 3 at 5-6. For detailed studies of the background to the conflict see for example, Newbury, *The Cohesion of Oppression: Clientship and Ethnicity in Rwanda, 1860-1960* (New York, NY: Columbia University Press, 1988); Prunier, *The Rwandese Crisis (1959-1994): From Cultural Mythology to Genocide* (London: C. Hurst & Co., 1995); O'Halloran, *Humanitarian Intervention and the Genocide in Rwanda* (London: Institute for the Study of Conflict & Terrorism, 1995).
159 African Rights, *Rwanda: Death, Despair and Defiance* (London: African Rights Publications, 1994) at iii.
160 O'Halloran, *supra*, note 158 at 3.
161 Destexhe, *supra*, note 158 at 6.

the Tutsi minority, and forcing another tens of thousands to seek refuge in Burundi, Tanzania and Uganda. In 1973, Habyarimana seized power in a military coup, establishing the National Revolutionary Movement for Development (MRND). Since then, Rwanda became a one-party state with the "Tutsi factor" mainly absent in Rwandese politics. Habyarimana put in place a system of ethnic quotas for jobs and educational opportunities. Power was mainly concentrated in a minority of northern Hutus.[162] Response to internal and external pressures led to opening up of the political system and the formation of other parties in June 1991.[163]

In October 1990, the Rwandan Patriotic Front (RPF), which was made up of Tutsi exiles who had sought refuge in neighbouring countries after the majority Hutu overthrew the rule of the minority Tutsi following independence, initiated a military offensive into Rwanda from Uganda. For the next three years, a low intensity civil conflict was waged between the Rwandan government and the RPF. The RPF demands included the return of all Rwandan refugees and the formation of a government that would promote ethnic reconciliation. The RPF achieved limited success. The Rwandan government began a security crackdown. Around this time, the international community started protesting human rights violations in Rwanda and threatening Kigali with sanctions.

Pressure from the international community resulted in the signing of the Arusha Accords in August 1993 between Habyarimana and the RPF.[164] This agreement offered the prospect for peace, democracy and national reconciliation. Yet it also encountered strong opposition from

---

162 Jones, *supra*, note 158 at 227.
163 *Supra*, note 159 at iv.
164 The Accords dealt with some of the most important issues underlying the conflict such as the return of Rwandan refugees and resettlement of displaced people, power sharing, and integration of the armed forces. This UN-brokered peace had an implementation program that called for the deployment of what became known as the United Nations Assistance Mission for Rwanda (UNAMIR I), to guarantee peace and the transition to democracy; creation of a transitional government involving the parties in power, the opposition parties and the RPF; and, the holding of multi-party elections no later than 1995. See *supra*, note 159 at 32-33.

Hutu extremists who feared an end to their hitherto privileged status in Rwandan society. These extremists were bent on derailing implementation of the Arusha Accords and its supporters including moderates within the Rwandan government.

With the peace plan in jeopardy, on April 6, 1994, President Habyarimana and the President of Burundi died in a plane crash caused by the firing of rockets at Kigali airport.[165] This incident not only renewed the civil conflict with the RPF but led to the creation of a political vacuum in which Rwandan government forces, the Presidential Guard, and the Hutu youth militias (the *interahamwe* and the *impuzamugbmi*) engaged in killing Tutsis and moderate Hutu leaders. The wave of terror unleashed resulted in the most brutal and systematic slaughter of civilians ever witnessed on the African continent.[166] In the wake of this tragedy, the RPF launched a fresh offensive from Uganda. It finally defeated the remnants of the Hutu-dominated government forces in July 1994, and unilaterally declared a ceasefire.

Although about 2,700 troops constituting UNAMIR had maintained a presence in Rwanda at the time to oversee implementation of the Arusha Accords, they were powerless in stopping the massacres. The Rwandan Prime Minister, members of her government, along with Belgian UN guards assigned to protect her, were brutally killed. Belgium withdrew its military contingent serving with UNAMIR following this incident, and urged the Security Council to withdraw continuation of the UNAMIR operation given the circumstances of chaos and mayhem in the country.[167] It is estimated that up to one million Rwandans were killed. Furthermore, an estimated 1.3 million fled to neighbouring countries with a further 2.2 million people internally displaced. In a nutshell, over half Rwanda's total population estimated at 8.1 million

---

165 Although the source of the attack has not been determined, Hutu extremists are suspected of being responsible for the attack. The Rwandan military, however laid, the blame on the doorstep of the Tutsi. *Supra*, note 31 at 362.

166 *Supra*, note 83 at 155.

167 Hindell, "An Interventionist Manifesto" (1996) XIII: 2 *International Relations* 23 at 28-29.

before the genocide, has either been killed, annihilated by epidemics, or internally displaced as a result of the civil war.[168]

Despite the humanitarian crisis of almost unprecedented magnitude engendered by the civil conflict, the initial international response was less than enthusiastic. The initial Security Council reaction was to pass Resolution 912 on April 21, 1994, reducing the number of UNAMIR troops to 270 in order to prevent sustaining more casualties, and in the hope that the violence would end.[169] The situation, however, continued to deteriorate. On May 13, 1994, the UN Secretary General, in his report to the Security Council, stated:

> [t]he world community has witnessed with horror and disbelief the slaughter and suffering of innocent civilians in Rwanda. While the chances for a lasting peace are fundamentally in the hands of the political and military leaders of the country, the international community cannot ignore the atrocious effects of this conflict on innocent civilians.[170]

He urged the Security Council for a reexamination of Resolution 912 and a reconsideration of appropriate action to end the massacres. The Security Council appeared to adjust to the reality of what was going on in Rwanda. On May 17, 1994, the Security Council unanimously passed Resolution 918, increasing the strength of UNAMIR to 5, 500 troops. The Resolution called for an expanded mandate for UNAMIR which included protection of displaced persons, refugees and civilians. It also called for the creation and maintenance of secure humanitarian areas, and the provision of support for humanitarian relief operations. However, these troops were not deployed at the time, the reason being that member states made no commitments to provide the requisite number of troops for such an undertaking. The delay by member states meant

---

168 Martin, *International Solidarity and Cooperation in Assistance to African Refugees: Burden-Sharing or Burden-Shifting* (Paper presented at the Eighth Annual Meeting, Academic Council on the United Nations System, New York, 19-21 June 1995) at 14-15.

169 *Supra*, note 31 at 363.

170 UN Doc.S/1994/565, 13 May 1994.

little or no international action taken that might have prevented or
reduced the enormity of the refugee situation. As Robert Oakley observed "[a]t a minimum, an earlier response would have had many more
relief workers and supplies on the ground to start work at once rather
than after death and debilitation from disease and hunger had taken such
a heavy toll".[171] With media coverage of the escalating outrage, the
international community began to take action in what might be characterized as a typical case of "too little, too late".[172]

Given the absence of multilateral action, France unilaterally undertook a UN- authorised intervention in Rwanda. "Operation Turquoise"
began on June 22, 1994, and by July 2, the French concluded that the
most that could be accomplished was the setting up of a security zone
in southwestern Rwanda.[173] Having fulfilled its duty after two months,
and rejecting appeals to prolong its mission, French forces withdrew,
handing over control of the security zone to a UN peacekeeping force
composed primarily of African units. Giving reasons for the intervention
France stressed the strictly humanitarian nature of the operation. At the
Security Council, France maintained the aim of its

> initiative is exclusively humanitarian: the initiative is motivated by the
> plight of the people, in the face of which, we believe, the international
> community cannot and must not remain passive. It will not be the mis-
> sion of our soldiers in Rwanda to interpose themselves between the
> warring parties, still less to influence in any way the military and
> political situation. Our objective is simple: to rescue endangered civil-
> ians and put an end to the massacres, and to do so in an impartial man-
> ner.[174]

Also, the French Prime Minister argued that France was under an obligation to end "one of the most unbearable tragedies in recent his-

---

171 Oakley, "A Slow Response on Rwanda", *The Washington Post*, 27 July
    1994, at A27. Quoted in *supra*, note 168 at 15.
172 Martin, *ibid.*
173 Some 3, 000 French troops were involved in the operation and close to
    1.5 to 2 million people ended up in the security zone.
174 UN SCOR, 49th Sess., 3392d., at 5-6, UN Doc.S/PV.3392 (1994).

tory".[175] Similarly, the French Defence Minister emphasised that France was not in Rwanda for a national French action. It intervened to enforce a UN resolution to stop atrocities.[176]

In spite of these statements, France's motives for the intervention had been questioned. Posen for example, questions how much good the intervention did for the Tutsi inside the safe zone. To what extent was the intervention a way of protecting remnants of the extremist-dominated Hutu government of Rwanda from destruction by the RPF?[177] Skepticism was expressed about the French intervention since France had a long-standing relationship with, and supported the Habyarimana government that had engaged in massive human rights violations against Rwandans. It also supported that government militarily with troops and arms in its counter-offensives against the RPF in 1992 and 1993. Moreover, some observers argued that France was apprehensive of its credibility in Africa, particularly since an RPF victory meant a Rwanda under the control of Anglophones. The regional impact of an RPF victory would also mean curtailing the power of Mobutu Sese Sekou, a loyal ally of France, thereby weakening France's hold in the Central African region – traditionally an area under its sphere of influence.[178] For these reasons there was ambiguity surrounding French action given it had significant political and economic interests in Rwanda, and in the region, and might not have been wholly guided by humanitarian motivations.

Operation Turquoise nevertheless served a significant humanitarian purpose. It provided security and logistical support to humanitarian

---

175 Nundy, "Balladur Takes a Moral Stance on Intervention" *The Independent*, 23 June 1994. He had earlier stated five criteria that would form the basis for French action: the operation must have UN authorization and the support of other countries; all operations should be limited to humanitarian actions; troops should remain near the Zairean border; they should not enter into the heart of Rwanda, and finally, the mission should be limited to a maximum of weeks before handing over to a strengthened UNAMIR force. Quoted in *supra*, note 83 at 157-158.

176 *Ibid.*, at 158.

177 Posen, "Military Responses to Refugee Disasters" (1996) 21: 1 *International Security* 72 at 97

178 See *supra*, note 83 at 158-159; Destexhe, *supra*, note 158 at 11.

assistance operations both inside Rwanda and in the refugee camps in Zaire. It was prompt action that saved the lives of several thousand Tutsis in the period of frenzy, and before the full deployment of UNAMIR II.[179]

The moral considerations involving the genocide in Rwanda with regard to taking action either to prevent or suppress it are overwhelming. Once the genocide began in the wake of the assassination of the Presidents of Rwanda and Burundi, the international community took little or no action. Yet there was evidence to suggest that an impending disaster was in the making, not forgetting Rwanda's track record of previous massacres even dating back to its independence. Even in the period between October 1990 and April 1994 "it [was] possible to trace the evolution of the strategy of mass killing. Many military and civilian institutions were largely or entirely dedicated to mass murder, including the Presidential Guard, the Rwandese Armed Forces, the gendarmerie and the interahamwe militia".[180] The UN had knowledge and was warned that genocide was being planned but the information either got lost in the bureaucracy, or the Rwandan situation was considered one of low priority.[181] Once the reign of terror began, the inability of

---

179 Destexhe, *ibid.*, at 11.

180 *Supra*, note 159 at 42.

181 Hindell writes that "[i]n January 1994 the [UN] Force Commander General Romeo Dallaire, forwarded to the Secretariat information gained from a 'very important government official' turned informer. Dallaire's cable described a lurid but detailed plan to assassinate moderate politicians at a public ceremony with the expectation that it would provide an opportunity for a murderous attack on the Belgian UNAMIR soldiers protecting the government. The informer also estimated that his units could kill a thousand targeted Tutsi in twenty minutes".See *Supra*, note 167 at 27-28. The former UN Secretary General Boutros Boutros-Ghali has in retrospect acknowledged that the UN was slow to warn of plans for the genocide in Rwanda, and that greater notice should have been taken of the Dallaire message. He admitted that the Security Council should have been given an explicit warning about the possibility of genocide. One reason for not acting on the cable, according to him, was that "it was hard to believe ... ethnic slaughter could be organized systematically in one of the world's poorest countries". See Knox, "Boutros-Ghali admits Rwanda errors", *The Globe*

UNAMIR to cope with the crisis prompted a withdrawal. This withdrawal could be interpreted as a renunciation of the moral responsibility of the UN with a result that diminished its credibility in Rwanda even though many humanitarian NGOs continued to work at a risk to their lives caught in the throes of violence.[182] The UN Secretary General, however, cast the net widely in admitting the mistake of the UN and its responsibility. He stated that "we are all responsible for this disaster, not only the super-powers, but also the African countries, the non-governmental organizations, the entire international community. There has been a genocide and the world is talking about what it should do. It is a scandal".[183]

One of the reasons, if not the main reason, for the slow response to Rwanda lies in the lack of political will on the part of the US in showing its leadership, in terms of making any substantial commitment. As Iraq, Bosnia and Somalia show, American involvement was crucial. Hesitation in Rwanda is due to the absence of US geopolitical interests in the area. As well, the Somalia syndrome had a role to play regarding inaction on the part of the US. The situation in Rwanda was, however, different from Somalia. Unlike Somalia, Rwanda was not swamped with weapons, and the militias carried out attacks mainly armed with machetes. But the Somalia syndrome was still at work, so much so that America had to rethink its foreign policy.[184] It is instructive, however,

---

and Mail, September 10, 1998, at A9.

182 Tyagi, "The Concept of Humanitarian Intervention Revisited" (1995) 16 Michigan Journal of International Law 883 at 904.

183 Supra, note 167 at 30.

184 Destexhe, supra, note 158 at 10. The result was the Presidential Decision Directive on Reforming Multilateral Peace Operations (PDD25) issued on May 3, 1994, which spelled out strict guidelines for American military participation in multilateral military operations. These guidelines for US involvement include: impact on US national interests; availability of troops and funds; the necessity of US participation; congressional approval; a clear date for withdrawal; and, acceptable command and control agreements. It emphasizes American military non-involvement in operations in places where national security is not directly threatened. But, as Natsios has forcefully argued, "[h]umanitarian intervention applied carefully and with

to note that after months of hesitation the US launched a massive emergency relief operation for the Rwandan refugees and displaced persons that involved the airlift of food, medicine, and water.

Going back to the French intervention, even if the argument is made that it represents a case of selfish motives, the appalling situation in Rwanda morally required some form of action. Webster drives the point home by writing:

> [w]hen the aftermath of the Rwandan affair is analysed and the number of days when massacres were averted totalled up, an answer might emerge to the question of whether it was better to do something, even in self-interest, as the French have done, or whether it was better to stand aside in hesitation and indifference like the rest of the world.[185]

The legal basis for the French intervention can be found in Security Council Resolution 929. This Resolution authorized member states of the UN to establish "a temporary operation under national command and control aimed at contributing, in an impartial way, to the security and protection of displaced persons, refugees and civilians at risk in Rwanda".[186] Acting under Chapter VII of the Charter, it authorized "Member

---

restraint is as much in the self-interest of the United States as is geopolitical intervention. Most of the world expects moral leadership by the United States in humanitarian crises and to fail to provide it would damage the moral authority of the United States – at untold cost". More importantly, he continues, "Great powers should not always act on the basis of their narrow geopolitical interests but should venture beyond parochialism when the moment requires it. Chaos, the distinguishing characteristic of humanitarian emergencies ... .is the ground on which political fanaticism is built and tyrants raised. It seldom brings civilized democratic leadership to power but most often brutes who can suppress the violence but can do little else. And it is as systematically destructive to the economy and infrastructure of a country as full-scale war". Natsios, "Food Through Force: Humanitarian Intervention and US Policy" (1993) 17: 1 *The Washington Quarterly* 129 at 143.

185 Webster, "France Ducks as the Shells Whistle in" *The Guardian*, 7 July, 1994. Quoted in *supra*, note 83 at 160.

186 SC Res. 929, 49 UN SCOR (1994). UN Doc. S/RES/929 (1994).

States cooperating with the Secretary-General to conduct the operation ... using all necessary means to achieve the humanitarian objectives".[187] This resolution authorized the use of force on grounds that the human rights situation in Rwanda constituted a threat to international peace and security. While this threat was manifested in the large influx of refugees into neighbouring African countries due to the civil strife, it was also quite clear that the French intervention was designed to end the commission of further atrocities.

The scene of carnage, desolation and deprivation in Rwanda was evidence of the commission of genocide under the Genocide Convention. The ruthlessness of the Hutu massacres against the Tutsi and the objectives of those attacks undoubtedly confirmed the gravity of the crime. Yet, quite unfortunately, the UN failed to take timely decisive action by way of putting a stop to it. In the event of UN or other multilateral failure to act, it is imperative that unilateral action be undertaken to assert the right of intervention for humane purposes. In this context, the legitimacy of the French action would have been enhanced if it had come earlier than later.

In sum, the issue of intervention in Rwanda seems to be one of timely reaction. It raises questions whether UN intervention in preventing internal conflict has been successful. Could it be successful if better managed? Would it have been successful in preventing genocide in Rwanda? When should the UN force have intervened and with what force?[188] Although success does not impair the legitimacy of UN or French action in Rwanda, and is not a requirement of right action, [189]it is important that such questions be raised and addressed by the UN, if only in terms of lessons to guide future action.

The deployment of force early in a crisis situation can save not only lives but also money. In many cases it offers the best hope to prevent the escalation of violence.[190] Major-General Dallaire, commander of UNAMIR, has remarked: "[i]n Rwanda, the international community's

---

187 *Ibid.*
188 *Supra*, note 167 at 34.
189 *Supra*, note 31 at 365.
190 Destexhe, *supra*, note 158 at 16.

inaction ... contributed to the Hutu extremists' belief that they could carry out their genocide ... UNAMIR could have saved the lives of hundreds of thousands of people ... A force of 5, 000 personnel rapidly deployed could have prevented the massacres ... that did not commence in earnest until early May, nearly a month after the start of the war".[191] Thus, early robust intervention could have prevented or dissuaded genocide, or would at least have prevented the heavy casualties sustained. Rwanda is a prime example for the international community to direct increasing efforts towards early warning, preventive diplomacy, and proper conflict management.

Rwanda demonstrates the tenuous commitment of states to humanitarian intervention. The French response insisted on a duty of intervention to alleviate human suffering. The rest of the international community expressed shock and condemnation of the massacres that bordered on genocide. However, there was less commitment of physical resources to undertake a humanitarian intervention when it was most needed.

6   LIBERIA

The civil war in Liberia, which began in December 1989, witnessed a disturbing number of atrocities, and created a refugee crisis in the West African sub-region prompting regional military intervention.

---

191 See, *Towards a Rapid Reaction Capability for the United Nations* (Ottawa: Government of Canada, 1995) at 7, quoted in Schwartzberg, "A New Perspective on Peacekeeping: Lessons from Bosnia and Elsewhere" (1997) 3: 1 *Global Governance: A Review of Multilateralism and International Organizations* 1 at 2. Hindell also notes "[t]he Secretary-General originally recommended 7500 troops and the Canadian Commander 5500. Either figure would have saved thousands of lives if dispatched in October 1993 as originally requested, particularly if properly briefed, generously empowered and courageously led. Even a force sent after 6 April 1994 could have done more, as Operation Turquoise proved. Rwanda should have rated a much stronger force, such as was sent to Bosnia and Somalia. Such an intervention would have been expensive but the bill would not have approached the $1.3 billion spent on humanitarian relief and rehabilitation in the eight months from April to December 1994". *Supra*, note 167 at 35.

Liberia was created in the early nineteenth century as a settlement of emancipated slaves from the United States. These freed slaves, known as Americo-Liberians, are the elite that ruled the country for the next 150 years. Even though the Americo-Liberians constitute about 5% of the total population, they dominated the country's political, economic and social life.[192] In 1980, Master Sergeant Samuel Doe seized power in a bloody military coup that was initially welcomed by the indigenous majority of the population. The military government promptly tried and summarily executed some of the country's top politicians, bringing to an end a chapter in Americo-Liberian rule.

Throughout the 1980s, the Doe regime was sustained mainly by US foreign aid. Faced with increasing pressure for political reform after five years of military rule, the regime agreed to a program of democratization. In elections that were widely believed to have been rigged, Doe emerged as the President of the new Republic. Despite the affirmation of a commitment to democratic governance, human rights abuses were rampant under the Doe civilian administration.[193] These widespread human rights violations coupled with increasing economic difficulties precipitated the outbreak of civil conflict.[194]

---

192 For a detailed historical background of Liberia see Nelson ed., *Liberia: A Country Study* (Washington, DC: American University Foreign Area Studies, 1984).

193 For a catalogue of human rights abuses under the Doe government see for example, *Amnesty International Report* (1985) at 59-61; *Amnesty International Report* (1987) at 66-68; *Amnesty International Report* (1989) at 62-64.

194 One observer traces the cause of the war to withdrawal of foreign aid, the demise of the cold war, and the breakdown of patron-client politics that had bound the politicians of Liberia to one man. He observes that during the 1980s US aid to Liberia amounted to some $500 million – which made that country the largest per capita recipient of American aid in Africa. With the demise of the Soviet Union, Doe's role as host of American emergency military base and communications facilities no longer attracted that aid which had held together Doe's patronage network. Thus, with the invasion of Taylor's forces from the Ivory Coast in 1989, few, if any, associates of Doe saw any personal advantage in defending his government. See Reno, "The Business of War in Liberia" (May 1996) *Current History: A Journal*

The civil war began in December 1989 when Charles Taylor, leader of the National Patriotic Front of Liberia (NPFL), invaded the country from the Ivory Coast with the objective of overthrowing the Doe government.[195] By August 1990, civil authority had ceased to exist as the NPFL forces controlled the entire country except for the capital city of Monrovia. Around this time a splinter group of the NPFL emerged to form the INPFL led by Prince Johnson. This group, which initially aimed at ousting the Doe government from power, reached a deal with Doe and subsequently directed its attacks on the NPFL.[196] As the war continued, all sides to the conflict were accused of torturing and murdering innocent civilians.[197] Thousands of civilians faced starvation, more than 700, 000 people fled the country seeking refuge in neighbouring West African states and a further 500, 000 were internally displaced.[198] The general breakdown of law and order and the increasing loss of life led to a decision by the Economic Community of West African States (ECOWAS) to intervene.

The ECOWAS interventionary force, known as the ECOWAS Monitoring Group (ECOMOG) were deployed on August 23, 1990 in a bid to try to end the fighting.[199] In its attempt to impose peace on Liberia, ECOMOG came under attack by the NPFL which opposed any foreign intervention in the conflict. In September 1990, Doe was killed by INPFL forces which then directed their attacks at the NPFL. The situation over the next few months was one of fighting among the factions and skirmishes between

---

of Contemporary World Affairs at 212.

195 *West Africa Magazine*, January 8-14, 1990, at 33-34.

196 Ofodile, "The Legality of the ECOWAS Intervention in Liberia" (1994-95) 32 *Columbia Journal of Transnational Law* 381 at 383.

197 For a chronology of gruesome crimes committed against the civilian population see, for example, "Litany of Atrocities" *West Africa Magazine*, June 14-20, 1993.

198 Scott, *Humanitarian Action and Security in Liberia 1989-1994* (Providence: Watson Institute for International Studies, 1995) Occasional Paper No.20, at 2.

199 Johnson and Doe welcomed the ECOWAS intervention which they saw as an opportunity to prevent Taylor from claiming victory in the civil war. See *supra*, note 195 at 384.

ECOMOG and the NPFL. By November 1990, ECOMOG was in control of Monrovia and a precarious truce was established. A transitional government which controlled the Monrovia area was installed with protection from ECOMOG. In response to this, Taylor, who was in de facto control of most of the country, declared the establishment of his own government. These two governments each claimed legitimacy and struggled for control of the country. This state of affairs led ECOWAS to look for a viable means of unifying the country under a freely elected government.[200]

Liberia proved to be a frustrating experience for ECOMOG. There were cycles of cease-fires, renewed violence and negotiations. A series of agreements had been signed dating back to November 1990 between the increasingly numerous Liberian factions and ECOWAS member states, which over time were divided over the objectives of their action in Liberia. In October 1991, the Yamoussoukro IV agreement was signed, which provided for ECOMOG's deployment throughout the country, the confinement of armed forces to camp and the holding of multiparty elections at the end of one year.[201] Renewed fighting, however, shattered this ceasefire with the entry into Liberia from Sierra Leone of the United Liberation Movement for Democracy in Liberia (ULIMO) made up of the remnants of Doe's army. This force attacked the NPFL stronghold in Western Liberia which in turn provoked an NPFL attack on Monrovia in October 1992.[202]

In the summer of 1993, a peace agreement was reached under the auspices of ECOWAS, the OAU, and the UN. This became known as the Cotonou agreement. It provided for the expansion of the ECOWAS force, the establishment of a United Nations Observer Mission in Liberia (UNIMIL, which subsequently was created by the Security Council) to monitor the ceasefire and disarmament, the creation of a multifactional transitional government, and a peaceful environment for elections. With

---

200 Wippman, "Enforcing the Peace: ECOWAS and the Liberian Civil War" in Damrosch ed., *supra*, note 59 at 158.

201 For details of the Yamoussoukro Accord see *Africa Research Bulletin (Political Series)*, September 1991, at 10274-10276.

202 Jean ed., *supra*, note 99 at 54-56.

an increase in the number of ECOWAS troops and the involvement of
the UN, it was hoped that peace would be achieved. While the three main
factions continued to disagree over the agreements, two other factions
emerged and started attacks on NPFL and ULIMO controlled areas. This
scenario held back implementation of the agreement as the factions were
unwilling to disarm under the threat of force from the new factions.[203]

The parties subsequently signed three other supplementary agreements. These were the Akosombo Agreement of September 24, 1994;
the Accra Agreement of December 21, 1994; and, the Abuja Agreement
of August 19, 1995. The Akosombo Agreement provided a more detailed
scheme for the disengagement, disarmament and demobilization of
forces. It also called for a more active role for the Liberian National
Transitional Government in collaboration with ECOMOG and UNOMIL
to ensure its provisions were carried out. The Accra Accord primarily
called for a reorganization of the Liberian Armed Forces. The Abuja
Accord mainly addressed the composition of the Liberian Council of
State and called on ECOWAS, the OAU, and the UN to monitor operations
of the Ad Hoc Elections Commission.[204] Prospects for peace were,
however, dim with continuing disagreement among the parties, and
within ECOMOG, on details of the peace accords and power sharing.[205]

The initial international response to ECOMOG's intervention in Liberia
was one of cautious approval. Before Resolution 788 was passed, the
UN, OAU, EC and other nations adopted a 'wait and see' attitude, but
nonetheless encouraged ECOWAS to find a settlement to the Liberian
conflict. Apart from Burkina Faso, which had earlier on condemned the
action as an unlawful intervention in the internal affairs of a sovereign

---

203 The portion of the accord that was implemented related to the creation of
a collective presidency, a transitional government and a transitional parliament. *Supra*, note 196 at 387.
204 (1996) XXXIII: 1 *UN Chronicle*, at 17-18.
205 Reno for one, notes that the prospects for peace will remain in danger until
its guarantors (especially the US) reduce what he calls "the relative advantages of warlord politics". For him, since "illicit warlord trade is notor-
iously difficult to control, the most viable option is to rebuild Liberia's non-
warlord economy, and provide financial support and retraining to integrate
warlord fighters into that economy". *Supra*, note 194 at 215.

country, most states said little or nothing about the means employed by ECOWAS to bring about peace in that country.[206] In November 1992, the Security Council adopted Resolution 788.[207] It determined that the deterioration of the situation in Liberia constituted a threat to international peace and security, particularly in the West African region. This resolution commended efforts by ECOWAS to find a lasting peaceful solution to the conflict. It called on all the parties to the conflict to respect the Yamoussoukro IV agreement which established a framework for settlement of the civil strife. It also imposed an embargo on the delivery of weapons and military equipment to Liberia. An interpretation of the Resolution and the subsequent collaborative efforts on the part of the UN indicated a broad approval of the ECOWAS decision to use force in the Liberian civil war. At the Security Council, the US maintained:

> we must not lose sight of what ECOWAS has accomplished through intervention and negotiation. The dispatch of a six-nation West African peace-keeping force in August 1990 demonstrated unprecedented African determination to take the lead in regional conflict resolution. ECOMOG ended the killing, separated the warring factions, allowed relief assistance to flow to avert starvation and established a cease-fire and framework for peaceful negotiations ... .Although the dispatch of peace-keeping forces to Liberia was a decision taken by the ECOWAS Governments on their own initiative, we supported this effort from its inception.[208]

Giving reasons for the intervention, various leaders from ECOWAS cited the humanitarian basis for the action. The President of Gambia stated that ECOMOG was not an invasion force. Its task is strictly humanitarian,

---

206 *Supra*, note 200 at 175.
207 UN Doc.S/RES/788 (1992).
208 UN SCOR, 47th Sess., 3138th mtg. at 74-76. UN Doc.S/PV.3138 (1992). Quoted in Murphy, *Humanitarian Intervention: The United Nations in an Evolving World Order* (Philadelphia: University of Pennsylvania Press, 1996) at 156.

helping civilians caught in the civil war get relief supplies.[209] Similarly, the Nigerian Head of State claimed "[w]e are in Liberia because events in that country have led to massive destruction of property, the massacre by all parties of thousands of innocent civilians including foreign nationals, women and children ... contrary to all standards of civilised behaviour and international ethics and decorum".[210] The ECOWAS Standing Mediation Committee, in its Final Communique, justified the decision to intervene as follows:

> [t]he failure of the warring parties to cease hostilities has led to the massive destruction of property and the massacre by all the parties of thousands of innocent civilians, ... contrary to all recognized standards of civilized behaviour ... The civil war has also trapped thousands of foreign nationals, including ECOWAS citizens, without any means of escape or protection. The result of all this is a state of anarchy and the total breakdown of law and order in Liberia. Presently, there is a government in Liberia which cannot govern and contending factions which are holding the entire population as hostage, depriving them of food, health facilities and other basic necessities of life. These developments have traumatised the Liberian population and greatly shocked the people of the sub-region and the rest of the international community. They have also led to hundreds of thousands of Liberians being displaced and made refugees in neighbouring countries, and the spilling of hostilities into neighbouring countries.[211]

In effect the basis for the ECOWAS intervention was grounded in the need to end the atrocities and the mass killing of civilians in Liberia; the need to protect foreign nationals; the need to protect regional peace and security; and, lastly, the need to restore some order given the anarchic state of affairs in Liberia.

---

209 *West Africa Magazine*, November 26-December 2, 1990, at 2895.
210 *Ibid.*
211 Final Communique of the First Joint Meeting of the ECOWAS Standing Mediation Committee and the Committee of Five, paras.6-9. Quoted in *supra*, note 200 at 176.

Besides its mandate relating to the restoration of order, and in the long run, promoting a lasting peace, ECOWAS had also focused on the delivery of humanitarian assistance. It took practical measures to alleviate human suffering, started and encouraged the creation of refugee camps where much needed relief supplies were distributed to refugees. Its members had also taken in the large influx of refugees as a result of the war.[212]

The legal basis of the ECOWAS intervention in the Liberian civil conflict may be justified as an instance of collective humanitarian intervention. Some commentators examining the ECOWAS' justifications for the intervention have concluded that it was contrary to principles of international law since the intervention did not satisfy many of the requirements for a valid humanitarian intervention.[213] However, it is argued that if unilateral humanitarian intervention survived the Charter as a rule of customary international law as shown in the previous chapter, then a state or group of states, in this case ECOMOG, was legally justified in intervening to remedy the extreme human rights violations. It seemed at the time there was no viable peaceful means for resolving the conflict. Wippman for instance has explained why intervention to put an end to the violence was not forthcoming from either the UN, or the US, despite calls by Liberian politicians for intervention at the time. Apart from the fact that the international community's attention was focused on developments subsequent to the Iraqi invasion of Kuwait, the US did not see any post-Cold War strategic interest in Liberia. It also did not want to assume responsibility for assisting any of the warring factions, all of which Washington considered undesirable, into power. It thus characterized the situation as an internal matter to be left for Africans to resolve. This view was soon shared by members of the Security Council. Particularly, Ethiopia and Zaire, who were members

---

212 Kufuor, "Starvation as a Means of Warfare in the Liberian Conflict" (1994) XLI *Netherlands International Law Review* 313 at 316.

213 See Kufuor, "The Legality of the Intervention in the Liberian Civil War by the Economic Community of West African States" (1993) *African Journal of International and Comparative Law* 523. See also, *supra*, note 196 (questioning the legality of the ECOWAS intervention).

of the Council, sought to avoid the creation of a precedent for future intervention in African affairs. Consequently, the Security Council was reluctant to become seized of the matter.[214] It was in this context that ECOWAS took the initiative to put an end to the carnage, given the prevailing disinterest by the international community in addressing the volatile situation in Liberia – a situation that threatened regional stability. "To the extent that attention was focused on the legality of the intervention" as Murphy notes, "it would appear that the intervention was not viewed as violative of international law".[215]

The legality of the ECOWAS action has also been subject to debate with regard to the issue of enforcement action undertaken by a regional organization acting under Chapter VIII of the Charter. Article 52 states: "Nothing in the present Charter precludes the existence of regional arrangements or agencies dealing with matters relating to the maintenance of international peace and security" under the condition that "their activities are consistent with the Purposes and Principles of the United Nations". It encourages states to use such arrangements before directing their conflicts to the Security Council. It also recommends that the Council make use of regional organizations. Articles 53 and 54 seek to define relations between the UN and regional arrangements by prohibiting the latter from taking international peace and security measures without Council authorization and by insisting that the Council be kept fully informed of such activities. The question is whether such organizations have an independent authority to authorize military action (beyond self-defense) whenever they reach the conclusion that such a measure is necessary to avert or bring to an end a threat to peace and security, or to other collective regional interests?[216] Some commen-

---

214 Wippman, in Damrosch ed., *supra*, note 59 at 164-165.

215 Murphy, *supra*, note 208 at 163.

216 Farer, "The Role of Regional Collective Security Arrangements" in Weiss ed., *Collective Security in a Changing World* (Boulder: Lynne Rienner Publishers, 1993) 153 at 162. Some scholars have even questioned whether a subregional organization such as ECOWAS falls within the meaning of a Chapter VIII regional organization. However, it should be noted that the Charter does not define what a regional arrangement or agency is, and no consensus exists on what constitutes such an organization.. It would appear

tators have asserted that ECOWAS did not have the legal authority to determine the existence of a threat to peace and security, and to subsequently embark on an enforcement action without Security Council authorization. The Security Council in this case did not give its authorization for the enforcement action since the operation commenced before the Council's involvement in the situation. However, it is argued that the ECOWAS intervention was consistent with the broad purposes and principles of the UN – to restore peace and security and to remedy gross human rights violations. Even if the initial action was considered unlawful, its subsequent approval by the Security Council conferred legitimacy on the intervention within the meaning of Chapter VIII.[217] ECOWAS had reported its efforts to the Security Council consistent with the provisions of the Charter.[218] Infact, the Secretary General of the UN was of the view that ECOWAS did not need the consent of the Security Council before the intervention.[219] Elsewhere, the Secretary General noted:

> Liberia continues to represent an example of systematic and effective cooperation between the United Nations and regional organizations, as envisaged in Chapter VIII of the Charter. The role of the United Nations has been a supportive one. Closest contact and consultation

---

that ECOWAS qualifies as such an organization since "most geographically concentrated group of states that habitually act in concert under a governing charter or similar set of rules can qualify as a regional organization". Wippman, in Damrosch ed., *supra*, note 59 at 183-184.

217 See Wippman, *ibid.*, at 184-185.

218 Article 54 of the Charter states: "The Security Council shall at all times be kept fully informed of activities undertaken or in contemplation under regional arrangements or regional agencies for the maintenance of peace and security".

219 See da Costa, "Peacekeepers Run to UN as Mediation Runs Out of Steam" Inter Press Service, September 23, 1992, available in LEXIS, News Library, Inpres File. Cited in *supra*, note 196 at 413-414. Ofodile argues the Secretary General's statement that ECOWAS did not need the consent of the Security Council is contrary to the UN Charter. For him, ECOWAS would have been under no legal obligation to obtain the consent of the Council if the mission had been a purely peacekeeping operation. See, *ibid.*, at 414.

have been maintained with ECOWAS, which will continue to play the
central role in the implementation of the [Cotonou] peace agreement.[220]

Given the enormity of loss of life coupled with the fact that mass starvation and deprivation were imminent there is no doubt that intervention
was required to reverse the deplorable state of affairs in Liberia. Moreover, continuation of the conflict posed a clear threat to regional security.
This was manifested first in the conflict spreading to other countries
in the region, as it did when it spread to Sierra Leone. Secondly, a large
exodus of refugees into neighbouring countries did occur to worsen the
situation in those countries, which were not well equipped to handle
the large refugee populations.

Furthermore, the ECOWAS intervention respected the sovereignty of
Liberia. It did not impose a government on Liberia but encouraged the
formation of a transitional government through the involvement of all
parties to the conflict. The various peace accords discussed earlier
offered clear evidence of attempts by the interventionary force to move
the parties closer to finding a lasting political settlement to the conflict,
in the face of the intransigence of the various factions.

The precedential value of the intervention as an example in regional
or sub-regional collective action for meeting the challenge of humanitarianism is particularly significant. This is so for the following reason.
It shows many African states are becoming amenable to the idea that
egregious human rights violations, whether arising from governments
or the result of civil war, have been removed from the domestic sphere
and have become matters of international concern. These human rights
violations and the cross-border refugee situations that they engender are
significant indicators in the determination of the use of force. As Wippman correctly observes, "several prominent African leaders endorsing
ECOMOG's role in Liberia would have been unthinkable just a few years

---

220 UN Department of Public Information Reference Paper, *The United Nations
   and the Situation in Liberia* (April 1995). Quoted in Murphy, *supra*, note
   208 at 164. Murphy, however, notes the Liberian case was not representative of a "systematic and effective cooperation between the UN a regional
   organizations for various reasons. See *ibid.*

ago".[221] In his defence that ECOMOG's role in Liberia was consistent with the OAU Charter, the OAU Secretary General stated that "non-interference should not be taken to mean indifference".[222] For him, the OAU Charter cannot be interpreted to mean ignoring massive human rights violations in member states. He continues:

> ... for an African government to have the right to kill its citizens or let its citizens be killed, I believe there is no clause in the charter that allows this. To tell the truth, the charter was created to preserve human dignity, and the rights of the African. You cannot use a clause of the charter to oppress the African and say that you are implementing the OAU charter. What has happened is that people have interpreted the charter as if to mean that what happens in the next house is not one's concern. This does not accord with the reality of the world.[223]

Other African leaders notably, Museveni of Uganda and Mugabe of Zimbabwe have voiced similar sentiments.[224] Even though most African leaders would probably not endorse the Secretary General's interpretation of the OAU Charter, nevertheless, the fact that such proposals receive serious attention in Africa is indicative of an important shift in thinking.[225] It is a realization that an absolute norm of non-intervention does not protect, or does little to protect the values of state sovereignty in the situation of a civil war that results in continuing anarchy with its attendant humanitarian crisis. In situations such as Liberia, intervention to restore order and to address the humanitarian problems promotes rather than undermines state sovereignty. Thus, notwithstanding the commitment of the OAU to the principle of nonintervention, the ECOWAS intervention in Liberia was hailed throughout Africa, and the international community, as appropriate and offering hope for the restoration of order in that country.

---

221 *Supra*, note 200 at 181.
222 quoted in *ibid.*
223 Quoted in *ibid.*
224 See the sources cited in *ibid.*, at footnote 70.
225 *Ibid.*

In furtherance of the continuing concern of the Liberian situation, a 1996 OAU summit resolution produced some serious tough talk. It had warned the faction leaders that should the ECOWAS assessment of the Liberian peace process turn out to be negative, the Organization will help sponsor a draft resolution in the UN Security Council for the imposition of severe sanctions on them, including the possibility of the setting up of a war crimes tribunal to try the leadership of the warring factions on the gross violations of human rights of Liberians. In July 1997 however, peaceful elections were held under the supervision of ECOWAS and other international observers. Charles Taylor emerged as the winner and has formed a constitutional government. Whether democratic rule in post-war Liberia will be sustained and its socio-economic and political structures rebuilt remains to be seen.[226]

In sum, ECOMOG was a West African sub-regional initiative to end the Liberian civil war and the consequent humanitarian crisis, but it enjoyed the full regional support of the OAU,[227] and the UN. Recent proposals for a permanent ECOWAS force in light of its successful intervention in Liberia is an indication of the regional grouping's efforts to remain at the forefront of dealing with internal conflict situations in the future. This will be a new development pointing to less dependence on the West in developing indigenous mechanisms to ending conflicts in the region.

7   HAITI

The case of Haiti, although distinct in many aspects from the earlier cases examined, shares with them the ingredient of massive human suffering in a situation of egregious violation of human and political rights. The immediate crisis precipitating international action began with the ouster of President Jean Bertrand Aristide in a military coup in

---

226 "The OAU Summit", *West Africa Magazine*, July 22-28, 1996 at 1139. For details of the election results, see Butty, "Liberia – A Resounding Victory" *West Africa Magazine*, August 4-10, 1997 at 1252-1253.

227 See "Salim Salim Speaks", *ibid.*, at 1140.

September 1991 and subsequent widespread human rights violations by the new military rulers.

Haiti achieved its independence in 1804 and since then has had a tradition of dictatorial rule.[228] This state of affairs seemed to have become more pronounced when Francois "Papa Doc" Duvalier became the country's leader after winning elections that were considered fraudulent in 1957. His term of office was marked by violence and intimidation as tools of controlling the Haitian people. In 1971, Jean-Claude "Baby Doc" Duvalier succeeded his father as President and proceeded to govern in a similar manner.[229] He was overthrown in 1986 and succeeded by the National Council of Government, a civilian-military junta. In 1987, the Organization of American States (OAS) urged Haiti to move towards democratization by holding free and fair elections. However, the period from 1986 to January 1991 was marked by a series of short-term governments each of which came to power either through a military coup or through elections fraught with irregularities.[230]

The political uncertainty in Haiti, however, ended with internationally supervised elections on December 16, 1990. Aristide became the first democratically elected President on February 7, 1991, after securing 67% of the popular vote.[231] Aristide's populist approach to governance was

---

228 Violence has always been the means of settling conflicts and selecting leaders since its independence. Haiti has had over 20 Constitutions and was always ruled by authoritarian rulers since its independence. See "Electoral Assistance to Haiti" UN Doc.A/45/870 at 9. Cited in Acevedo, "The Haitian Crisis and the OAS Response: A Test of Effectiveness in Protecting Democracy" in Damrosch ed., *supra*, note 59 at 124, footnote 13.

229 His administration was characterised by gross human rights violations in which government forces, notably the Volunteers for National Security (known as the Tonton Macoutes) were reportedly involved in harassment, persecution, kidnapping and killing of political opponents, labour activists, lawyers, journalists and human rights activists. Acevedo, *ibid.*, at 124-126. Smith points out that successive United States administrations tolerated the Duvaliers as the alternative to possible communist penetration. Smith, "Haiti: From Intervention to Intervasion" (1995) 94: 589 *Current History: A Journal of Contemporary World Affairs* 54 at 56.

230 See Acevedo, *ibid.*, at 126-129.

231 *Ibid.*, at 130.

seen as a threat by certain entrenched groups in Haiti, and on September 30, 1991, the Haitian military led by General Raoul Cedras overthrew the Aristide government in a violent coup.[232]

The initial Security Council response to the coup was to consider it as a domestic jurisdiction issue which did not constitute a threat to the peace.[233] The Council only issued a nonbinding statement exercising caution not to encroach upon the domestic jurisdiction of Haiti. However, in a formal statement, the foreign ministers of the OAS meeting on October 2, 1991, condemned the coup and recommended the imposition of economic and diplomatic sanctions on Haiti, as well as the prohibition of arms deliveries. They demanded "full restoration of the rule of law and of the constitutional regime, and the immediate reinstatement of President Jean Bertrand Aristide in the exercise of his legitimate authority".[234] Although this resolution was not without precedent, Acevedo notes that it "was undoubtedly the strongest resolution the OAS had adopted against any government".[235] On October 3, 1991, President Aristide addressed the Security Council. Although members condemned the coup and expressed strong support for the OAS effort, the Council did not adopt a formal resolution dealing with the coup in Haiti. This attitude was taken because China and certain third world states had reportedly expressed concern about the Council's in-

---

232 See "Haiti's Military Assumes Power After Troops Arrest President" *New York Times*, October 1, 1991 at A1; Friedman, "US Suspends Assistance to Haiti and Refuses to Recognize Junta" *New York Times*, October 2, 1991 at A1.

233 A report in the New York Times stated: "Haiti's representative at the United Nations expressed disappointment ... over the failure of the Security Council to discuss the coup. The Haitian official ... said at a news conference that he was disturbed by the Security Council's reaction, which he described as 'unfair and a denial of Haitian rights'. The President of the Security Council had informed him that a majority of the delegations felt there should not be a meeting on what was seen as 'an internal matter'". Friedman, *ibid.*

234 See "Support of the Democratic Government of Haiti", OAS resolution MRE/ Res.1/91, Doc. OEA/Ser.F/V.1, October 3, 1991. Quoted in Acevedo, *supra*, note 228 at 132.

235 *Ibid.*

volvement in matters traditionally considered within the domestic jurisdiction of states and beyond the concern of the UN.[236]

At the forty-sixth session of the UN General Assembly, Honduras
requested that the question of human rights and democracy in Haiti be
included on the agenda. On October 10, 1991, the General Assembly
"strongly condemn[ed] both the illegal replacement of the constitutional
President of Haiti and the use of violence, military coercion and the
violation of human rights" in Haiti. It urged UN member states "to
consider the adoption of measures in keeping with those agreed on by
the Organization of American States".[237]

In May 1992, the OAS ad hoc Meeting of Consultation of Foreign
Ministers again passed a resolution which called upon member states
"to adopt whatever actions may be necessary for the greater effectiveness
of the measures referred to" in the ministers' earlier resolutions in
response to the coup. Additionally, they recommended the immediate
freezing of all assets of the Haitian State held in any OAS member
state.[238]

By December 1992, the OAS seemed to have exhausted its efforts
as the coup leaders remained intransigent in relinquishing power. A
different approach was necessary as it became obvious the OAS had
failed to achieve its objective. The focus of concerted action thus shifted
to the UN. Invoking Chapter VII of the Charter at the request of the
Haitian delegation, the Security Council unanimously adopted Resolution
841 in June 1993. This Resolution imposed wide-ranging sanctions on
Haiti, targeting both its state and non-state entities responsible for the
deplorable state of affairs in that country.[239] The immediate effect of

---

236 *Supra*, note 31 at 355.
237 GA Res. 46/7, October 11, 1991. On December 17, 1991, and again on
December 2, 1992, the General Assembly passed resolutions regarding the
human rights situation in Haiti. See GA Res. 46/138 and UN Doc. A/C.3/47/
L.73. Cited in *supra*, note 228 at footnote 55.
238 See Restoration of Democracy in Haiti, Res. MRE/RES.3/92, May 17, 1992.
Cited in *ibid.*, at 133-134.
239 S.C. Res.841, UN Doc.S/RES/841 (1993). With regard to this Resolution,
Damrosch maintains that " ... [it] goes farther than any other to date in
applying universal, mandatory, and severe economic sanctions to influence

this Resolution was to speed up the movement towards restoring democracy in Haiti. In July 1993, a UN-brokered accord was reached known as the Governors Island Agreement. This agreement was to return Haiti to democratic rule under President Aristide.[240] The economic sanctions were partially suspended in August 1993 when it seemed that the military dictators were implementing the Governors Island Agreement. They were reinstated two months later under Resolution 873[241] in the wake of violence against Aristide supporters and when it became obvious that the de facto military authorities in Haiti were not implementing the settlement in good faith.

As the pressures for international action continued to mount in the wake of the de facto government's brutal treatment of its people and the flight of refugees from Haiti, the Security Council passed Resolution 940 by a vote of 12-0 in July 1994. It authorized member states "to form a multinational force [and] ... to use all necessary means to facilitate the departure from Haiti of the military leadership".[242] Pursuant to this resolution, the US and other member states turned the heat on the Haitian military rulers to relinquish power. US warships were positioned off the Haitian coast, heightening the imminence of military action, if necessary, to return Aristide to power. A settlement was finally reached with US representatives in September 1994 after the junta's leadership discovered a US invasion force was on its way to Haiti. US-led multinational forces landed in Haiti within days, paving the way for Aristide's return to power in October 1994.

---

a domestic political crisis over democratic governance. Its cautious wording (stressing more than once the 'unique and exceptional' circumstances) cannot hide its precedential significance". Damrosch, "Epilogue" in Damrosch ed., *supra*, note 59 at 375.

240 According to Haiti's ambassador to the US, the agreement "contain[ed] elements of democracy, the return of the truly elected President of the Republic [on October 30, 1993] and the retirement from command of the coup leaders". "Pact Signed to Return Aristide to Power", *Globe and Mail*, July 5, 1993, at A7.

241 UN Doc. S/RES/873 (1993).

242 UN Doc. S/RES/940 (1994).

The international community welcomed the September 1994 settlement and the ensuing US occupation of Haiti.[243] The OAS Secretary-General expressed "deep satisfaction over the agreement, which assumes that political measures and diplomacy will prevail".[244] Venezuela was the only Latin American state to condemn the US mission in Haiti.[245]

The US-led Multinational Force in Haiti (MNF) was replaced with the United Nations Mission in Haiti (UNMIH) in March 1995 charged with a mandate to assist Haiti in: sustaining a secure and stable environment; protecting international personnel and key installations; creating the conditions for holding elections; and, establishing a new professional police force.[246] This force has made some progress in fulfilling its mandate.[247] In December 1995, Presidential elections were held with Rene Preval, a close associate of Aristide emerging as the winner.[248] He was sworn into office in February 1996.

The UN-authorized US-led multilateral involvement in Haiti signals a precedent in support of multilateral humanitarian intervention, and for some commentators, an emerging principle of democratic governance.[249] The moral and legal dimensions of international action in Haiti

---

243 *Supra*, note 31 at 357.
244 Quoted in *ibid*.
245 *Ibid*.
246 *UN Chronicle*, Spring 1996, at 4.
247 *Ibid*.
248 Preval had received 87.9% of the popular vote with his runner up getting only 2.5%. An estimated 28% of the registered voters took part in the elections. See *ibid*.
249 The case of Haiti as a paradigm of what some publicists refer to as "pro-democratic intervention" is beyond the scope of this work. In finding a basis for this kind of intervention, Scheffer, for example, argues that "where the United Nations or a regional organization has been instrumental in developing a democratic government ... such as has occurred in ... Haiti, ... there arises a legitimate basis for the United Nations and the regional organization to guarantee the survival of democracy in that nation when it has been overthrown by a military coup ... which typically leads to internal violations of the collective human rights of the people". He goes on to state that "we do need to understand the growing possibility that a humanitarian intervention may serve not only the purpose of responding

are defensible. The US-led action is justified partly as action to put a stop to the human rights violations of the Cedras regime. In offering reasons for the intervention, the US President, Bill Clinton held the de facto military authorities in Haiti responsible for human rights abuses that included the execution of children, the raping of women, and the rampant killings that were going on. The President stated: "[l]et me be clear, General Cedras and his accomplices alone are responsible for this suffering and terrible human tragedy".[250] Despite harrowing scenes of government brutality against the Haitian people which were regularly flashed across television screens, and repeated references by the American President to atrocities committed in Haiti, some commentators have raised concerns about the US-led action, and thus question its legitimacy as a case of humanitarian intervention.[251] Weber, for one, argues that

---

to a humanitarian crisis but also of facilitating the restoration of democracy in a state where that form of government previously has been guaranteed by the United Nations or a regional organization. For in most cases it would be the collapse of democracy and the rise of totalitarianism that would lead to human rights atrocities". Scheffer, *supra*, note 6 at 292. For a detailed discussion of "pro-democratic" interventions or interventions against illegitimate regimes, see for example, Damrosch & Scheffer eds., *Law and Force in the New International Order* (Boulder, Colo: Westview Press, 1991); Farer, *Collectively Defending Democracy in a World of Sovereign States: The Western Hemisphere Prospect* (International Centre for Human Rights and Democratic Development, 1993); Fox, "The Right to Political Participation in International Law" (1992) 17: 2 *Yale Journal of International Law* 609; Franck, "The Emerging Right to Democratic Governance" (1992) 86: 1 *American Journal of International Law* 81; *Supra*, note 31 at 325-335.

250 Federal News Service at 3.Quoted in Weber, "Dissimulating Intervention: A Reading of the US-Led Intervention in Haiti" (1995) 20 *Alternatives* 265 at 271.

251 See for example, Gordon, *supra*, note 38 at 52 (asserting that the intervention in Haiti was arguably not a humanitarian one); Regensburg, "Refugee Law Reconsidered: Reconciling Humanitarian Objectives with the Protectionist Agendas of Western Europe and the United States" (1996) 29: 1 *Cornell International Law Journal* 225 at 253 (suggesting international law played a minute, if any, role in the American decision to intervene in Haiti, and that history may judge Resolution 940 to be an unwise decision).

the September agreement brokered just before the intervention suggests that human rights violations were not a priority for the US. She writes:

> it seems ... the focus on the protection of Haitian human rights served as a false cover for an issue closer to home – immigration. Viewing human rights through immigration concerns suggests that the population at risk in US-Haitian relations was not so much the Haitian population but the US citizenry ... Focusing on one issue like human rights in order to cover a concern with another issue like immigration is not a particularly new move. One finds this frequently in intervention discourses. I want to suggest that the US discourse on Haiti ... was ... an example of dissimulation understood as the escalation of the fake. US intervention justifications amounted to projecting the US population's own fears (real or imagined) onto the Haitians (a 'false') location.[252]

The existence of mixed motives regarding US involvement cannot be ruled out in this case. The Clinton administration was certainly concerned about the continued mass exodus of Haitian refugees seeking asylum in the US and seeking methods to bring the refugee situation to an end. US national interests were thus affected by the intolerable situation in Haiti that created the refugee problem. The national interest, must be construed broadly as being affected because the Haitian situation was morally reprehensible. The fact that mixed motives were present should not nullify this intervention since the humanitarian motive was clearly evident.[253] Moreover, the US-led action indicates that humanitarian crises can become internationalized pointing the way to action against a government in power.[254]

The legal basis for humanitarian intervention in Haiti can be found in Resolution 940. The Security Council expressed grave concern regarding the "significant further deterioration of the humanitarian situation".

---

252 Weber, *supra*, note 250 at 272.
253 See for example, *supra*, note 31 at 359.
254 Mills, "Eclipsing Sovereignty: The Legitimacy of Humanitarian Intervention" *Paper Presented at the Academic Council on the United Nations System/American Society of International Law Summer Workshop*, Providence, Rhode Island, July 28-August 9, 1996, at 26.

In addition it referred to the Haitian authorities' "systematic violation of civil liberties". The Security Council thus used the grave human rights violations and the removal of the de facto government in Haiti as the justification for authorizing military action. The Haitian paradigm thus seems to reinforce the proposition that states have accepted egregious human rights violations as the basis for action by the Security Council under Chapter VII.[255]

Some lessons emerge from the Haitian experience. Although the OAS was less effective[256] in taking action against Haiti, its immediate reaction in the wake of the crisis by applying diplomatic and economic sanctions must be commended. It suggests a willingness on the part of the regional organization to respond to similar situations in the future. The Organization's initiative prompted the UN to lend its support to find a solution to the crisis. In the same breath, this action also reveals the ambiguities that characterize the international community efforts to arrive at some consensus on when and how to intervene in a humanitarian crisis. It took two years for the UN to take its first decisive action. Even then, it was only after mandatory sanctions were in effect that the Haitian military dictators began taking the UN or OAS seriously.[257] It took another year for the Security Council to authorize action that proved effective in returning Aristide to power. By the time those other remedies had proved quite ineffective, it was too late to save those who could have been rescued by an earlier intervention. The point here is that an

---

255 *Ibid.*, at 358. See however, Gordon, *supra*, note 38 at 53. (arguing Resolution 940 did not authorize the use of force specifically to deal with the humanitarian aspects of the crisis).

256 Pastor suggests reasons for failure of the OAS: first, Haiti had no prior experience with democracy, and the fact that its newly elected leaders failed to uphold the constitution in a manner that was consistent with maintaining a democratic tradition; secondly, the OAS looked on its role as judge rather than as a problem-solver: and lastly, it failed to back its diplomacy with the credible threat of force which rather worsened the situation in Haiti rather than achieving its aim. Pastor, "Forward to the Beginning: Widening the Scope for Global Collective Action" in Reed & Kaysen eds., *Emerging Norms of Justified Intervention* (Cambridge, Mass: American Academy of Arts and Sciences, 1993) 133 at 144.

257 Damrosch, *supra*, note 239 at 375.

early use of force may have been desirable in preventing further worsening of the crisis.[258]

In conclusion, it is significant to note that a number of states in the Latin American region supported various measures ranging from mediation, economic sanctions, to the use of force to reinstall Aristide, although some of the larger states were reluctant to support military force.[259] Despite the lack of unanimity for forceful action, the very fact of expression of support to some extent represents a shift on the part of governments in the Latin American region from their previous absolute non-intervention stance.[260]

8   CONCLUSION

An overall assessment of the case studies suggests a number of cross-cutting issues but points to the growing support for the use of force in aid of humanitarian objectives and the debate over the conditions required for its legitimate use. Post-Cold War practice suggests that the international community is ready to implement a broader conception of humanitarian intervention. The cumulative effect of the number of Security Council Resolutions relating to the various cases discussed in the chapter has reinforced the observance of human rights as a significant underpinning for international peace and security. Internal conflicts producing human suffering, as in most of the cases examined, and massive human rights violations by governments, as in the case of Haiti, constitute a threat to international peace and security. These situations have provided the basis for international action including the employment

---

[258] *Supra*, note 109 at 39, 44. See also, Smith, "In Defense of Intervention" (1994) 73: 6 *Foreign Affairs* 34 at 35 (observing that although the Haitian intervention is to be welcomed, the decision to act was so late and characterized by hesitation that it hardly would appear to set the sort of precedent that would deter others).

[259] Brazil, for example, abstained from the vote on Resolution 940. See UN Doc. S/PV.3413.

[260] See *supra*, note 250 at 30.

of economic sanctions, the use of protection forces to watch over minority enclaves, and the use of military force in securing the supply of humanitarian assistance.

These recent cases demonstrate a growing support for humanitarian intervention, and a significant shift in the manner in which states respond to humanitarian crises. The degree to which this change has occurred is manifest especially in comparison to the cases of humanitarian intervention discussed in the preceding chapter where support or condemnation varied in the context of the Cold War, and state response was mainly apathetic. The cases have also shown the international community re-evaluating and taking seriously assumptions concerning human rights and state sovereignty. Emphasis on notions of absolute state sovereignty and nonintervention are beginning to give way to a more responsible view of state sovereignty. The responsibilities which accrue to states include the protection of human rights. Thus, massive human rights violations open the state to intervention on humanitarian grounds.

4

ASSESSING HUMANITARIAN INTERVENTION IN THE POST-COLD WAR PERIOD: SOURCES OF CONSENSUS

1   INTRODUCTION

Developments in the post-Cold War era regarding intervention to protect human rights suggest a gradual change in attitudes and challenges to state sovereignty and its corollary principle of nonintervention.[1] With the end of the Cold War, the UN has been less inclined to permit concern for human rights to end at a state's territorial borders. In a speech at the University of Bordeaux in 1991, Perez de Cuellar stated "...we are clearly witnessing what is an irresistible shift in public attitudes towards the belief that the defence of the oppressed in the name of morality should prevail over frontiers and legal documents". The fact that sovereignty is continually evolving and that absolute notions of sovereignty

---

[1]   As stated earlier, this is, however, not to suggest that state sovereignty and nonintervention are no longer important norms in international relations. They still are. After a comprehensive review of recent cases Damrosch, for instance, concludes "[i]nstead of the view that interventions in internal conflicts must be presumptively illegitimate, the prevailing trend today is to take seriously the claim that the international community ought to intercede to prevent bloodshed with whatever means are available ... arguments now focus not on condemning or justifying intervention in principle, but rather on how best to solve practical problems of mobilizing collective efforts to mitigate internal violence". Damrosch, "Concluding Reflections" in Damrosch ed., *Enforcing Restraint: Collective Intervention in Internal Conflicts* (New York: Council on Foreign Relations Press, 1993) at 364.

are no longer defensible is increasingly becoming evident.[2] As the UN's

2   As noted in the last chapter, former UN Secretary-General Boutros-Ghali,
     in his "Agenda for Peace", stressed that the time of absolute and uncon-
     ditional sovereignty has passed. Scholarly writings have also taken account
     of these developments. Esman argues "[n]ormative expectations seem to
     be shifting in favour of limiting absolute state sovereignty when inter-
     national peace and stability are threatened, human rights are flagrantly
     abused, and humanitarian disasters are created by ethnic conflict". Esman,
     "A Survey of Interventions" in Esman and Telhami eds., *International Or-
     ganizations and Ethnic Conflict* (Ithaca: Cornell University Press, 1995)
     21 at 47. Similarly, Parekh has remarked that "[s]overeignty does not inhere
     in the state, it is an achievement made possible by the continuing support
     of *both* its own citizens and the outside world. Since it has both an internal
     and an external basis, the state is accountable not only to its own citizens
     but also to outsiders for the conduct of its affairs. Its citizens are not cut
     off from the rest of mankind but form an integral part of it, and are objects
     of its legitimate moral concern". Parekh, "Rethinking Humanitarian Inter-
     vention" (1997) 18: 1 *International Political Science Review* 49 at 63. See
     also, Chopra and Weiss, "Sovereignty is no Longer Sacrosanct: Codifying
     Humanitarian Intervention" (1992) 6 *Ethics & International Affairs* 95;
     Scheffer, "Toward a Modern Doctrine of Humanitarian Intervention" (1992)
     23: 2 *University of Toledo Law Review* 253 at 259-261; Lyons and Mastan-
     duno eds., *Beyond Westphalia: State Sovereignty and International Interven-
     tion* (Baltimore: The Johns Hopkins University Press, 1995) ; Makinda,
     "Sovereignty and International Security: Challenges for the United Nations"
     (1996) 2: 2 *Global Governance: A Review of Multilateralism and Inter-
     national Organizations* 149 (examining how the UN has approached notions
     of state sovereignty and international security in the post-Cold War period,
     and explaining the changing nature of sovereignty); Hehir, "Expanding
     Military Intervention: Promise or Peril" (1995) 61: 1 *Social Research* 41-51
     (arguing the pattern of world politics has changed sufficiently that traditional
     notions of absolute sovereignty and nonintervention serves neither states
     nor their citizens); Schacter, "Sovereignty and Threats to Peace" in Weiss
     ed., *Collective Security in a Changing World* (Boulder: Lynne Rienner
     Publishers, 1993) at 19, 23 (observing contemporary events have tended
     to show the limits of sovereignty as a principle of international order, and
     that juridical thought while differing, have tended to "agree that sovereignty
     in law, as in fact, cannot be absolute"); Hoffmann, "Sovereignty and the
     Ethics of Intervention" in Hoffmann et al., *The Politics and Ethics of
     Humanitarian Intervention* (Notre Dame: University of Notre Dame Press,

Independent Commission on International Humanitarian Issues has stated: "sovereignty need not conflict with humanitarian concerns if States can be brought to define their interests beyond the short term....The interests of common humanity which transcend national boundaries are not a menace to the vital interests of States".[3] This position is also supported by the International Court of Justice.[4] Sovereignty is and will remain an important organizing principle in international relations, but, as Nanda remarks, "to insist on adherence to its 'absolute' dimensions flies in the face of international realities".[5] The conclusions of a 1992 international conference on human rights protection for internally displaced persons made up of human rights experts, humanitarian organizations, international lawyers, officials from UN and regional organizations, and government representatives, are that sovereignty confers responsibility on governments to protect the inhabitants of their territories. Failure to meet

---

1996) 12-37; Griffths, Levine and Weller, "Sovereignty and Suffering"in Harriss ed., *The Politics of Humanitarian Intervention* (London: Pinter Publishers, 1995), 32-90 (arguing that despite the absence of any declared international consensus on the limits of sovereignty, there is nevertheless a consistent trend emerging from recent practice); Ryan, "Sovereignty, Intervention, and the Law: A Tenuous Relationship of Competing Principles" (1997) 26: 1 *Millennium: Journal of International Studies* 77 at 86-87; Mills, *Human Rights in the Emerging Global Order: A New Sovereignty?* (London: Macmillan Press, 1998).

3   See Independent Commission on International Humanitarian Issues, *Modern Wars: The Humanitarian Challenge* (London: Zed Books, 1988) at 189-190. Quoted in Haas, "Beware the Slippery Slope: Notes Toward the Definition of Justifiable Intervention" in Reed & Kaysen eds., *Emerging Norms of Justified Intervention* (Cambridge, Mass: American Academy of Arts and Sciences, 1993) at 64.

4   See *Nicaragua* v. *United States* (Merits) (1986) International Court of Justice Reports 14. The Court held in this case that giving "strictly humanitarian assistance ...cannot be regarded as unlawful intervention, as in any other way contrary to international law". See also comments by Haas on the application of this principle by UNICEF during the Sudanese civil war. Haas, *ibid.*, at 85, footnote 3.

5   Nanda, "Humanitarian Intervention and International Law" in Conference Report, *The Challenge to Intervene: A New Role for the United Nations?* (Uppsala: Life & Peace Institute, 1992) at 38.

those obligations means that governments risk undermining their legitimacy.[6] In essence there is the tendency to restore notions of responsibility
to state sovereignty.[7] When humanitarian tragedies of grave proportions
occur, be it in situations of civil strife, or when a government persistently
and systematically tramples upon the human rights of its citizens, such
as causes outrage in the international community, outside intervention
is often one of the most important instruments that can be employed
to halt these tragedies. Yet, it remains unclear whether the international
community will support such action in every case.

The trend towards collective intervention discussed in the last chapter, and as reflected in statements and decisions of the UN Security Council, while a welcome development, has sometimes, to use the words of
Weiss, tended to be surrounded by more heat than light. In light of the
varying international responses to the various humanitarian tragedies,
the debate surrounding the legitimacy of humanitarian intervention continues unabated. In 1993 Roberts, was prompted to observe that

'[h]umanitarian war' is an oxymoron which may yet become a reality.
The recent practice of states, and of the United Nations, has involved
major uses of armed force in the name of humanitarianism ... These

---

6   See Refugee Policy Group, *Human Rights Protection for Internally Dis-
    placed Persons: An International Conference* (Washington, D.C.: 1991) cited
    in Deng, "Reconciling Sovereignty with Responsibility: A Basis for Inter-
    national Humanitarian Action" in Harbeson and Rothchild eds., *Africa in
    World Politics: Post-Cold War Challenges* (Boulder: Westview Press, 1995)
    295 at 298. This view is consistent with an approach that maintains that
    "sovereignty carries humanitarian duties and responsibilities that, when
    breached, eviscerate sovereignty and open the state to intervention on
    humanitarian grounds". See Arnison, "International Law and Non-Interven-
    tion: When Humanitarian Concerns Supersede Sovereignty?" (1993) *Flet-
    cher Forum* 199 at 207. See also Caney, "Human Rights and the Rights
    of States: Terry Nardin on Nonintervention" (1997) 18: 1 *International Po-
    litical Science Review* 27-37 (arguing human beings as human beings have
    certain entitlements and interests which are not contingent nor affected by
    national origins, and a state that denies them forfeits its rights to autonomy.
    Thus, intervention is justified when it has the aim of protecting these rights).
7   Deng, *ibid.*, at 299.

humanitarian activities in situations of conflict raise many awkward questions.

More importantly, he highlighted two questions:

1. Is humanitarian involvement in conflicts – in the form of provision of food, shelter, and protection, under international auspices – a step on a ladder which can or should lead to much more direct military involvement, even to participation in hostilities?
2. Can we conclude from recent and contemporary practice that a new consensus is emerging on humanitarian intervention, that is, military intervention in a state, without the approval of its authorities, and with the purpose of preventing widespread suffering or death among the inhabitants?[8]

---

8   Roberts, "Humanitarian War: Military Intervention and Human Rights" (1993) 61 *International Affairs* 429. Similarly, Nanda has posed the question whether there is "an emerging right, and perhaps even a duty, on the part of the world community to intervene in the internal affairs of a state when egregious violations of basic human rights occur..." Nanda, Tragedies in Northern Iraq, Liberia, Yugoslavia, and Haiti – Revisiting the Validity of Humanitarian Intervention under International Law-Part I" (1992) 20 *Denver Journal of International Law and Policy* 305 at 306. Ramsbotham and Woodhouse have observed that core issues regarding human rights violations during the Cold War remain the same now, although "the centre of gravity has shifted. The fundamental question during the Cold war was: [i]f governments violate the basic human rights of their citizens, should other governments intervene forcibly to remedy the situation? In the post-Cold War period the basic question has been: "[i]f internal wars cause unacceptable human suffering, should the international community develop collective mechanism for preventing or alleviating it"? Ramsbotham and Woodhouse, *Humanitarian Intervention in Contemporary Conflict: A Reconceptualization* (Cambridge: Polity Press, 1996) at 139. With regard to Roberts' remark about humanitarian war being an oxymoron, Weiss and Campbell contend that military humanitarianism as part of a new agenda for international security in the post-Cold War is not an oxymoron. See Weiss and Campbell, "Military Humanitarianism" (1991) 33: 5 *Survival* 451 at 463.

It is in this context that differing views have been put forth. Some observers argue a significant change seems to be underway in terms of the establishment of precedents in the post-Cold War period regarding intervention to protect human rights. Others maintain the possibilities for collective action under Security Council authorization will not be forthcoming in every instance. Yet still, for some, this is an errant period that is unlikely to continue in the future. This chapter assesses contemporary developments in the principle and practice of humanitarian interventions in the post-Cold War period and argues that a notable shift seems to be underway.

2   ASSESSMENT OF POST-COLD WAR PRACTICE

Recent practice seems to suggest a shift that has implications for sovereignty and humanitarian intervention. Humanitarian crises resulting either from governmental acts or internal conflict have become amenable to outside intervention. What emerges from these cases in terms of the various UN Security Council Resolutions, as Damrosch puts it, "evidence a newly emerging consensus that the Security Council's enforcement powers may be invoked ... in ... purely domestic situation[s]".[9] On the

---

9   Damrosch, "Changing Conceptions of Intervention in International Law" in Reed and Kaysen eds., *supra*, note 3 at 105. Writing in 1973, Reisman and McDougal, had argued that "[b]oth natural and analytical international legal jurisprudence cojoin, in humanitarian intervention, in viewing the jurisdictional exclusivity of any nation State as conditional rather than absolute. The conditionality of the jurisdiction is most obvious in respect to minimum human rights". Reisman and McDougal, "Humanitarian Intervention to Protect the Ibos" in Lillich ed., *Humanitarian Intervention and the United Nations* (Charlottesville: University of Virginia Press, 1973) at 169. Rodley has commented "while there remain protagonists, especially among affected governments, of the traditional strict doctrine that a human rights problem concerns none but the state where it takes place, " this according to him "is becoming an increasingly eccentric position". Rodley, "Collective Intervention to Protect Human Rights and Civilian Populations: The Legal Framework" in Rodley ed., *To Loose the Bands of Wickedness: International Intervention in Defence of Human Rights* (London: Brassey's,

basis of these developments significant conclusions can be discerned or reached on the principles of humanitarian intervention and their application in the post-Cold War period.[10] First, these emerging principles suggest that massive or widespread violations of human rights or humanitarian law arising from governmental acts or internal conflicts and the magnitude of human suffering that they engender, can constitute a threat to international peace and security that governments can no longer afford to ignore. These are matters that do not fall within the domestic domain of states. The Security Council, in those circumstances, can take appropriate measures, including the use of force, grounded in Chapter VII of the Charter for the protection of humanitarian relief operations and the creation of a secure environment for such operations.

Second, abandonment of victims of man-made or natural disasters, especially the deliberate withholding or impeding of food and medical supplies necessary for survival of civilians trapped in the throes of internal conflict, constitutes a threat to human life, and ultimately peace and security. In those situations, necessary measures including force can be employed to get much needed humanitarian relief supplies to such victims.

Third, states have a duty to lend support to international organisations or humanitarian organisations working to provide humanitarian assistance to the victims of complex emergencies like situations of starvation, widespread suffering, and death.

Fourth, state sovereignty will not bar action to protect and sustain the lives of large numbers of civilians trapped in situations of internal conflict. Added to this is the principle of individual responsibility for

---

1992) 14 at 21-22. But see Donnelly, who argues "human rights are ultimately a profoundly *national* – not international – issue". [Emphasis in original]. Donnelly, "Human Rights, Humanitarian Crisis, and Humanitarian Intervention" (1993) XLVIII *International Journal* 607 at 639-640.

10 See for example, Schindler, "Humanitarian Assistance, Humanitarian Interference and International Law" in Macdonald ed., *Essays in Honour of Wang Tieya* (Dordrecht: Martinus Nijhoff Publishers, 1994) 689 at 693.

war crimes, and grave breaches of international humanitarian law, including interference with humanitarian assistance.[11]

Although these principles emerge from the cases, international
responses to the various humanitarian tragedies were less consistent.
Multilateral response to one situation "served as a benchmark for evaluating the response or lack of response to others".[12] The emerging pic-
ture has thus been varied international responses and mixed results. For
some, this casts doubts on the legitimacy of humanitarian interventions.
Nonetheless, the various responses have been grounded in the principle
that massive human rights deprivations do constitute a threat to international peace and security either through transboundary refugee flows
or spillage of internal strife across borders. On this basis, international
action, including the use of force, can be justified to address these problems.

However, the euphoria generated in the aftermath of the Gulf War
subsided with the expression of frustrations and disillusionment by the
mid-1990s regarding vigorous international action to deal with these
humanitarian crises. This problem was summed up by Boutros-Ghali
when he admitted that "we are still in a time of transition ... unforseen
or only partly forseen difficulties have arisen ... the different world that
emerged when the Cold War ceased is still a world not fully understood".[13] Even though there is a clear indication that the post-Cold War
era is still unfolding, nevertheless it is important that the emerging
international principles and practice, be sorted out, if only, to serve as
signposts into the future.

---

11 Falk, for instance, notes the "emergence of a highly articulated international
    law of human rights, reinforced psychologically by ideas about government
    and individual accountability for their gross violation". Falk, "The Com-
    plexities of Humanitarian Intervention: A New World Order Challenge"
    (1996) 17: 2 *Michigan Journal of International Law* 491 at 493.
12 *Supra*, note 1 at 360.
13 See, Boutros-Ghali, *Supplement to An Agenda for Peace: Position Paper
    of the Secretary-General on the Occasion of the Fifthtieth Anniversary of
    the United Nations*, UN Doc. A/50/60-5/1995/1, 3 January 1995. at 2, 3,
    24.

Various actors and writers have sought to place interpretations on these trends. First, an increasing number of scholars view these developments as establishing the right to international intervention for humanitarian purposes, and thus establishing significant precedents.[14] In a comprehensive survey of state practice, UN law, and most commentators, Ajaj reaches the conclusion that the theory of humanitarian intervention has never enjoyed as much legitimacy as it does today.[15] Scheffer interestingly summarizes the new sense of urgency with regard to the need for international response by stating that

> In the post-Cold War world ... a new standard of intolerance for human misery and human atrocities has taken hold ... Something quite significant has occurred to raise the consciousness of nations to the plight of peoples within sovereign borders. There is a new commitment – expressed in both moral and legal terms – to alleviate the suffering of oppressed or devastated people. To argue today that norms of sovereignty, non-use of force, and the sanctity of internal affairs are paramount to the collective human rights of people, whose lives and well-being are at risk, is to ignore the march of history.[16]

In that light, Greenwood has asserted "the law on humanitarian intervention has changed both for the United Nations and for individual states. It is no longer tenable to assert that whenever a government massacres its own people or a state collapses into international anarchy international law forbids military intervention altogether".[17] Ethically, Hoffmann has argued, military intervention is justified when domestic unrest threatens regional or international security and massive abuses of human rights occur. He points out, however, "[i]n most, but not necessarily all

---

14 See for example, Weiss, "Triage: Humanitarian Interventions in a New Era" (1994) *World Policy Journal* 11; Barzani, "Hope Restored: Benefits of Humanitarian Intervention" (1993) *Harvard International Review* at 18-19.

15 See Ajaj, "Humanitarian Intervention: Second Reading of the Charter of the United Nations" (1993) *Arab Law Quarterly* at 215-236.

16 Scheffer, *supra*, note 2 at 259.

17 Greenwood, "Is there a Right of Humanitarian Intervention?" (1993) 49: 2 *The World Today* at 40.

cases the intervention should be organised or at least authorised by the UN Security Council, which should be given autonomous means and reorganised to enhance both its legitimacy and the capacity for action".[18] While Roberts notes, with respect to the questions posed earlier, that "international thought and practice seem to be changing",[19] Tesón forcefully argues that "the doctrine of humanitarian intervention has experienced a dramatic revival with the end of the Cold War" and concludes "that the international community has a right to intervene to uphold human rights is supported by recent practice".[20] Even though Falk suggests that humanitarian intervention since 1989 has been a failure, and attributes reasons for the failure, he nevertheless argues that "with the end of the Cold War there has been a notable shift in interventionary diplomacy away from purely geopolitical interventionism in the direction of support for humanitarian claims to alleviate human suffering" and "from a purely normative perspective of law and morality, this shift in interventionary practice is a welcome development".[21]

---

18 Hoffmann, "The Politics and Ethics of Military Intervention" (1995-96) 37: 4 *Survival* 29.

19 Roberts, *supra*, note 8. Wheeler and Morris, in their examination of the cases of Iraq, Somalia and Rwanda, come to the conclusion the post-Cold War interventions "provide no more than the most tentative support for the descriptive claim that the concept of humanitarian intervention is now seen by the international community as legitimate". See Wheeler and Morris, "Humanitarian Intervention and State Practice at the End of the Cold War" in Fawn and Larkins eds., *International Society after the Cold War* (London: Macmillan Press, 1996) at 135 at 160.

20 See Tesón, "Collective Humanitarian Intervention" (1996) 17: 2 *Michigan Journal of International Law* 323.

21 *Supra*, note 11 at 511, 512. For other writers supportive of humanitarian intervention in the post-Cold War period see for instance, Duke, "The State and Human Rights: Sovereignty versus Humanitarian Intervention" (1994) 12 *International Relations* 25 (examining justifications for intervention and concluding that legal grounds exist when adequate proof of gross violations of fundamental human rights can be established); Arnison, *supra*, note 6 (noting how events in the cases examined illustrate the growing need for humanitarian intervention when armed conflict, egregious human rights violations or starvation put countless lives at risk); Nanda, *supra*, note 8 at 344 (discussing post-Cold War practice and concluding "'humanitarian

Opponents of humanitarian intervention, however, remain sceptical, by insisting that sovereign states and their prerogatives remain fundamental even when humanitarian issues arise. For Donnelly, "[w]e should not expect – hopefully or fearfully – the imminent emergence of an international practice of humanitarian intervention".[22] Others have also expressed concerns about the viability of humanitarian intervention as a mechanism for enforcement of the will of the international community.[23] Ayoob distinguishes between two kinds of humanitarian inter-

---

intervention' remains a viable alternative.That it should be sparingly used is appropriate. But that it can be used should prove a powerful deterrent to oppressive regimes"); Harff, "Rescuing Endangered Peoples: Missed Opportunities" (1995) 62: 1 *Social Research* 23 (arguing in favour of humanitarian intervention as a last resort to correct massive violations of human rights like genocide and political mass murder); Burmester, "On Humanitarian Intervention: The New World Order and Wars to Preserve Human Rights" (1994) *Utah Law Review* 269; Delbruck, "A Fresh Look at Humanitarian Intervention Under the Authority of the United Nations" (1992 67 *Indiana Law Journal* 887; Nafziger, "Humanitarian Intervention in a Community of Power Part II" (1994) 22 *Denver Journal of International Law and Policy* 219; Walzer, "The Politics of Rescue" (1995) 62: 1 *Social Research* 53; Dowty and Loescher, "Refugee Flows as Grounds for International Action" (1996) 21: 1 *International Security* 43 (arguing whatever the theoretical debates, international intervention as a response to refugee flows is quietly becoming a de facto norm in state declaration and practice) ; Chopra and Weiss, *supra*, note 2; Higgins, *Problems and Process: International Law and How We Use it* (Oxford: Clarendon Press, 1994) at 247-248; Parekh, *supra*, note 2 at 49-69; Lillich, "The Role of the UN Security Council in Protecting Human Rights in Crisis Situations: UN Humanitarian Intervention in the Post-Cold War World" (1994) 3 *Tulane Journal of International and Comparative Law* at 1-17.

22 *Supra*, note 9 at 607.

23 As noted earlier, Roberts, questions whether "'humanitarian war' is not an oxymoron". He points out that armed intervention "may come to involve a range of policies and activities which go beyond, or even conflict with, the label 'humanitarian'". The use of force with the objective of saving lives is likely to lead to more loss of lives. The lives of intervenors as well as innocent civilians are likely to be endangered through such operations. Booth has noted in this regard "[t]he desire to 'do something' has to be

ventions: the politically motivated and politically innocent varieties. The former take place when the political interests of a major power are evident, and this affects the legitimacy of the action. The latter type of intervention fails to consider and address the political causes of conflict from the onset. He questions the selective nature of humanitarian interventions even among the many candidates for intervention in the third world which reinforces doubts about the real motives of intervenors, and concludes:

> [f]or many reasons humanitarian intervention, in any effective sense of the term, can be considered a nonstarter. Both politically motivated and politically innocent varieties of intervention may be counterproductive. Moreover, lack of resources and will could make such intervention selective, detracting further from its credibility as a legitimate instrument for the enforcement of the will of the international community as a whole.[24]

However, as Whitman argues, "the deployment of military force is always founded on a hard-headed calculation of risk, and there is nothing to preclude humanitarian objectives on an agenda framed by a more determinedly self-interested motivation".[25] It is argued that if states conduct their affairs based on national interest, then the trends in post-Cold War humanitarian interventions can be explained on the basis that national interest is being redefined in such a way that humanitarian crises cannot be ignored since they affect all nations. This is especially evident

---

tempered by the knowledge that not only may it not be possible to 'solve' a historic conflict by a short and dramatic military intervention, but it may make matters worse". For him, "[t]he injection of military force to impose a resolution on a bitter conflict is likely to be a slippery slope, and probably an ineffective instrument". See Roberts, *supra*, note 8 at 429, 448; Booth, "Human Wrongs and International Relations" (1995) 71: 1 *International Affairs* 103 at 120-121.

24 Ayoob, "The New-Old Disorder in the Third World" (1995) 1: 1 *Global Governance: A Review of Multilateralism and International Organizations* 59 at 70-71. See also Conference Report, *supra*, note 5 at 6.

25 Whitman, "A Cautionary Note on Humanitarian Intervention" (1995) *Journal of Humanitarian Assistance* 1.[http: //www-jha.sps. cam.ac.uk]

when humanitarian tragedies result in wider regional conflicts, and when the flow of refugees destabilizes states. Thus, states have begun to redefine national interests more broadly, and in ways which acknowledge the relationship between humanitarian crises, national, political, and economic security. Instances of less consistent responses to humanitarian crises or the selection bias in these cases of intervention can be explained by the assignment of various priorities to other interests at any particular time.

Having said that, though, it seems to be the case that not all states are supportive or in favour of a proactive international interventionist stance. International support has been forthcoming mainly from Western states. France has been in the forefront, and champion of a new human-itarian intervention,[26] and to this end has even created a ministry of humanitarian affairs to deal exclusively with those issues. In a speech

---

26 France has advocated a new *droit et devoir d'ingerence* (the right and duty of intervention). This discourse has its foundations in ethical concerns grounded in human rights conceived as minimum standards. Bettati and Kouchner have been its foremost proponents. Kouchner has argued "[h]umanitarian intervention, backed by UN resolutions, has become our duty. And little by little, under the impetus of war, catastrophe and the awakening of the World's conscience, this duty should become our right; to intervene wherever victims are calling out for help, where human beings are suffering and dying, regardless of borders". Kouchner, "A Call for Humanitarian Intervention" UNHCR, (December 1992) Refugee Magazine, quoted in Harriss ed., *supra*, note 2 at 61. Even though this position has not been accepted as common practice, international opinion seems to be moving in that direction. For a detailed discussion of d'ingerence see for example, Bettati, "The Right of Humanitarian Intervention or the Right of Free Access to Victims?" (1992) 49 *The Review: International Commis-sion of Jurists* 1; Sandoz, "'Droit' or 'Devoir d'Ingérence' and the Right to Assistance: The Issues Involved" (1992) 49 *The Review: International Commission of Jurists* 12; Garigue, "Intervention-Sanction and 'Droit D'Ingérence in International Humanitarian Law" (1993) XLVIII *International Journal* 668; Bowring, "The 'Droit et Devoir D'Ingérence': A Timely New Remedy for Africa?" (1995) 7: 3 *African Journal of International and Comparative Law* 402 at 499; Guillot, "France, Peacekeeping and Human-itarian Intervention" (1994) 1: 1 *International Peacekeeping* 30-43.

in July 1991, President Mitterand stated "France had taken the initiative of this new right, rather extraordinary in the history of the world, which is in a way the right of intervention within a country, when parts of its population is a victim of persecution".[27] Humanitarian issues have thus become a major theme of French diplomacy within the UN. French initiatives led to the adoption of UN General Assembly Resolution 43/131 (1988), which recognized the right of humanitarian assistance to victims of natural disasters and similar emergency situations, and Resolution 45/100 (1990) which reaffirmed these rights and the endorsement of the "corridors of tranquillity" concept in order to facilitate the work of humanitarian agencies.[28] It is therefore not surprising that given the context of collective efforts aimed at alleviating human misery and suffering, France was actively involved in UN operations in Northern Iraq, Bosnia and Somalia, and took the initiative, albeit too late, in responding to the humanitarian tragedy in Rwanda. Thus, with regard to the justification for the French intervention in Rwanda, its Foreign Minister claimed a legal duty to intervene for humanitarian reasons.

Appalled by the response to the Rwandan crisis, the Danish Foreign Ministry convened a study group to jointly evaluate the emergency assistance to Rwanda, which has resulted in a report that Hindell charac-

---

27 Quoted in Bettati, *ibid.*, at 5. Elsewhere, French Foreign Minister Dumas has commented "France believes that the law of humanity takes precedence over the law of nations and should always serve as a basis for the latter; and that the duty to provide humanitarian assistance, ever more an integral part of today's universal conscience, should be embodied in international legislation in the form of a "right to intervene on humanitarian grounds". Quoted in Torrelli, "From Humanitarian Assistance to 'Intervention on Humanitarian Grounds'?" (1992) *International Review of the Red Cross* 228 at 229.

28 France was also responsible for the origins of GA Res.A/RES/46/182 (1991), requesting the UN Secretary-General to establish the position of an emergency assistance coordinator to work with governments and insurgents to provide more effective humanitarian assistance. This ultimately led to the establishment of the United Nations Department of Humanitarian Affairs in early 1992.

terizes as essentially an interventionist manifesto.[29] Germany and Belgium have expressed similar sentiments. Genscher, the former German Foreign Minister, in his speech at the UN General Assembly expressed Germany's conviction that "where human rights are trampled upon, the family of nations cannot be confined to a role of spectator".[30] The Belgian Foreign Minister also declared that "the international community should help States to respect human rights, and to force them to do so, if necessary".[31] This statement emphasizes the idea that governments must be held accountable for the human rights violations of their citizens. Thus, forcible measures should, if necessary, be employed in extreme situations that warrant its use. Following the intervention in Northern Iraq the British Foreign Secretary Douglas Hurd proclaimed that "recent international law recognises the right to intervene in the affairs of another state in cases of extreme humanitarian need".[32] Britain has consistently supported Security Council resolutions dealing with various humanitarian crises discussed earlier. The Canadian government laid the foundation for a significantly different approach in dealing with sovereignty, internal conflicts and human rights violations abroad. Former Canadian Prime Minister Brian Mulroney drew an analogy between internal violence and international violence by saying "just as it is no longer acceptable for society, the police, or the courts to turn a blind eye to family violence, so it is equally unacceptable for the international community to ignore violence and repression within national borders".[33] The new approach in Canadian foreign policy has been sup-

---

29   For a review of the five-volume report titled "The International Response to Conflict and Genocide: Lessons from the Rwanda Experience", see Hindell, "An Interventionist Manifesto" (1996) XIII *International Relations* 23-35.

30   *Ibid.*

31   *ibid.*

32   Quoted in *supra*, note 25 at 2.

33   Notes for an Address by Prime Minister Brian Mulroney on the Occasion of the Centennial Anniversary Convocation, Stanford University, California, September 29, 1991. Cited in Gillies, "Human Rights or State Sovereignty? An Agenda for Principled Intervention" in Charlton and Riddle-Dixon eds., *International Relations in the Post-Cold War Era* (Scarborough: Nelson

portive of humanitarian intervention, although this has not been without controversy.[34] At the outset of the Clinton administration, a policy of "assertive multilateralism" was put forth. This policy was to see the US working closely with international institutions like the UN in addressing intractable problems like ethnic conflicts, aggression, genocide, and the survival of democracy in the face of tyranny, among others. The then US Permanent Representative to the UN, Madeleine Albright, outlined the relationship that the US will forge in the UN. She pointed out the fusion of peace-keeping and peace enforcement operations with the delivery of humanitarian assistance as examples of what the US will support.[35] The US experience in Somalia resulted in the passage of PDD 25 which had implications for ruling out the deployment of ground troops in Bosnia until after the Dayton Accord made that possible, the refusal to act in Rwanda other than sending humanitarian relief after the massacres had stopped, and hesitation about intervention in Haiti, although a US-led intervention was finally authorized. With the recent American involvement in Haiti, and in Bosnia, the US sought to define

---

Canada, 1993) at 463. Similarly, the Canadian permanent representative to the UN in an address points out "[t]he principles of sovereignty and non-intervention in internal affairs of states no longer reign supreme in the UN. Indeed the pressure felt in the UN is for more intervention, not less and the debate of the future may revolve less around the question of whether the UN has the right to intervene than whether it has a duty to do so". "Lessons From Recent UN Operations in Yugoslavia, Cambodia and Somalia" (Address to the Sixth Annual Meeting of the Academic Council on the United Nations System, Montreal, June 18, 1993) at 2. Quoted in Weiss, "Intervention: Whither the United Nations" (1993) 17: 1 *The Washington Quarterly* 109 at 124.

34 See Department of Foreign Affairs and International Trade, *Towards a Rapid Reaction Capability for the United Nations* (1995). For a fuller discussion of Canadian initiatives and controversies surrounding her policy of humanitarian intervention which have been criticized as being spontaneous, inconsistent, and without adequate planning and material support, see, Keating and Gammer, "The "New Look' in Canada's Foreign Policy" (1993) XLVIII *International Journal* 720-748.

35 Albright, "The Use of Force in a Post-Cold War World" in (1993) 4: 39 *US Department of State Dispatch*, at 667.

new forms of participation in global conflict management which Blech-man has described as "combining UN peace operations with parallel, but separately managed, multilateral interventions".[36] Although American foreign policy was less consistent, characterized by a range of responses from doing something to doing very little, this multilateral approach in using international institutions has benefited the UN in terms of its capacity for dealing with the humanitarian problems it has been confronted with.

At the UN Security Council summit meeting in 1992, Russian President Boris Yeltsin intimated support for the primacy of human rights and the need for a rapid response mechanism to consolidate the rule of law throughout the world.[37] At the very least, Russia and other former Soviet Republics have explicitly expressed their intention to participate actively in international institutions, [38]or at least acquiesce in the international community's efforts towards such ends. This development has permitted the UN to take actions that it would previously not have taken.

In Northern Iraq, Resolution 688 was passed to protect the Kurdish population through the creation of no-fly zones and Kurdish enclaves. In this case, the Security Council emphasised the link between respect for human rights and the maintenance of international peace and security. In Somalia, UNOSOM was created by Resolution 751 to monitor a cease-fire and escort delivery of humanitarian supplies. Resolution 794 authorized the use of "all necessary means" to establish a secure environment for humanitarian relief operations which provided the basis for the US-led

---

36 For a detailed explanation of why the US hesitated in taking on the leader-ship role promised by the rhetoric of the new world order, see Daalder, "The United States and Military Intervention in Internal Conflict" in Brown ed., *The International Dimensions of Internal Conflict* (Cambridge, Mass: MIT Press, 1996), 461-488. See also Blechman, "Emerging from the Inter-vention Dilemma" in Crocker, Hampson, Aall eds., *Managing Global Chaos: Sources of and Responses to International Conflict* (Washington, D.C.: United States Institute of Peace Press, 1996), 287-295.
37 Cited in Scheffer, *supra*, note 2 at 283.
38 Evangelista, "Historical Legacies and the Politics of Intervention in the Former Soviet Union" in Brown ed., *supra*, note 36 at 119.

deployment of UNITAF. Under Resolution 814, the UN assumed transitional authority in Somalia, where the use of force was authorized to restore law and order and to deal with bandits. Moreover, in the case of the former Yugoslavia, Resolution 743 established UNPROFOR with a mandate "to create the conditions of peace and security required for the negotiation of an overall settlement of the Yugoslav crisis". In a series of Resolutions, the Security Council demanded an unimpeded delivery of humanitarian supplies for the populations of Sarajevo and other parts of the country. Resolution 770 called on states and regional organisations to take "all measures necessary", which did not exclude the use of force, to protect humanitarian convoys in Bosnia. Furthermore, in Rwanda the UN mandate before the genocide broadly related to monitoring implementation of the Arusha Accords. Resolution 912 reduced the number of troops with a mandate to act as intermediary between the government and rebel forces, and to assist in humanitarian relief operations. By Resolution 918, the mandate was expanded to include protection of refugees through the establishment of safe humanitarian zones and the provision of security for relief operations. Resolution 929 eventually authorized member states to use "all necessary means" to carry out humanitarian operations. In Liberia, ECOWAS troops intervened in that country in a bid to end the civil strife, restore law and order, and prevent further loss of life. The Security Council in Resolution 788 commended the ECOWAS effort to find a lasting peace to the conflict. Finally, in Haiti, Security Council Resolution 841 imposed wide-ranging sanctions in 1993 on the Haitian military authorities. Resolution 940 called on member states to form a multinational force and to use "all necessary means" to return Aristide to power. The United Nations Mission in Haiti (UNMIH) was finally deployed to replace US forces. These resolutions reflect the UN's willingness, at least in principle, to find massive human rights violations as constituting threats to, or breaches of international security, and thus taking action not excluding military measures to redress those violations.

Opposition to humanitarian intervention has mainly come from Third World states. Many non-Western states view with scepticism the motives of Western countries in advocating humanitarian intervention. States like China, India[39] and Zimbabwe[40] have been at the forefront in arguing that it is not within the domain of the Security Council to handle human rights issues. China is very important in this regard since it has a veto in the Security Council. However, it has proceeded cautiously. It has so far gone along with other Security Council members, albeit reluctantly, in authorizing UN-directed humanitarian interventions, or abstained from voting in that regard.[41]

Furthermore, concerns have been expressed about the expanding definition of "international peace and security" by the Security Council.[42] Scepticism is expressed regarding the interpretation of what amounts to "a threat to the peace, breach of the peace, or act of aggression" to include issues which were previously considered to be within the domestic affairs of states. The Security Council can become involved in issues ranging from peace building and peace enforcement; early-

---

39 India, however, has intimated its readiness to develop "general principles and guidelines for such intervention". See UN S/PV.3046 31 January 1992). Cited in Childers and Urqhart, *Renewing the United Nations System* (Uppsala: Dag Hammerskjold Foundation, 1994) at 18.

40 Zimbabwe seems to be retreating from this position. In reaction to ECOMOG's intervention in Liberia, Zimbabwe's President Mugabe stated the "'domestic affairs' of a country must mean affairs within a peaceful environment, but ... when there is no government in being and there is just chaos in the country, surely the time would have come for an intervention to occur". Ephson, "Right to Intervene", quoted in Wippman, "Enforcing the Peace: ECOWAS and the Liberian Civil War" in Damrosch ed., *supra*, note 1 at 182. See also, *ibid.*

41 Wheeler and Morris comment that the reason for Chinese caution remains unclear, though it seems her experience with colonial powers, and a radically different notion of human rights grounds a policy that places sovereignty and nonintervention as sacrosanct principles. Although its sensitivity over Article 2 (7) of the UN Charter acts as a strong brake on Security Council-mandated humanitarian intervention, her options are limited by wider political constraints. This dictates not stepping too far out of line with a Security Council dominated by its three Western permanent members, especially the US. Wheeler and Morris, *supra*, note 19, at 162-163.

42 See Weiss, "On the Brink of a New Era? Humanitarian Interventions, 1991-1993" (1994) *The Brown Journal of World Affairs* 235 at 240.

warning systems; protection of human rights to nonmilitary threats to peace and security in the economic, social, humanitarian and ecological fields.[43] The ever-increasing powers of the Security Council have created an apprehension among certain third world states of being subject to, in the words of Dallmeyer, a "hegemonic directorate", or what Nafziger describes as "the spectre of a modern Holy Alliance of the Great Powers" that could dispense with the principle that the basis for UN action in a state's domestic affairs must be subject to that state's consent.[44] Some of these states perceive a greater threat from the per-

---

43 See generally, Boutros-Ghali, *An Agenda for Peace: Preventive Diplomacy, Peacemaking and Peace-keeping*, Report of the Secretary-General pursuant to the statement adopted by the Summit Meeting of the Security Council on 31 January 1992 (New York: United Nations, 1992).

44 Dallmeyer provides an example of reaction by certain third world states towards a proposal to provide emergency humanitarian assistance following major disasters. The Moroccan representative stated "[w]e believe also that any international assistance in this area must be subject to consent, following a request by a state, and must be compatible with needs and priorities. This consent and the appeal of the State concerned must be respected ... [O]ur country cannot go along with any undertaking designed to create autonomous machinery that, if not properly defined and strictly controlled, could result in interference in the internal affairs of States". The Indian representative stated: "The Charter of the United Nations stresses the domestic jurisdiction of states; nobody can or should dilute this aspect of national sovereignty, even if the stakes are high". The Pakistani delegate observed: "First, no attempt should be made to compromise national sovereignty when providing emergency assistance. We agree with those who have categorically rejected the use of humanitarian relief as a disguise for political intervention". Finally, the representative of Tunisia stated: "First, there must be consensus on this important and complex question. Emergency humanitarian assistance necessarily involves the participation of several parties, including donor and recipient countries ... Secondly, the main responsibility for disaster management rests with the Governments of the stricken countries. Humanitarian assistance ... should in no case violate the principle of national sovereignty. Any reform in this field should, in our view, fully respect national sovereignty as embodied in the consent given or the request made by the country concerned". See UN/46/PV.41 at 19-56. Quoted in Dallmeyer, "National Perspectives on International Intervention: From the Outside Looking In" in Daniel & Hayes eds., *Beyond*

manent members of the Security Council than existed during the Cold War contest between the superpowers.[45] Some Third World states have

---

Traditional Peacekeeping (London: Macmillan Press Ltd., 1995) 20. See also, Nafziger, "Humanitarian Intervention in a Community of Power Part II" (1994) 22 *Denver Journal of International Law and Policy* 219 at 230.

45 A publication by the United Nations Association in the United States, notes "[t]he East-West rapprochement and the invigoration of the Security Council have left many developing countries deeply concerned about their vulnerability to international intervention in the post-cold war era. There is now no counterbalancing political bloc to discourage Western countries from using economic pressure to force a developing- country government to make the sort of internal changes they believe desirable; and the big powers have now demonstrated the potential for forceful intervention under the aegis of the Security Council. Governments of weak and poor states, acutely aware of the limited nature of their 'sovereignty' in confronting the global tides of economic, social, environmental, and communication changes, have drawn the line to assert at least their political sovereignty. They have blocked efforts by Western powers to add to the Security Council agenda such issues as environment, drugs, and democratization – issues that, they fear, might be used to justify international intervention in their affairs – insisting that such matters are the province of the General Assembly, whose one-state/one-vote rule of decision-making embodies the Charter principle of the 'sovereign equality of states'". UNA-USA, *The Common Defense; Peace and Security in a Changing World* (1992) at 34, quoted in Nafziger, *ibid.*, at 230-231, footnote 54. A detailed discussion of specific proposals, and the pros and cons of Security Council reform is beyond the scope of this work. On these issues see The Report of the Independent Working Group on the Future of the United Nations, *The United Nations in its Second Half-Century*; Sutterlin, "United Nations Decisionmaking: Future Initiatives for the Security Council and the Secretary-General" in Weiss ed., *Collective Security in a Changing World* (Boulder: Lynne Rienner Publishers, 1993) 121-138; Russet, O'Neill & Sutterlin, "Breaking the Security Council Logjam" (1996) 2: 1 *Global Governance: A Review of Multilateralism and International Organizations* 65; Smith, Comment, "Expanding Permanent Membership in the UN Security Council: Opening a Pandora's Box or Needed Change?" (1993) 12 *Dickinson Journal of International Law* 173; Bills, Note, "International Human Rights and Humanitarian Intervention: The Ramifications of Reform on the United Nations' Security Council" (1996) 3: 1 *Texas International*

thus argued that the General Assembly should maintain a greater involvement in decisionmaking processes regarding humanitarian intervention lest the UN becomes dominated by the major powers using it for their own ends.[46] In cautioning against an expansion of the definition of humanitarian intervention, the Chairman of the Group of 77 noted:

> the Group of 77 is slightly worried that some ... may not be sensitive to certain pleas for an abiding respect for the sovereignty of nations. Our concern stems from our historical past, when many of us, as colonial subjects, had no rights. The respect for sovereignty which the United Nations system enjoins is not an idle stipulation that can be rejected outright in the name of even the noblest gestures ... An essential attribute of that sovereignty is the principle of consent, one of the cornerstones in the democratic ideal itself.[47]

In essence, international intervention is viewed with suspicion and fear since it conjures up memories of imperialism, colonialism, racism and humiliation which militates against any broadly based formulation of principles regarding intervention.[48] Nevertheless, this attitude of outright hostility to humanitarian intervention seems to be changing. As noted in the last chapter, comments by several prominent African leaders endorsing ECOMOG's role in Liberia demonstrate shifting attitudes and thinking about sovereignty and under what circumstances intervention may be appropriate. This seems to be consistent with Childers and Urqhart's findings of a growing readiness among third world states to

---

Law Journal 107; Caron, "The Legitimacy of the Collective Authority of the Security Council" (1993) 87 *American Journal of International Law* 552; Weiss, "Whither the United Nations" (1993) 17: 1 *The Washington Quarterly* 109.

46 Nafziger, *ibid.*, at 231.

47 UN/46/PV.41, at 34-36. (Statement of Mr. Kofi Awoonor, representative of Ghana speaking on behalf of the Group of 77). Quoted in Dallmeyer, *supra.*, note 44 at 26.

48 Dallmeyer, *ibid.*

find ways for "genuinely disinterested and UN-directed humanitarian intervention".[49]

Moreover, international organization inertia appears to open the door to a more vigourous approach to humanitarian interventions. Within institutional secretariats, the former UN Secretary-General Boutros Ghali's *Agenda for Peace,* and the Supplement to the *Agenda* offer a useful starting point. Boutros-Ghali observed that respect for sovereignty and integrity is "crucial to any common international progress", but "the time of absolute and exclusive sovereignty ... has passed" and it was necessary for governments "to find a balance between the needs of good internal governance and the requirements of an ever more interdependent world".[50] During his tenure of office, Boutros-Ghali regularly urged the Security Council to devote equal attention to less prominent trouble spots of the world when it seemed the Council would not discuss, or even act in certain situations. As one commentator notes, the fast pace of change "turned on its head the long-standing question of whether the United Nations could do anything useful" to "whether the United Nations can do everything".[51]

The theme of a more assertive humanitarianism was commented on by other prominent Secretariat officials. The former UN representative in Somalia, Mohamed Sahnoun, observed that "[g]overnments cannot invoke sovereignty to prevent humanitarian access to the population ... If there is a humanitarian catastrophe, the international community is morally bound to intervene".[52] In a similar vein, Jan Eliasson, Undersecretary-General of the UN Department of Humanitarian Affairs, in response to a question as to whether there is a moral obligation for the international community to respond to humanitarian crises, asserted: "[c]ertainly there is a moral obligation, and now also an obligation that

---

49 See *supra,* note 39.
50 *Supra,* note 43 at 5.
51 Pastor, "Forward to the Beginning: Widening the Scope for Global Collective Action" (1993) XLVIII *International Journal* at 642.
52 Sahnoun, "An Interview with Mohamed Sahnoun" (1994) 2-3 *Middle East Report* 29.

is accepted by ... member states [of the UN]". He went on to admit that "the concept that solidarity does not end automatically at a border but rather with a human being in need has broken through in the humanitarian area".[53] Commenting on the role of the Security Council in the post-Cold War era, the present UN Secretary-General, Kofi Annan, then Undersecretary-General for peacekeeping operations stated that "[t]he ... Council is moving towards greater interventionism because in many tragedies public opinion perceives a human imperative that transcends anything else. We are using more force because we are encountering more resistance".[54] Writing about concerns leading to an effort to better define conditions under which humanitarian intervention could be undertaken, the Undersecretary-General for Political Affairs sums it up as follows:

> [i]n interviews with representatives of member states at the United Nations and in discussions at various seminars, there is no objection to humanitarian intervention where there is overwhelming evidence that many people are starving and those involved in the conflict are deliberately preventing the international community from delivering humanitarian assistance to those who need it.
>
> There is a consensus that under such conditions efforts must be made to overcome obstacles and to override the objections of the warring parties. There is also a consensus that these efforts should not be carried out unilaterally – either by one country or a coalition of countries – but that such a situation should be brought to the attention of the international community to obtain a clear mandate for humanitarian intervention.[55]

Thus, it appears the consensus supports multilateral intervention in situations of extreme human rights deprivations and suffering.

---

53 Eliasson, "Interview – The UN and Humanitarian Assistance" (1995) 48: 2 *Journal of International Affairs* at 492-493.
54 Quoted in Martin, "Peacekeeping as a Growth Industry" (1993) 32 *The National Interest* at 3.
55 Jonah, "Humanitarian Intervention" in Weiss and Minear eds., *Humanitarianism Across Borders: Sustaining Civilians in Times of War* (Boulder: Lynne Rienner Publishers, 1993) 69 at 70.

With regard to regional organizations, international enforcement action involved their use, for example, in the former Yugoslavia. Security Council authorization to states "acting nationally or through regional organizations" to enforce a no-fly zone over Bosnia, to enforce economic sanctions, and to protect the Bosnian Muslims through the concept of safe havens were undertaken through NATO and the Western European Union. As Javier Solana, NATO Secretary-General, points out, "NATO helped bring the war to an end through its support over several years to the United Nations through its limited, but effective use of airpower". He continues, "not to meet the challenge of Bosnia would have been a profound failure of collective will and an abdication of moral responsibility by the entire international community".[56] These statements suggest NATO had in the past complemented UN efforts, and that where necessary, the organization will support future UN efforts when called upon.

The Haitian problem served as a trigger for the OAS to overcome its reservations regarding interference in the domestic affairs of states. The Santiago commitment of June 1991, in which the OAS resolved that any "sudden or irregular interruption of democratic political institutional process" in any one of the member states would result in the convening of an emergency meeting to decide what to do, was vital in establishing "a normative trigger" to deal with Haiti, even though "articulation of the response was too weak to constitute a deterrent".[57] Nevertheless, more significantly, the Declaration "internationalizes issues of domestic governance, stating that democracy and human rights are essential to regional identity".[58] If the lessons of Haiti are anything to go by, then it seems the OAS will be prepared to take similar kinds of action in future, even if they fall short of the use of force where democratic rule – and the consequent violations of human rights – is truncated.

---

56 Solana, "NATO's role in Bosnia: Charting a New Course for the Alliance" (1996) XLVII *Review of International Affairs* 1.
57 Damrosch, *supra*, note 1 at 351.
58 Wedgwood, "Regional and Subregional Organizations in International Conflict Management" in Crocker et al., *supra*, note 36 at 279.

The Somalian tragedy has influenced the OAU in rethinking its approach to issues of sovereignty, human rights and intervention. Prior to the Somali catastrophe, African states were reluctant ot allow foreign intervention in internal strife on the continent. However, a change of viewpoint seems to be underway. At the OAU foreign ministers meeting in Addis Ababa in February 1992, and at its summit meeting in July 1992, African states were prepared to approve intervention in circumstances such as Somalia.[59] OAU commendation of the ECOWAS action in Liberia has already been noted. Since the tragedy of Somalia, the Organization's Secretary-General, Salim Salim, has made bold proposals for an OAU mechanism for conflict prevention and resolution. He has observed that "if the OAU is to play the lead role in any African conflict" then "it should be enabled to intervene swiftly". He goes on to suggest that the OAU should be a leader in transcending the traditional notion of sovereignty, building on African values of kinship, solidarity, and the view that "every African is his brother's keeper".[60] It is also interesting to note that African leaders gave their support for a military intervention to dislodge leaders of the recent coup in Sierra Leone. A Nigerian-led alliance took military action in that country which eventually led to the return of the ousted President. Reacting to the events, the UN Secretary-General noted there was general African acceptance of the military intervention. The Nigeria-led move had also enjoyed the apparent, if not explicit support of the OAU, and the Commonwealth, whose General Secretary called a military intervention "totally justified".[61] As noted earlier, these developments suggest an increasing recognition by many African states, and the OAU, that a total prohibition on intervention in a state's internal affairs as a result of suffering caused by war, or widespread human rights violations is no longer feasible, or necessarily in their interest.

---

59 *Supra*, note 55 at 74.
60 OAU Council of Ministers, Report of the Secretary-General on Conflicts in Africa, quoted in Deng, *supra*, note 6 at 299.
61 *The Globe and Mail*, June 4, 1997 at A13.

Nongovernmental organizations (NGOs)[62]are also becoming central to international responses to internal conflicts, and have performed important humanitarian tasks alongside other actors in the post-Cold War period. This increasing importance of NGOs is becoming evident in the fact that "some control programmatic resources that rival or dwarf those of many governments and UN agencies".[63] During the Cold War,

---

62 Anderson has stated that "[n]ongovernmental organizations are privately organized and privately financed agencies, formed to perform some philanthropic or other worthwhile task in response to a need that the organizers think is not adequately addressed by public, governmental, or United Nations efforts". These NGOs receive private contributions or are founded with funds from private sources. Some rely on funding from their national governments, and others completely avoid any government funding. Anderson, "Humanitarian NGOs in Conflict Intervention" in Crocker et al., *supra*, note 36, at 344. A distinction is usually made between national and international NGOs. The latter, may however, be described as national NGOs that extend their activities internationally. Anderson identifies four different mandates that NGOs mainly based in Europe and North America, and operating internationally, carry out. These are: 1. The provision of humanitarian relief to people in emergencies. 2. The promotion of long-term social and economic development in countries where poverty persists. 3. The promulgation and monitoring of basic human rights, and 4. The pursuit of peace, including the promotion of the philosophy and techniques of negotiation, conflict resolution, and nonviolence. NGOs have grown over the last forty years from 832 in 1951 to 16, 208 in 1990. It is estimated that some 400 to 500 international NGOs are currently involved in humanitarian activities world-wide. Beigbeder, *The Role and Status of International Humanitarian Volunteers and Organizations: The Right and Duty to Humanitarian Assistance* (Dordrecht: Martinus Nijhoff Publishers, 1991) at 80-82. Cited in Martin, "International Solidarity and Cooperation in Assistance to African Refugees: Burden-Sharing or Burden-Shifting?" (Paper presented at the Eighth Annual Meeting of the Academic Council on the United Nations System, New York City, 19-21 June 1995) at 12. On the changing nature of NGOs, see for example, Aall, "Nongovernmental Organizations and Peacemaking" in Crocker et. al., *ibid.*, at 433-443.

63 Examples of these NGOs include: World Vision International, Save the Children, CARE, International Rescue Committee, *Medecins Sans Frontières,* Oxfam, and Catholic Relief Services. These organizations engage in various activities in almost all humanitarian crises. Others, however, operate in

when UN agencies' operations were limited due to political considerations, NGOs mostly became the conduit through which relief reached
suffering populations. NGOs have been more flexible, less partial, and
operate to some extent on rules of neutrality in their delivery of relief
supplies in situations of conflict.

The rise of NGOs in emergency relief throughout the 1980s was spec-
tacular. In 1991, European-based NGOs delivered about 450, 000 tonnes
of food aid to Africa, in comparison with about 180, 000 tonnes in
1989.[64] In 1994 NGOs accounted for over 10% of total public development aid which amounted to some $8 billion. They earmarked about
half of the ever-growing percentage of their resources to emergency
relief.[65] According to Weiss, "about one-quarter of US development
aid is being channelled through NGOs as of the mid-1990s", and this
is expected to "increase to one-half by the end of the 1990s".[66] The
reasons for NGO success in emergency relief work according to Griffiths,
Levine and Weller lie in their "flexibility, speed of reaction, comparative
lack of bureaucracy, operational and implementational capacity, commitment and dedication of the usually young staff". Additionally, "the
political independence of the NGOs ... gives them a strong comparative
advantage in increasingly complex internal conflicts".[67] Their "low
overhead operations help victims that governmental and intergovern-
mental aid programs often fail to reach".[68] Thus, bilateral and multilateral organizations are increasingly relying on NGOs as sub-contrac-

---

specific countries or continents, sectors, or population groups. The International Committee of the Red Cross (ICRC), which Weiss places in a
category by itself, assists and protects individuals in both international and
non-international armed conflicts. This organization consists of
governmental and nongovernmental members, with donor governments
funding about 90% of its $500 million budget. Weiss, "Nongovernmental
Organizations and Internal Conflict" in Brown ed., *supra*, note 36 at 439.

64 Griffiths et al., *supra*, note 2 at 72.

65 Weiss, in Brown ed., *supra*, note 36 at 441-442.

66 *Ibid.*, at 442. See also, Bennet et al., *Meeting Needs: NGO Coordination
in Practice* (London: Earthscan Publications, 1995) at xi.

67 Griffiths et.al., *supra*, note 2 at 72.

68 *Ibid.*

tors. While this trend will allow for expansion of the scope of their activities, some NGOs have expressed concern about the possibility of being exploited by governments or international institutions with a consequent loss of autonomy in their operations.[69]

The provision of humanitarian relief by NGOs has become a vital supplement to the efforts of governments and international institutions to rebuild societies torn apart by war. NGOs response to the humanitarian crises spawned by internal conflicts in the post-Cold War era has meant that they are often trapped in the midst of this violence. Thus, it becomes important to assess their views on the use of force in addressing these crises.

NGO support for the use of military forces in the complex humanitarian emergency situations of the 1990s appears to be mixed. UN military actions have been the "objects of a loud chorus of criticism or mixed messages from parts of the NGO community – some calling for military intervention one day and then castigating it the next".[70] Given the pacific nature of humanitarian NGOs, it is not surprising that many of them have been critical of the use of force in the various UN missions. However, as Keen, Curtis and Slim suggest there is a tendency among the NGO community, where "it has certainly been almost de rigueur to concentrate on the failings of UN military humanitarianism rather than to identify what military forces can do well in such situations".[71] While African Rights, for instance, has described UN and NGO missions in this period as one of liberating humanitarian organizations from "the Cold War straight-jacket", it has nevertheless been critical of these missions. It has characterized these missions as "a reckless period of humanitarianism unbound in which assertive humanitarian policies have often done

---

69   See Weiss, in Brown ed., *supra*, note 36 at 442. Also, see generally Weiss ed., *Beyond UN Subcontracting: Task-Sharing with Regional Security Arrangements and Service-Providing NGOs* (London: Macmillan Press, 1998).

70   Slim, "Military Humanitarianism and the New Peacekeeping: An Agenda for Peace?" (1995) *Journal of Humanitarian Assistance* at 3.[http://www-jha.sps.cam.ac.uk]

71   Keen, Curtis, and Slim, *Calling in the Cavalry: A View of the Literature on Military Humanitarianism 1991-1994* (CENDEP: Oxford Brookes University, 1995 in press), quoted in *ibid*.

more harm than good".[72] Some NGOs like Save the Children Fund (SCF) believe that the injection of UN military forces in humanitarian emergencies actually worsens the situation. SCF has stated that

> military intervention is no panacea ... greater [military] intervention by the international community should not be automatically equated with rapid and durable solutions ... once the United Nations intervenes militarily in a humanitarian emergency, as in Somalia, its actions can all too easily become part of the problem – another complicating ingredient.[73]

Slim and Visman have argued UN military operation in Somalia in early 1993 made NGOs less secure with the disarming of armed guards hired by the NGOs whilst leaving the rest of the country still armed.[74] Once the UN had decided that it was embarking upon disarming these armed guards, a more persistent and appropriate level of force should have been used to disarm other armed bandits who were left to roam the countryside, and who carried out attacks on relief consignments targeted for the civilian population.

There seems to be a dilemma among the NGO community on the use of force regarding situations of intense levels of violence and acute human suffering. As Wheeler asks, in cases where NGO operations are overwhelmed given the level of violence and human suffering, should they appeal to states to use force knowing that such use of force, while unlikely to offer a lasting solution, might save a lot of lives in the short term?[75] In answering this question, Cuny has noted how NGOs operating

---

72 African Rights, *Humanitarianism Unbound: Current Dilemmas Facing Multi-Mandate Relief Operations in Political Emergencies* (London: November, 1994), quoted in *ibid.*

73 Save the Children, *The United Nations and Humanitarian Assistance: A Position Paper* (London: Save the Children, 1994) at 3. Quoted in *ibid.*, at 3-4.

74 Slim and Visman, "Evacuation, Intervention and Retaliation: United Nations Operations in Somalia, 1991-1993" in Harriss ed., *supra* note 2, 145 at 156-157.

75 Wheeler, "Agency, Humanitarianism and Intervention" (1997) 18: 1 *International Political Science Review* 9 at 22.

in the Former Yugoslavia and Somalia "resented their sponsoring governments' willingness to place them in harm's way without providing adequate security, either by peacekeeping forces or direct intervention".[76]
Luck, head of the United Nations Association of the United States, has
stated that when "a national government collapses, leaving chaos and
widespread domestic violence in its place" the UN is justified in authorizing a multilateral military intervention.[77]

In the former Yugoslavia, NGOs were initially hostile to the idea of
armed protection for humanitarian convoys, but as the situation deteriorated, they finally succumbed to the idea.[78] Having resisted since
its inception to advocate the use of force for humanitarian purposes,
Médecins Sans Frontières eventually called for it in response to the
genocide in Rwanda in 1994.[79] Other NGOs like the International Commission of the Red Cross (ICRC) argue that the use of force has a role
to play in preventing massive violations of human rights. It notes military forces were effective when ordered to protect civilians in Rwanda,
and that far more lives could have been saved had the UN employed
military force to stop the genocide.[80] The capability of even the small
UN force to save lives in Rwanda in May 1994, and the French action
to secure the chaotic situation in Southwestern Rwanda subsequently,
according to Weiss, led Oxfam to conclude "that the policy of caution
about UN peacekeeping, induced by experiences in Somalia, should now
be reviewed".[81] Thus, it appears to be the case with NGOs, as Hermet

---

76 Cuny, "Humanitarian Assistance in the Post-Cold War Era" in Weiss and
    Minear eds., *supra*, note 55 at 162.
77 Luck, "Making Peace" (1992-93) 89 *Foreign Policy* at 145.
78 Guillot, *supra*, note 26 at 33.
79 *Supra*, note 73 at 22.
80 International Federation of Red Cross and Red Crescent Societies, *World
    Disasters Report 1996* (Oxford: Oxford University Press, 1996) at 80. Cited
    in Farrell, "Book Reviews" (1997) 73: 1 *International Affairs* at 162.
81 Vassal-Adams, *Rwanda: An Agenda for Action* (London: Oxfam Publishers,
    1994) at 59, cited in Weiss, "Overcoming the Somalia Syndrome" (1995)
    1: 2 *Global Governance: A Review of Multilateralism and International
    Organizations* 171 at 179.

suggests, that the level of human suffering has come to mean "there could be no qualms about the methods used".[82]

In sum, there is a shift underway in terms of the principle and practice of humanitarian intervention in the post-Cold War era.[83] There is the belief that state sovereignty connotes responsibility and cannot be used as a shield to perpetrate massive and systematic violations of human rights. Human rights have been a recurring normative theme in international relations. From the inception of the state system, the Peace of Westphalia, which marked the ideas of the sovereign authority of the state, and subsequent peace treaties noted in chapter one, contained significant clauses limiting sovereign prerogatives vis-a-vis the rights of populations inhabiting their territories. Contemporary post-1945 developments have also seen an elaborate international human rights regime starting from the UN Charter, the Universal Declaration of Human Rights, to the 1966 UN Covenants on Human Rights, the Genocide Convention, and beyond. These documents spell out responsibilities of governments toward their citizens in terms of promoting and protecting their human rights. Recent innovations such as the OAS's Santiago Declaration, the OSCE's Copenhagen Document, and the Harare Commonwealth Declaration[84] contain notable human rights provisions. Even states applying to join NATO's "Partnership for Peace" are required to commit to the Universal Declaration on Human Rights. Similarly, international financial institutions like the World Bank and the IBRD have since the 1980s imposed various political conditionalities, including

---

82 Hermet, "Rwanda: Why Médecins Sans Frontières made a Call for Arms" in Forbes and Francois eds., *Populations in Danger 1995: A Médecins Sans Frontières Report* (London: Medecins Sans Frontieres) at 91-96. Quoted in *supra*, note 77 at 22.

83 Blechman observes "the belief that governments have a right, even obligation, to intervene in the affairs of other states seems to have gained great currency in recent years". Blechman, in Crocker et. al. *supra*, note 36 at 288.

84 For a discussion of this Declaration as well as an overall renewed commitment by the Commonwealth to human rights issues, see for example, Duxbury, "Rejuvenating the Commonwealth – The Human Rights Remedy" (1997) 46: 2 *International and Comparative Law Quarterly* 344-377.

respect for human rights, as a prerequisite for receiving financial loans and aid. Most western countries in their dealings with third world countries have as well incorporated the linking of aid and trade to human rights in their foreign policies. The Commission on Global Governance has recently acknowledged that

> global security extends beyond the protection of borders, ruling elites, and exclusive state interests to include the protection of people ... To confine the concept of security exclusively to the protection of states is to ignore the interests of people who form the citizens of a state and in whose name sovereignty is exercised. It can produce situations in which regimes in power feel they have the unfettered freedom to abuse the right to security of their people ... All people, no less than states, have a right to a secure existence, and all states have an obligation to protect those rights.[85]

As Jackson argues "human security presupposes the sovereignty of the people, and where those conditions are not met a human right of security can be invoked to protect people endangered by that development".[86]

These policies and practices suggest adherence by governments to certain principles in their domestic practices. Interventions to protect human rights should thus not be seen as incompatible with state sovereignty but rather affirming it. Support for humanitarian intervention is on the rise among scholars, states (to a lesser degree among Third World states), in institutional secretariats, and it seems in the NGO community, at least in cases of intense violence and human suffering. The trend, however, is still unfolding, and if the international community should move towards an entrenched notion of humanitarian intervention, the UN can use recent cases to provide a framework for laying down some general principles or guidelines, on when an internal situation warrants

---

85   *Our Global Neighbourhood: The Report of the Commission on Global Governance* (Oxford: Oxford University Press, 1995) at 81-84.

86   Jackson, "Human Security in a World of States", Paper presented at the Annual Conference of the International Studies Association, Toronto, March 18-22, 1997, at 16.

international action, either through authorization by the Security Council
or regional organization.

It is apparent that although support for humanitarian intervention
is gaining currency, there are still various actors opposed to its use. In
order to get closer to an international consensus, a clear articulation of
principles is necessary to further enhance the legitimacy of humanitarian
interventions. To this end, some analysts have proposed the Security
Council and the General Assembly jointly adopt a standard operating
procedure for humanitarian intervention.[87] At the very least, some kind

---

87   In Adam Roberts' view "one might even say that if a coherent philosophy
     and practice of humanitarian intervention could be developed, it could have
     the potential to save the nonintervention rule from its own logical absur-
     dities and occasional inhumanities". Roberts, ""The Road to Hell': A Criti-
     que of Humanitarian Intervention" (1993) 16: 1 *Harvard International
     Review* at 11. Nafziger, for example, proposes that "the General Assembly
     and the Security Council might jointly adopt a resolution on humanitarian
     intervention. It should preempt unilateral actions. Accordingly, member
     states would be authorized, *only* [emphasis in original] under the resolution,
     to undertake measures in other states that are deemed necessary to vindicate
     fundamental human rights. Such measures might include the use of force,
     unless [emphasis in original] the target state agreed within a reasonable
     period of time to submit immediately to fact-finding and conciliation
     procedures, and in good faith to carry out any resulting recommendations
     or decisions. Under Articles 98 and 99 of the UN Charter, the Secretary-
     General might continue to play a central role. Rescue missions requiring
     an immediate response would be an exception; these would be governed
     primarily by customary rules of law, such as immediacy, proportionality,
     and necessity. Thus, humanitarian intervention by one state would be
     permissible only under two circumstances: first, if a target state had declined
     to submit a dispute to impartial review within a reasonable period or time;
     second, if after agreeing to do so, the target state failed to comply in good
     faith with resulting recommendations or decisions. Humanitarian interven-
     tion would be subsumed within a process of community decision, and would
     be authorized only as a last resort when Article 33 procedures have failed.
     Effective community deliberations and collective initiatives, rather than
     unilateral argument and doctrinal justification of intervention, would become
     the hallmark of a new process of multilateral dispute resolution". See
     Nafziger, *supra*, note 44 at 229. Burton also proposes codification of a
     limited doctrine of unilateral humanitarian intervention in one of three

of general declaration or statement analogous to the Copenhagen Document or the Santiago Declaration would be appropriate.[88] While international consensus, understood not necessarily to mean unanimity but eliciting the widest possible support to bring this about, will be a dif-

---

forms: 1. an amendment to the UN Charter; 2. a multilateral treaty; or 3. a General Assembly resolution. He assesses the merits of each form as well as an acknowledgement of the political obstacles to codification. See Burton, "Legalizing the Sublegal: A Proposal for Codifying a Doctrine of Unilateral Humanitarian Intervention" (1996) 85: 2 *The Georgetown Law Journal* 417 at 440-448.

88 The Copenhagen Document recognises a responsibility to protect democratically elected governments, if these are threatened by acts of violence or terrorism. Document of the Copenhagen Meeting of the Conference on the Human Dimension of the Conference on Security and Co-operation in Europe (CSCE), reprinted in (1990) 29 *International Legal Materials* 1305. For comments on the Document see Halberstam, "The Copenhagen Document: Intervention in Support of Democracy" (1993) 34 *Harvard International Law Journal* 163. A similar declaration is the Moscow Concluding Document. This document affirms the CSCE's (now OSCE) power to conduct investigations of human rights violations in member states without their consent. See *Conference on Security and Co-Operation in Europe: Document of the Moscow Meeting on the Human Dimension, Emphasizing Respect for Human Rights, Pluralistic Democracy, The Rule of Law, and Procedures for Fact-Finding*, reprinted in (1991) 30 *International Legal Materials* 1670. The Santiago Declaration calls for an automatic meeting of the OAS Permanent Council "...in the event of any occurrences giving rise to the sudden or irregular interruption of the democratic political institutional process or of the legitimate exercise of power by the democratically elected government in any of the Organization's member states, in order, within the framework of the Charter, to examine the situation, decide on and convene an ad hoc meeting of the Ministers of Foreign Affairs, or a special session of the General Assembly, all of which must take place within a ten-day period". It further stipulates the purpose of any such meeting should be "to look into the events collectively and adopt any decisions deemed appropriate, in accordance with the Charter and international law". Resolution on Representative Democracy adopted June 5, 1991, OAS AG/RES.1080 (XXI-0/91). It was pursuant to these provisions that the OAS adopted economic sanctions against Haiti following the coup that toppled President Jean-Bertrand Aristide.

ficult undertaking, it is nevertheless worth exploring. It is in this regard
that the notion of epistemic communities becomes important.

3   THE ROLE OF EPISTEMIC COMMUNITIES IN FORGING CONSENSUS

Epistemic communities have been employed in altering perceptions and
framing the context for collective responses to various international
problems. Examples of specific issue-areas in which epistemic community roles have had significant influence include arms control, where
a US based epistemic community framed the issue and cultivated an interest in superpower cooperation around the theme of nuclear arms control.
In pollution control, ecologic epistemic community activities have engendered joint decisions emphasizing environmental protection. In telecommunications, epistemic community activity has been relevant in
framing the context of a telecommunications regime and influencing
state choices in the direction of multilateral agreements. In structuring
the Law of the Sea regime, epistemic consensus on the economics of
seabed mining produced a broader set of possible bargaining aimed at
promoting a broader arrangement of interest-based negotiation. It also
aided in the identification of specific compromises on which international
policy coordination could be based.[89] In post-World War II economic
management, policymakers were alerted to the possibilities of mutual
gain and the need for strategic, coordinated action.

   Ikenberry shows how the underlying structures of power and interest
alone do not fully explain the postwar economic order. He looks instead
at how the many conflicting political interests were reconciled in
reaching agreement by laying emphasis on the community of experts,
and how consensus was arrived at within the larger political environment, and within and across both the United States and British govern-

---

89   The articles in (1992) 46: 1 *International Organization* by Drake, Kalypso,
     Nicolaidis, Adler, Peterson and Haas all investigate the ways in which epis-
     temic communities provided an initial framework of issues for collective
     debate, which influenced subsequent negotiations and brought about pre-
     ferred outcomes to the exclusion of others in the examples outlined.

ments. For him, what mattered in structuring this economic regime was that it was not based on policy ideas put forth by an expert community, but that "the policy ideas resonated with the larger political environment". The ideas of the experts, however, "ultimately carried the day because they created the conditions for larger political coalitions within and between governments...". He argues that the group of economists and policy specialists did not entirely constitute an epistemic community by a strict definition of the term, "nor did the manner in which these experts influenced the terms of settlement conform to the strict logic of epistemic community influence...". The community of experts in this instance was not "an independently existing scientific community".[90] Rather, the expert community was created by the process of Anglo-American negotiations. Thus, he points out, to that extent

> ...the Anglo-American experts were, at best, a primitive epistemic community, a collection of professional economists and policy specialists who shared a set of general and technical views which concerned the proper functioning of the world economy and distilled contemporary economic thought and lessons of recent economic history.[91]

The application of Ikenberry's notion of primitive epistemic communities to efforts aimed at codifying humanitarian intervention can potentially yield fruitful results. In the realm of humanitarian intervention, one has to identify, heuristically, analogous actors at the international level that could be considered epistemic communities given the role of these communities in other issue areas. It is a recognized fact of international political life today that human rights have been internationally recognized and made the object of varied international action. This development

---

90   Ikenberry, "A World Economy Restored: Expert Consensus and the Anglo-American Postwar Settlement" (1992) 46 *International Organization* 289 at 292, 293.

91   *Ibid.*, at 293. The application of the epistemic community concept here is exploratory. It is only a research strategy and an invitation to academics and groups working in the area of international human rights seriously to consider this approach in terms of its potential contribution to speeding up the process of codification of humanitarian intervention.

has been possible in recent times, due partly to the activities of certain groups. It would seem that groups such as the ICRC, Amnesty International, Human Rights Watch, Oxfam, Médecins Sans Frontières, to name a few, and the International Commission of Jurists, the International Law Commission, the Academic Council on the United Nations System (ACUNS) have all been active and significant catalysts in the process of international governance and have played varying roles in the institutionalization of human rights norms. These groups potentially fall within the category of constituting at least primitive epistemic communities, for purposes of consolidating the present support for humanitarian intervention. These various groups have performed useful roles in the past and will be expected to do so in the future.

NGOs have demonstrated the ability to influence policymakers and have tried to effect change at the national and international levels by working with and beyond the governmental framework.[92] As Weiss notes, "[b]oth through formal statements in UN fora and through informal negotiations with international civil servants and members of national delegations, many NGOs seek to ensure that their views, and those of their constituencies, are reflected in international texts and decisions".[93] Their influence on state responses to humanitarian crises vary from one organization to another and from case to case. Their efforts can affect the timing and configuration of international responses to humanitarian crises.[94] In the US, for instance, NGO efforts aided the favourable domestic climate that existed for the Bush administration's decision to intervene in Northern Iraq in support of the Kurds. A similar climate existed for the US-led decision to intervene in Somalia. Key personnel within the humanitarian NGO community such as the President of CARE-US, who had been seconded to the UN, pressed for the use of force in Somalia. With regard to Rwanda, NGO advocacy was less effective in

---

92 On the contributions of Humanitarian Nongovernmental Organizations to humanitarian action see for example, Aeberhard, "A Historical Survey of Humanitarian Action" (1996) 2: 1 *Health and Human Rights: An International Quarterly Journal* 31-44.

93 Weiss, in Brown ed., *supra*, note 36 at 443.

94 *Ibid.*, at 444.

persuading the Clinton government to act in stopping the genocide in April and May 1994. Eventually, however, they were successful in urging the government to act in support of relief operations in the refugee camps of Zaire and Tanzania.[95]

Additionally, NGOs have drawn attention of the media to crisis situations, particularly, as in the case of the Sudan and in Ethiopia, where the governments were part of the humanitarian crises that engulfed those countries. Thus, their influence on public opinion, reports and activities, as Helman notes, "puts pressure on Western democracies to act, regardless of the nonintervention principle".[96] In France, NGOs championed an assertive humanitarian policy that was adopted by the French government which subsequently influenced debates in the UN, leading to the passage of the General Assembly Resolutions on humanitarian assistance referred to earlier. Thus NGOs can have an impact on how the international community will respond to various humanitarian crises, as well as the ability to influence the creation of new norms for international action.

Humanitarian NGOs operate on a political logic shaped almost entirely by moral considerations, and as Falk points out, on "an ethos of responsibility and solidarity – that is very different from the statist outlook that guides most governments when they are engaged in humanitarian missions".[97] Where governments are stymied by political considerations and unwilling to act, humanitarian NGOs can become significant catalysts, at least, in efforts directed towards non-use of force in humanitarian tragedies, and prompting states to use force when all else fails. Humanitarian NGO operations historically have been dependent upon interstate organizations for the provision of channels of action. However, in recent times, international NGOs not only transcend national boundaries but

---

95 *Ibid.* See also, Ramsbotham and Woodhouse, *supra*, note 8 at 204.
96 Helman, "Humanitarian Intervention: The De Facto Record" in Scheffer, Gardner and Helman, *Post-Gulf War Challenges to the UN Collective Security System: Three Views on the Issue of Humanitarian Intervention* (Washington, D.C.: United States Institute of Peace, 1992) at 34.
97 Falk, *supra*, note 11 at 499.

have also created a direct and independent form of non-governmental diplomacy through networks of their own.[98] In the words of one writer:

> [t]he economic, informational and intellectual resources of NGOs have garnered them enough expertise and influence to assume authority in matters that, traditionally, have been solely within the purview of state administration and responsibility ... [Furthermore], the relative influence of NGOs is not a static phenomenon. [T]heir impact on state policies has changed and is changing with time.[99]

In sum, apart from the important roles humanitarian NGOs play in humanitarian crises, they are also engaged in education and advocacy. Given these functions and first-hand knowledge and experience in different humanitarian crises situations, it is possible that NGOs can be instrumental in any endeavour to convince governments of the benefits of formulating agreeable principles of humanitarian intervention through a combination of conferences, publicity, including making recommendations, and governmental diplomacy.

Since the 1940s, the International Law Commission has played a significant role in generating ideas and making proposals to the General Assembly for the development of consistent and coherent rules on various aspects of international law. It was, for example, instrumental in formulating the Law of the Sea regime, and has been prominent in putting forward proposals for the establishment of an international criminal court and criminal code. Based on the experience of the Commission in those areas, it is feasible that it could have a pivotal role in establishing the nature of a collective debate on humanitarian intervention.

The Academic Council on the United Nations System (ACUNS) is an international association of scholars, teachers, practitioners and others

---

98 See Sikkink, "Human Rights, Principled Issue Networks, and Sovereignty in Latin America" (1993) 47 *International Organization* 411 at 441. Also, see generally, Weiss & Gordenker eds., *NGOs, The UN and Global Governance* (Boulder: Lynne Rienner Publishers, 1996).

99 Clark, "Non-Governmental Organizations and their Influence on International Society" (1995) 48 *Journal of International Affairs* 507 at 508.

active in the work and study of international organizations. This group shares a professional interest in encouraging and supporting education and research which deepen and broaden understandings of international cooperation. In implementing its goals, the Council focuses special attention on the programs and agencies of the United Nations system. It also forges close working relationships with the UN Secretariat and other institutions within the UN system, as well as with other inter-governmental and non-governmental organizations. The Council's program consists of promoting research and organizing conferences and workshops to deliberate salient issues affecting the international community. Individual members of this group have been at the forefront in advocating humanitarian intervention and pertinent issues or considerations for its exercise. Based on the experience of these members in humanitarian crises situations and their writings, it is possible to disseminate these views among the wider membership that come from different parts of the world. Members from various countries may then articulate the advantages of codifying humanitarian intervention, with the ultimate goal of influencing governments towards that end.

The various groups, humanitarian NGOs, and publicists discussed here bear evidence of a primitive epistemic community or an epistemic-like community. Based on the experience of these actors in other issue-areas, it is suggested that identification of these groups and a simultaneous coordination of their activities at the national and international levels is sufficient to demonstrate the utility of epistemic communities in furthering the principle of humanitarian intervention as well as helping in its international institutionalization.[100]

In addition to the issues examined above, other important considerations that can be taken into account by epistemic communities in the effort towards providing a consolidated framework for collective humanitarian intervention should include, among others: the establishment of a permanent international criminal court; defining the respective roles of the UN and regional organizations in humanitarian intervention; and

---

100 See, Adler & Haas, "Conclusion: Epistemic Communities, World Order, and the Creation of a Reflective Research Program" (1992) 46 *International Organization* 367 at 371-372.

the conditions under which humanitarian intervention may be legitimately exercised.

First, issues relating to the possibility for the creation of a permanent international criminal court to try, among other international crimes, egregious human rights violations must be seriously considered.[101] Advances have been made under the auspices of the UN in declaring human rights deserve special protection. The many governmental actions adversely affecting human rights which are now prohibited through the UN Charter, the Universal Declaration of Human Rights, and several other international instruments examined in chapter two are indicative of this progress. Many states are increasingly demonstrating a willingness to accept international norms in an effort to create and maintain a more peaceful and stable international order. In this context, there is growing international recognition of the pressing need for such an institution as an essential means for reducing many of the sources of tension and

---

101 A detailed examination of issues is beyond the scope of this work. There is however a voluminous literature on the subject. See for example Tutorow ed., *War Crimes, War Criminals and War Crimes Trials – An Annotated Bibliography and Source Book* (1986); Ferencz, "An International Criminal Code and Court: Where they Stand and Where they're Going" (1992) 30 *Columbia Journal of Transnational Law* 375; Scharf, "The Jury is Still Out on the Need for an International Criminal Court" (1991) 135 *Duke Journal of International and Comparative Law* 135; Gianaris, "The New World Order and the Need for an International Criminal Court" (1992-1993) 16 *Fordham International Law Journal* 88; Greenberg "Creating an International Criminal Court" (1992) 10 *Boston University International Law Journal* 119; Anderson, "An International Criminal Court -An Emerging Idea" (1991) 15 *Nova Law Review* 433; McCormack and Simpson, "The International Law Commission's Draft Code of Crimes against the Peace and Security of Mankind: An Appraisal of the Substantive Provisions" (1994) 5: 1 *Criminal Law Forum: An International Journal* 1. See generally the articles in (1997) 60: 1*Albany Law Review* (Annual Symposium on Conceptualizing Violence: Present and Future Developments in International Law); Cassese, "On the Current Trends towards Criminal Prosecution and Punishment of Breaches of International Humanitarian Law" (1998) 9: 1 *European Journal of International Law* 2.

conflict among states, and to make individuals responsible for their crimes.[102] Although the Security Council has demonstrated some activism in creating ad hoc international criminal tribunals for the former Yugoslavia and Rwanda, with the object of punishing those suspected of committing war crimes and other grave breaches of international humanitarian law, these ad hoc measures are problematic. Inherent in ad hoc measures dealing with international criminality, apart from political and procedural flaws, is the question of selective adjudication.[103] The reported atrocities that were committed, for example,

---

102 The need for an international criminal court assumes importance when one assesses developments in international law pertaining to international or transnational crimes. The existing international law and practice is largely dependent on numerous international conventions addressing particular crimes, and require states to enact legislation criminalizing certain acts, prosecute or extradite offenders. These conventions cover crimes such as crimes against peace, aggression, war crimes, crimes against humanity, torture, genocide, apartheid, drug offences, counterfeiting, slavery, piracy, traffic in women and children, maritime terrorism, aircraft hijacking, aircraft sabotage, crimes against diplomatic agents and other internationally protected persons, and hostage taking. Bassiouni, for example, lists the existence of 22 categories of international crimes representing 315 international instruments between 1815-1988. See, Bassiouni, *International Crimes: Digest/Index of International Instruments 1815-1985*, Vols. I & II (1986). For a general exposition on state jurisdictional competence see Brownlie, *Principles of Public International Law*, 4th.ed., (Oxford: Clarendon Press, 1990) at 298-317; Shaw, *International Law* 3rd.ed., (Cambridge: Grotius Publications Ltd., 1991) at chapter 11.

103 The creation of an ad hoc tribunal for the former Yugoslavia for example, was viewed by some as politically driven and discriminatory. In a letter addressed to the UN Secretary-General, the Minister of Foreign Affairs of the Federal Republic of Yugoslavia noted: "Yugoslavia is one of the advocates of the idea concerning the establishment of a permanent international tribunal and respect for the principle of equality of States and universality and considers, therefore, the attempts to establish an ad hoc tribunal is discriminatory, particularly in view of the fact that grave breaches of international law of war and humanitarian law have been committed and are still being committed in many armed conflicts in the world, whose perpetrators have not been prosecuted or punished by the international

in Liberia and Burundi have gone unpunished. In other areas where internal conflicts are still continuing, with alleged crimes against international humanitarian law being perpetrated, there seems to be

---

community ... War crimes are not committed in the territory of one State alone and are not subject to the statute of limitations, so that the selective approach to the former Yugoslavia is all the more difficult to understand and is contrary to the principle of universality". A/48/170; S/25801 of 21 May 1993. Quoted in Perera, "Towards the Establishment of an International Criminal Court" (1994) 20 *Commonwealth Law Bulletin* 298 at 300. Wedgwood, for example, notes three potential problems that may limit the effectiveness of the Yugoslav War Crimes Tribunal. These are (1) the reluctance of the UN to proceed with war crimes trials in absentia, or effecting international arrest of the offenders; (2) the sources of applicable law for the war crimes trials; and, (3) the UN's failure to address the delicate relation between politics and criminal law after a civil war, particularly the absence of any pardoning power or amnesty power in the political organs of the UN. See Wedgwood, "War Crimes in the Former Yugoslavia: Comments on the International War Crimes Tribunal" (1994) 34 *Virginia Journal of International Law* 267. Rather generally, one commentator argues that "[h]owever impartial and incorruptible members of an ad hoc tribunal might be, the mere fact that the tribunal had been set up expressly to try crimes arising out of particular circumstances would suggest, however unjustly, that the tribunal is not impartial, that the matters to be tried have been prejudged and that the tribunal has been set up to give a false impression that justice is being done". Bridge, "The Case for an International Criminal Justice and the Formulation of International Criminal Law" (1964) 13 *International and Comparative Law Quarterly* 1255 at 1271. Crawford observes the creation of an ad hoc court carries with it the risk that it will be seen in a sense as part of the conflict. The establishment of special tribunals raise expectations that something will happen, which may divert attention from resolution of the conflict to the targeting and punishment of transgressors. Crawford, "The ILC Adopts a Statute for an International Criminal Court" (1995) 89 *American Journal of International Law* 404 at 415. See generally the articles in (1994) 5: 2-3 *Criminal Law Forum: An International Journal* (which is devoted to a critical study of the International Tribunal for the Former Yugoslavia); Scharf, "A Critique of the Yugoslavia War Crimes Tribunal" (1997) 25: 2 *Denver Journal of International Law and Policy* 313.

demonstrable inaction. Thus, the case for a standing court supported by the entire international community is strong.

UN activism surrounding humanitarian intervention also suggests an important role for regional and sub-regional organizations. Regional arrangements like the EU, OSCE, NATO, ECOWAS, and OAS played important roles in humanitarian operations in the Former Yugoslavia, Liberia, and Haiti respectively. Their role in the maintenance of international peace and security suggests that they can perform important functions in fostering or undertaking humanitarian interventions. Thus, their use in this context has certain advantages that may not be realized through UN action alone. Chapter VIII of the UN Charter provides the legal and institutional arrangements between these organizations and the UN.[104] Article 52 encourages states to use regional organizations before referring conflicts to the Security Council. It also recommends that the Security Council make use of such regional arrangements to facilitate the pacific settlement of disputes or to carry out enforcement measures. Regional organizations acting independently, but "consistently with the Purposes and Principles of the United Nations" may deal "with such matters relating to the maintenance of international peace and security as are appropriate for regional action". Articles 53 and 54 prohibit regional organizations from taking measures involving international peace and security without Security Council authorization and by insisting that regional organizations inform the Council. It is evident that the security structure of the international system is characterised by an overlapping jurisdiction between the UN, regional, and subregional organizations. This lack of specificity on the division of responsibility, however, allows states the flexibility to create mechanisms fostering international peace

---

104 Article 52 (1) of the Charter states: "Nothing in the present Charter precludes the existence of regional arrangements or agencies for dealing with such matters relating to the maintenance of international peace and security as are appropriate for regional action, provided that such arrangements or agencies and their activities are consistent with the Purposes and Principles of the United Nations".

and security,[105] or to shift responsibility when they do not to deal with an issue.

As the United Nations is overburdened in its ability to engage in enforcement action relating to international peace and security, then what role is there for regional organizations? Are regional organizations appropriate mechanisms for conflict management? Should they be viewed as a viable alternative to the UN? Should there be a possible division of labour? How could regional organizations work in tandem with the UN? These are all questions that must be considered in structuring a role for regional and sub-regional organizations vis-a-vis the UN. Some observers have a preference for collective action at the regional level, believing that humanitarian intervention should be the result of an expression of community standards and that regional organizations usually reflect the community better than a universal organization like the United Nations. The advantages of regional collective action are familiarity with the region, its people, its culture and the general environment; a regional organization should therefore be better adapted to take preventive measures and monitor potentially volatile situations. Proximity to a conflict situation is also likely to prompt regional entities to act in a timely manner since they are more directly affected than are distant states. Moreover, the local population caught in the throes of internal conflict is likely to view intervention by troops from a regional organization more favourably; they are seen as less foreign and thus are more welcome. Lastly, the parties to a dispute might prefer a regional forum for settlement.

There are, however, many problems associated with regional action. Weiss, Forsythe, and Coate, after examining the role of regional entities in conflict management, contend that "the apparent advantages of regional institutions exist more in theory than in practice". "In reality, these organizations are far less capable" they point out, "than the United

---

105 Weiss, Forsythe & Coate, *The United Nations and Changing World Politics* (Boulder: Westview Press, 1994) at 34.

Nations".[106] First, most regional entities, especially non-western regional organizations lack the organizational, financial, and military capacities either to carry out mandates in peace and security or to take effective action. NATO, which is an exception, was reluctant, at least initially, to act in cases where it should have acted, especially in the former Yugoslavia. Regional organizations may also have a particular stake in a conflict. One or more of the strong states in regional organizations may also be parties to a conflict or other humanitarian emergency, thus crippling the capacity of the organization to act as a neutral mediator, and rendering conflict resolution problematic. Furthermore, members of a regional entity may be so deeply divided as to make agreement on a particular course of action difficult to arrive at. Lastly, the leadership of a regional organization may be unwilling to approve a course of action lest it provides a precedent to be used against them in the future.[107] Regional collective action can thus have either positive or negative effects in a conflict situation. Although they may have the advantage or privilege to seek peaceful solutions within their regions, they do not necessarily have the institutional capabilities to do so.

In light of the difficulties associated with effective regional action, it is argued that "[a]lthough it makes sense to strengthen regional organizations where possible, ...they should not be viewed as a viable alternative to the United Nations in a conflict management role".[108] Rather, these regional arrangements should be viewed as a complement and not a replacement when it comes to dealing with issues relating to maintenance or restoration of international peace and security. In this era of multilateral diplomacy, the United Nations must clearly define

---

106 *Ibid.*, at 35. For a detailed historical account of global-regional competition in peacemaking see Henrikson, "The Growth of Regional Organizations and the Role of the United Nations" in Fawcett and Hurrell eds., *Regionalism in World Politics* (Oxford: Oxford University Press, 1995) at 122-168. On the role of regional organizations in enhancing global order, see Farer, "The Role of Regional Collective Security Arrangements" in Weiss ed., *supra*, note 2 at 153-186.

107 See *supra*, note 105 at 33-39.

108 MacFarlene & Weiss, "Regional Organizations and Regional Security" (1992) 2: 1 *Security Studies* 6 at 7.

its relationship with the various regional organizations. Issues relating to when the United Nations should address a particular problem, when a regional body should take up an issue, and under what circumstances both the UN and regional organizations should act in a particular situation need to be carefully re-examined. The modalities within which regional arrangements and the United Nations can best complement each other, especially regarding the taking of enforcement action, should be an important consideration.

The post-Cold War practice suggests new forms of inter-organizational cooperation in approaches to human security. It is encouraging that in his supplement to the *Agenda for Peace*, former UN Secretary-General Boutros-Ghali, identified at least five ways in which this cooperation can take place. First, there should be consultations with the object of exchanging views on conflicts and finding solutions to those conflicts. Second, mutual support must be gained through diplomatic initiatives. The United Nations can offer support to regional organization endeavours in peacemaking and other issues and vice versa. Third, operational support can be offered by regional organizations such as NATO air support for UNPROFOR troops during the conflict in the Former Yugoslavia. The United Nations, on the other hand, provides advice on technical or other aspects of peacekeeping operations carried out by regional organizations. Fourth, there should be co-deployment of UN and regional troops in enforcement actions such as in Liberia, or the former Soviet Republic of Georgia. Lastly, joint operations may be undertaken, as with the UN mission in Haiti.[109] The task ahead will be to build upon these principles, structuring a flexible UN-regional organizations relations. As Henrikson argues, "...at least some UN action is always necessary, if not to elicit regional-organizational efforts then to make them more fully accepted and effective; yet, without direct and deep regional involvement, international peacemaking is likely to lack continuity and consistency".[110]

If the present inconsistent stance on intervention is to improve, it is necessary to develop criteria for such interventions along with the

---

109 See *Supplement to an Agenda for Peace*, *supra*, note 13.
110 Henrikson, *supra*, note 106 at 125.

development of the means and the will to intervene. The conditions that would justify intervention to protect human rights have been enumerated in various scholarly works.[111] These deal with substantive and procedural issues and are considered either absolute or preferential prerequisites. The working standards that would trigger humanitarian intervention may be formulated to include the following. First, the unilateral or multilateral use of force should be contemplated or resorted to only in situations of gross, persistent and systematic violations of human rights.[112] This would include an imminent threat or widespread loss of life manifested in either mass killings, starvation, or other activities. Minear, for instance, suggests the number of persons affected should be expressed either as a percentage of a nation's population or as an absolute number. He also cites the severity of the threat to human life; the generation of substantial refugee flows or internally displaced persons and a demon-

---

111 See for example, Lillich, "Forcible Self-Help by State to Protect Human Rights" (1967) 53 *Iowa Law Review* 325; Fonteyne, "The Customary International Law Doctrine of Humanitarian Intervention: Its Current Validity under the UN Charter" (1974) 4 *California Western International Law Journal* 203; Bazyler, "Reexamining the Doctrine of Humanitarian Intervention in Light of Atrocities in Kampuchea and Ethiopia" (1987) 23 *Stanford Journal of International Law* 547; Hassan, "Realpolitik in International Law: After Tanzania-Ugandan Conflict "Humanitarian Intervention' Reexamined" (1980/81) 17 *Willamete Law Review* 859 at 897; Behuniak, "The Law of Unilateral Humanitarian Intervention by Armed Force: A Legal Survey" (1978) 79 *Military Law Review* 157; Nanda, "The United States' Action in the 1965 Dominican Crisis: Impact on World Order" (1966) *Denver Law Journal* 439; Krylov, "Humanitarian Intervention: Pros and Cons" (1995) 17 *Loyola of Los Angeles International and Comparative Law* 365.
112 See also, Moore, "The Control of Foreign Intervention in Internal Conflict" (1969) 9 *Virginia Journal of International Law* 209 at 264; Lillich, *ibid.*, at 348; Lauterpacht, ed., *Oppenheim's International Law* (8th ed.1955) at 312. Hoffmann, for instance, suggests "...massive violations of human rights, which would encompass genocide, ethnic cleansing, brutal and large-scale repression to force a population into submission, including deliberate policies of barbarism, as well as the kinds of famines, massive breakdowns of law and order, epidemics and flights of refugees that occur when a 'failed state' collapses..." *Supra*, note 2 at 38.

strated inability to cope with the magnitude of the crisis by the government in question.[113] It is difficult, however, to quantify the number of people whose lives must be threatened or lost before the use of force is justifiable. The more widespread the abuse, the easier it is to document and confirm its existence.

Secondly, there should be a preference for collective action wherever feasible. The unilateral use of force should only be undertaken by an interested state when the United Nations or relevant regional organizations fail to prevent extreme human right abuses to such an extent

---

113 Minear, Weiss and Campbell, *Humanitarianism and War: Learning Lessons from Recent Armed Conflicts, Occasional Paper no.8* (Providence: Watson Institute for International Studies, 1991) at 44-45. Minear and Weiss offer the 'Providence Principles of Humanitarian Action in Armed Conflict' to include the following: "1. Relieving Life Threatening Suffering: Humanitarian action should be directed toward the relief of immediate, life threatening suffering. 2. Proportionality to Need: Humanitarian action should correspond to the degree of suffering, wherever it occurs. It should affirm the view that life is as precious in one part of the globe as another. 3. Non-Partisanship: Humanitarian action responds to human suffering because people are in need, not to advance political, sectarian, or other extraneous agendas. It should not take sides in conflicts. 4. Independence: In order to fulfil their mission, humanitarian organizations should be free of interference from home or host political authorities. 'Humanitarian space' is essential for effective action. 5. Accountability: Humanitarian organizations should report fully on their activities to sponsors and beneficiaries. Humanitarianism should be transparent. 6. Appropriateness: Humanitarian action should be tailored to local circumstances and aim to enhance, not supplant, locally available resources. 7. Contextualization: Effective humanitarian action should encompass a comprehensive view of overall needs and of the impact of interventions. Encouraging respect for human rights and addressing the underlying causes of conflict are essential elements. 8. Subsidiarity to Sovereignty: Where humanitarianism and sovereignty clash, sovereignty should defer to the relief of life threatening suffering".See, "Humanitarian Values: Commentary" in Weiss and Minear eds., *supra*, note 55 at 4. For an elaboration of these principles see Minear and Weiss, *Humanitarian Action in Times of War: A Handbook for Practitioners* (Boulder: Lynne Rienner Publishers) at Chap. 1. For similar framework principles for humanitarian intervention see also, Ramsbotham and Woodhouse, *supra*, note 8 at 225-231.

that the humanitarian need is overwhelming and immediate action is needed. Where this is the case, there should be an immediate full reporting to the Security Council and the appropriate regional organization.[114]

Thirdly, great care must be taken to keep the use of force to a minimum where possible to prevent the escalation of violence. The intervention should be proportional to the triggering event. In other words, if the use of force should become necessary, it must be kept proportional to the nature and extent of the human rights violations. It is also important that the intervening forces stay as long as it takes to end the mass violence and loss of life.

Fourthly, the right of non-forcible humanitarian intervention by humanitarian nongovernmental organizations should arise when the following criteria are met: a) where man-made or natural disasters place large numbers of people at risk because of inadequate food or shelter, or acts of internal aggression lead to mass killings or casualties among the civilian population; b) where the local government is not capable of meeting or is unwilling to meet the humanitarian needs arising from the disaster or act of internal aggression; c) where the local government does not seek forcibly to prevent, and therefore acquiesces in, a non-forcible humanitarian intervention within its borders; and lastly, d) where the Security Council authorizes the intervention, and insists that the local government cooperate either with UN officials or other humanitarian aid agencies in the distribution of relief supplies.[115] It should be added that where action short of military force would be or have proven to be ineffective, the Security Council should in that situation consider authorizing the use of military force to achieve the humanitarian aims of the operation.[116]

Fifth, there should be an overriding humanitarian motive. Some scholars insist that the intervenor should be totally disinterested in the affairs of the target state, but this has been criticized as unrealistic where the decision to intervene falls upon a single state. Considerations of

---

114 Fonteyne, *supra*, note 111 at 264-265. See also, Moore, *supra*, note 112.
115 Scheffer, *supra*, note 2 at 288.
116 *Ibid.*

national interest should not, of themselves, render illegal or illegitimate an armed intervention so long as the overriding motive for the action is the protection of the most fundamental human rights.

Lastly, the exhaustion of alternative measures to protect victims is important. Intervenors must explore all other methods of bringing about a peaceful conflict resolution before embarking on the use of force. These would include the employment of diplomacy or the use of economic sanctions. However, where the threat is massive and the situation rapidly deteriorating, exhaustion of other remedies may not be required since delay is likely to exacerbate the situation. On balance, intervention should maximize the best outcome when weighed against other possible alternatives.[117]

In sum, the object of deliberating the issues discussed in this chapter is to reduce the dangers of abuse by proposing a standard against which to judge humanitarian interventions. As Minear suggests, the process of negotiating the new ground rules or trigger mechanism would help to de-politicize some of the post-Cold War conflicts and might gain the consent of a reluctant government or rebel group, or failing that, could help to isolate an entity unwilling to cooperate.[118] However, the establishment of such a standard is no guarantee that states would enforce it unless they considered it to be in their self-interest to do so.[119] Nevertheless, it is important that the issues and criteria discussed here should be seriously reconsidered with a view to improving them for acceptance by the international community.

The difficulty in making use of epistemic communities is the lack of consensus within the various bodies, even on the question of the desirability of codifying the principles of humanitarian intervention. At the very least, however, primitive epistemic communities or epistemic-like communities working within and outside the UN system could start to explore how a widespread consensus could be reached on the feasibility of such an undertaking. Here the dissemination and diffusion of

---

117 Dallmeyer, *supra*, note 44 at 25.

118 Minear, Weiss and Campbell, *supra*, note 113 at 43.

119 For a general discussion of arguments for and against codification see Chopra and Weiss, *supra*, note 2 at 99-101.

ideas on, among other things, the changing character of state sovereignty is important.

The nature of the increasing support for the the post-Cold War humanitarian interventions presents an opportunity to push forward the idea of codification. This undertaking is worth pursuing if the international community is to build upon the present practice of humanitarian intervention for the future. Epistemic communities can assist in this endeavour by laying the foundation through enlisting widespread support for the idea and its eventual reality.

5

CONCLUSION

This study has attempted to demonstrate a legitimate basis for humanitarian intervention through an examination of the evolution of the doctrine and its practice. The introduction briefly delineated the contours of the study. Chapter One outlined the historical development of the doctrine and practice of humanitarian intervention. It showed the doctrine coexisted with state sovereignty and that the meanings and interpretations of state sovereignty are not inconsistent with international intervention to protect human rights. Furthermore, it demonstrated that the doctrine of humanitarian intervention is grounded in international law, morality, scholarly writings on the subject, treaties, and state practice.

Chapter Two investigated the evolution and strength of humanitarian intervention under the UN Charter during the cold war era. It examined the norms of state sovereignty and nonintervention, the internationalization of human rights, and the UN Charter's effect on humanitarian intervention. It argued that the customary international law right of humanitarian intervention has survived the UN Charter. At least in principle, a norm of justified intervention to protect human rights can be found. Further, state practice relating to humanitarian intervention was discussed. It concluded that the extent of support or condemnation varied in each case depending on its impact on the wider geopolitical relationship between the superpowers, thus resulting in the doctrine not enjoying wide support in some cases. Nevertheless, the silent acquiescence on the part of majority of states and the UN, arguably, indicated a tacit acknowledgement of humanitarian intervention in the period under consideration.

Chapter Three examined the scope of collective humanitarian action in the post-Cold War period, the challenges and debates surrounding such intervention in their legal, moral, and practical dimensions in the cases of Northern Iraq, Somalia, the former Yugoslavia, Rwanda, Liberia, and Haiti. It suggested the cases show emergence of a wider support in the international community, albeit on a case-by-case basis around UN actions.

Chapter Four built on the preceding chapter by assessing contemporary developments in terms of sources of support for humanitarian intervention. It argued a notable shift seems to be underway. The principle has been invoked by the UN and regional institutions, by national governments, nongovernmental organizations, and publicists. Looking at the evidence, humanitarian intervention has gained wide support in the international community. It also articulated in this context the pertinent issues that need addressing in order to move towards consensus and enhanced legitimacy of humanitarian interventions. It utilized the notion of epistemic communities as vehicles to bring this about.

Some concluding remarks arising from the study are that intervention in support of human rights is grounded in the premise that it is the interests of humanity at large that are at stake, and not the interests of any particular state or group of states. From a legal perspective, the internationalization of human rights points to holding governments accountable for gross and systematic violations. Most governments that engage in violations of human rights tend to use state sovereignty and nonintervention as shields to protect them from scrutiny. Traditional notions of sovereignty, however, are beginning to give way to a growing international awareness grounded in international law, and under Chapter VII of the UN Charter, that states cannot ignore the consequences of internal conflicts and the attendant human rights violations that displace entire societies. State sovereignty means adherence to certain domestic practices, including protection of the human rights of citizens; thus the impediments that the concept has raised cannot, and should not, be used as a bar to international intervention in issues that are deemed international. Sovereignty has always been limited by human rights concerns. This is not something new. What we are witnessing in the post-Cold War era is an intensification and improvement of what has already been unfolding. This study suggests the scope of the 'international' is broadening to the point where the political authority of the UN and regional organizations has become more of a necessity.

Recent experience suggests the growth of authoritative claims to act in vindication of human rights. While the character of the UN's role has sometimes been ambiguous, and has been subject to criticism, nevertheless, the cases demonstrate an emerging international support for humanitarian interventions as legitimate activity. The cumulative effect of Security Council Resolutions relating to Iraq, Yugoslavia, Somalia, Haiti, Rwanda, and Liberia has been to establish the linkage between human rights violations and threats to, or breaches of international peace and security. It is equally plausible to argue that even if such link is not invoked, humanitarian intervention is still permissible or justifiable. In spite of problems that have plagued the UN, it has established protection forces to watch over the security of minority enclaves. It has also considered various means of securing the supply of humanitarian assistance to populations in distress as a result of internal conflicts. These developments constitute notable precedents for future international practice.

Even though post-Cold War practice reveals the UN is prepared to implement a broader conception of humanitarian intervention, there is a realization at the same time that some of the problems encountered do not lend themselves to short-term solutions. As Weiss points out, Security Council resolutions have not always matched the means to well-considered ends and objectives. Thus, a lack of commitment and resources has plagued some of the interventionary projects of this era. The result has been that UN humanitarian operations have suffered from operational and institutional shortcomings, and have not been translated into effective performance with any consistency, thus evoking mixed reactions.

The post-Cold War international order is still unfolding with its uncertainties. With the relaxation of East-West tensions and the demise of repressive regimes in many parts of the world, expressions of domestic tensions and grievances have come to the fore. Given this state of affairs, it is likely that internal conflicts will increasingly challenge what one analyst characterizes as "the ingenuity and resourcefulness of the international community".[1] If this is the case, then as Sadako Ogata remarks, "[t]he time has come for a major dialogue on the hard choices that will have to be made in the face of finite humanitarian resources and almost infinite humanitarian demands".[2] Pressure on the UN to engage in more humanitarian operations if this scenario unfolds will mean the assignment of priorities in light of limited capabilities to intervene effectively. As Weiss suggests, it would seem to be the case for now that "[c]onfronted with increasing chaos and a seemingly endless number of humanitarian emergencies, the choices are better prevention, better intervention, or triage".[3]

If the UN is to become more effective in the future regarding humanitarian interventions, then it must learn from its mistakes and build on its successes. This book suggests the necessity of establishing a comprehensive framework of general principles or statements to guide the UN in deciding when a domestic human rights situation or internal conflict warrants action by the Security Council, regional organization or a collectivity of states.[4] If future humanitarian interventions are to be successfully developed, then they must be collectively underwritten by

---

1   Minear, *Humanitarians and Intervention* (UN Programme, June 1994) at 9. See also, Schwartzberg, "A New Perspective on Peacekeeping: Lessons from Bosnia and Elsewhere" (1997 3: 1 *Global Governance: A Review of Multilateralism and International Organizations* 1 at 3 (providing figures suggesting hundreds of wars waiting to happen) .

2   Statement to the Economic and Social Council on Coordination of Humanitarian Assistance: Emergency Relief and the Continuum to Rehabilitation and Development, Geneva, July 1, 1993 at 4, quoted in Weiss, Intervention: Whither the United Nations? (1993) 17: 1 *The Washington Quarterly* 109 at 124.

3   Weiss, *ibid.*

4   But see Schachter, Commentary, (1992) 86 *American Society of International Law Proceedings* at 320 (cautioning against "a tendency on the part of those seeking to improve the United Nations to prescribe sets of rules for future cases, usually over-generalizing from past cases". For him, "[e]ach crisis has its own configuration. Governments will always take account of their particular interests and the unique features of the case. While they can learn from the past, it is idle and often counterproductive to expect them to follow 'codified' rules for new cases".

the international community as a whole. Epistemic communities may play a key role in this regard. The opportunity for developing a general framework towards successful humanitarian interventions has presented itself. How to improve collective responses still constitutes unfinished business of the international community.

BIBLIOGRAPHY

ARTICLES

Adelman, Howard. "Humanitarian Intervention: The Case of the Kurds" (1992) 4: 1 *International Journal of Refugee Law* 4.

Adler, Emmanuel & Haas, Peter. "Conclusion: Epistemic Communities, World Order, and the Creation of a Reflective Research Program" (1992) 46 *International Organization* 367.

Aeberhard, Patrick. "A Historical Survey of Humanitarian Action" (1996) 2: 1 *Health and Human Rights: An International Quarterly Journal* 31.

Ajaj, Ahmad. "Humanitarian Intervention: Second Reading of the Charter of the United Nations" (1993) *Arab Law Quarterly* 215.

Akhavan, Payam. "Lessons from Iraqi Kurdistan: Self-Determination and Humanitarian Intervention against Genocide" (1993) 1 *Netherlands Quarterly of Human Rights* 41.

Anderson, Stanley. "Human Rights and the Structure of International Law" (1991) 12 *New York Law School Journal of International and Comparative Law* 1.

Anderson, John B. "An International Criminal Court – An Emerging Idea" (1991) 15 *Nova Law Review* 433.

Arnison, Nancy. "International Law and Non-Intervention: When Humanitarian Concerns Supersede Sovereignty?" (1993) *Fletcher Forum* 199.

Augelli, Enrico & Murphy, Craig. "Lessons of Somalia for Future Multi-lateral Humanitarian Assistance Operations" (1995) 1: 3 *Global Governance: A Review of Multilateralism and International Organizations* 339.

Ayoob, Mohammed. "The New-Old Disorder in the Third World" (1995) 1: 1 *Global Governance: A Review of Multilateralism and International Organizations* 59.

Barkin, Samuel & Cronin, Bruce. "The State and Nation: Changing Norms and the Rules of Sovereignty in International Relations" (1994) 48 *International Organization* 107.

Bayefsky, Anne. "Cultural Sovereignty, Relativism, and International Human Rights: New Excuses for Old Strategies" (1996) 9 *Ratio Juris* 42.

Bazyler, Michael. "Reexamining the Doctrine of Humanitarian Intervention in Light of Atrocities in Kampuchea and Ethiopia" (1987) 23 *Stanford Journal of International Law* 547.

Behuniak, Thomas. "The Law of Unilateral Humanitarian Intervention by Armed Force: A Legal Survey (1987) 79 *Military Law Review* 157.

Benjamin, Barry. "Unilateral Humanitarian Intervention: Legalizing the Use of Force to Prevent Human Rights Atrocities (1992/93) 16 *Fordham International Law Journal* 120.

Benneh, E.Y. "Review of the Law of Non-Intervention" (1995) 7 *African Journal of International and Comparative Law* 139.

Beres, Louis R. "Iraqi Crimes and International Law: The Imperative to Punish" (1993) 21 *Denver Journal of International Law* 335.

Bettati, Mario. "The Right of Humanitarian Intervention or the Right of Free Access to Victims?" (1992) 49 *The Review: International Commission of Jurists* 1.

Betts, Richard K. "The Delusion of Impartial Intervention" (1994) 73: 6 *Foreign Affairs* 20.

Bilder, Rchard B. "Rethinking International Human Rights: Some Basic Questions" (1969) *Wisconsin Law Review* 170.

Bills, David. "International Human Rights and Humanitarian Intervention: The Ramifications of Reform on the United Nations' Security Council" (1996) 3: 1 *Texas International Law Journal* 107.

Booth, Ken. "Human Wrongs and International Relations" (1995) 71: 1 *International Affairs* 103.

Bowring, Bill. "The 'Droit et Devoir D'Ingerence': A Timely New Remedy for Africa?" (1995) 7: 3 *African Journal of International and Comparative Law* 402.

Bridge, John W. "The Case for an International Criminal Justice and the Formulation of International Criminal Law (1964) 13 *International and Comparative Law Quarterly* 1255.

Burmester, Byron F. "On Humanitarian Intervention: The New World Order and Wars to Preserve Human Rights (1994) *Utah Law Review* 269.

Burton, "Legalizing the Sublegal: A Proposal for Codifying a Doctrine of Unilateral Humanitarian Intervention" (1996) 85: 2 *The Georgetown Law Journal* 417.

Cabranes, J. "Human Rights and Non-Intervention in the Inter-American System" (1967) 65 *Michigan Law Review* 1147.

Caney, Simon. "Human Rights and the Rights of States: Terry Nardin on Nonintervention" (1997) 18: 1 *International Political Science Review* 27.

Caron, David. "The Legitimacy of the Collective Authority of the Security Council" (1993) 87 *American Journal of International Law* 552.

Cassese, Antonio. "On the Current Trends towards Criminal Prosecution and Punishment of Breaches of International Humanitarian Law" (1998) 9: 1 *European Journal of International Law* 2.

Chatterjee S.K. "Some Legal Problems of the Support Role in International Law: Tanzania and Uganda" (1981) 30 *International and Comparative Law Quarterly* 755.

Chopra, Jarat. "The Space of Peace-Maintenance" (1996) 15 *Political Geography* 335.

Chopra, Jarat & Weiss, Thomas G. "Sovereignty is no Longer Sacrosanct: Codifying Humanitarian Intervention" (1992) 6 *Ethics & International Affairs* 95.

Clark, Ann Marie. "Non-Governmental Organizations and their Influence on International Society" (1995) 48 *Journal of International Affairs* 507.

Clarke Walter & Herbst Jeffrey. "Somalia and the Future of Humanitarian Intervention" (1996) March/April *Foreign Affairs* 70.

Cobbah, Josiah A. "African Values and Human Rights Debate: An African Perspective" (1987) 9 *Human Rights Quarterly* 320.

Conference on Security and Cooperation in Europe, "Document of the Moscow Meeting on the Human Dimension", October 3, 1991. (1991) 30 *International Legal Materials* 1670.

Conference on Security and Co-Operation in Europe: Document of the Moscow Meeting on the Human Dimension, Emphasizing Respect for Human Rights, Pluralistic Democracy, The Rule of Law, and Procedures for Fact-Finding, reprinted in (1991) 30 *International Legal Materials* 1670.

Crawford, Susan. "U.N. Humanitarian Intervention in Somalia" (1993) 3 *Transnational Law and Contemporary Problems* 273.

Crawford, James. "The ILC Adopts a Statute for an International Criminal Court" (1995) 89 *American Journal of International Law* 404.

D'Amato, Anthony. "The Concept of Human Rights in International Law" (1982) 82 *Columbia Law Review* 1110.

D'Angelo, John R. "Resort to Force by States to Protect Nationals: The U.S. Rescue Mission to Iran and its Legality under International Law" (1981) 21 *Virginia Journal of International Law* 485.

Damrosch, Lori Fisler. "Politics Across Borders: Nonintervention and Nonforcible Influence over Domestic Affairs" (1989) 83 *American Journal of International Law* 1.

De Schutter, B. "Humanitarian Intervention: A United Nations Task" (1972) 3 *California Western International Law Journal* 21.

Delbruck, Jost. "A Fresh Look at Humanitarian Intervention Under the Authority of the United Nations" (1992 67 *Indiana Law Journal* 887.

Destexhe, Alain. "The Third Genocide" (1994-95) 97 *Foreign Policy* 3.

Document of the Copenhagen Meeting of the Conference on the Human Dimension of the Conference on Security and Co-operation in Europe (CSCE), reprinted in (1990) 29 *International Legal Materials* 1305.

Donnelly, Jack. "Human Rights and Human Dignity: An Analytic Critique of Non-Western Conceptions of Human Rights" (1982) 76 *American Political Science Review* 303.

Donnelly, Jack. "Human Rights, Humanitarian Crisis, and Humanitarian Intervention" (1993) XLVIII *International Journal* 607.

Dowty, Alan & Loescher, Gil. "Refugee Flows as Grounds for International Action" (1996) 21: 1 *International Security* 43.

Duke Simon, "The State and Human Rights: Sovereignty versus Humanitarian Intervention" (1994) XII *International Relations* 25.

Duxbury, Alison. "Rejunevating the Commonwealth – The Human Rights Remedy" (1997) 46: 2 *International and Comparative Law Quarterly* 344.

Eisner, Douglas. "Humanitarian Intervention in the Post-Cold War Era" (1993) 11 *Boston University International Law Journal* 195.

Eliasson, Jan. "The U.N. and Humanitarian Assistance" (1995) 48: 2 *Journal of International Affairs* 491.

Ermacora, Felix. "Human Rights and Domestic Jurisdiction (Article 2 (7) of the Charter)" (1968) 124 *Recueil Des Cours* bk.II, 371.

Fairley, Scott H. "State Actors, Humanitarian Intervention and International Law: Reopening Pandora's Box" (1980) 10 *Georgia Journal of International and Comparative Law* 29.

Falk, Richard. "The United States and the Doctrine of Nonintervention in the Internal Affairs of Independent States" (1959) *Howard Law Journal* 163.

Falk, Richard. "The Complexities of Humanitarian Intervention: A New World Order Challenge" (1996) 17: 2 *Michigan Journal of International Law* 491.

Farer, Tom. "Intervention and Human Rights: The Latin American Context" (1982) 12 *California Western International Law Journal* 503.

Farrell, Theo. "Book Reviews" (1997) 73: 1 *International Affairs* 161.

Feinberg, Nathan. "International Protection of Human Rights and the Jewish Question (An Historical Survey)" (1968) 3 *Israel Law Review* 487.

Fenwick, Charles G. "Intervention: Individual and Collective" (1945) 39 *American Journal of International Law* 645.

Ferencz, Benjamin. "An International Criminal Code and Court: Where they Stand and Where they're Going" (1992) 30 *Columbia Journal of Transnational Law* 375.

Fields, Belden & Narr, Wolf-Dieter. "Human Rights as a Holistic Concept" (1992) 14: 1 *Human Rights Quarterly* 1.

Figa-Talamanca, Nicolo. "The Role of NATO in the Peace Agreement for Bosnia and Herzegovina" (1996) 7: 2 *European Journal of International Law* 164.

Flinterman, C. "Humanitarian Intervention" (1978) 26 *Chitty's Law Journal* 284.

Fonteyne, Jean-Pierre L. "The Customary International Law Doctrine of Humanitarian Intervention: Its Current Validity Under the UN Charter" (1974) 4 *California Western International Law Journal* 203.

Fox, Gregory. "The Right to Political Participation in International Law" (1992) 17: 2 *Yale Journal of International Law* 539.

Franck Thomas, & Rodley, Nigel. "The Law, The United Nations and Bangla Desh" (1972) 2 *Israel Yearbook on Human Rights* 142.

Franck Thomas, & Rodley, Nigel. "After Bangladesh: The Law of Humanitarian Intervention by Military Force" (1973) 67 *American Journal of International Law* 275.

Franck, Thomas. "The Emerging Right to Democratic Governance" (1992) 86: 1 *American Journal of International Law* 81.

Freeman, Michael. "The Philosophical Foundations of Human Rights" (1994) 16 *Human Rights Quarterly* 491.

Gaeta, Paola. "The Dayton Peace Agreements and International Law" (1996) 7: 2 *European Journal of International Law* 147.

Garigue, Philippe. "Intervention-Sanction and 'Droit D'Ingerence in International Humanitarian Law" (1993) XLVIII *International Journal* 668.

Gianaris, William N. "The New World Order and the Need for an International Criminal Court" (1992-1993) 16 *Fordham International Law Journal* 88.

Goodman, Louis. "Democracy, Sovereignty, and Intervention" (1993) 9 *American University Journal of International Law and Policy* 27.

Gordon, Edward. "Article 2 (4) in Historical Context" (1985) 10 *Yale Journal of International Law* 279.

Gordon, Ruth. "Humanitarian Intervention by the United Nations: Iraq, Somalia, and Haiti" (1996) 31: 1 *Texas International Law Journal* 43.

Gray, Christine. "After the Ceasefire: Iraq, the Security Council and the Use of Force" (1994) 65 *British Yearbook of International Law* 135.

Green, Leslie C. "Rescue at Entebbe – Legal Aspects" (1976) 6 *Israel Yearbook on Human Rights* 312.

Green, Leslie C. "Humanitarian Intervention – 1976 Version" (1976) 24 *Chitty's Law Journal* 217.

Green, Leslie C. "General Principles of Law and Human Rights" (1955-56) 8 *Current Legal Problems* 162.

Green, Leslie C. "The Little Assembly" (1949) 3 *The Yearbook of World Affairs* 169.

Green, Leslie C. "Rescue at Entebbe-Legal Aspects" (1976) 6 *Israel Yearbook on Human Rights* 312.

Green, Leslie C. "Institutional Protection of Human Rights" (1986) 16 *Israel Yearbook of Human Rights* 69.

Green, Leslie C. "Group Rights, War Crimes and Crimes against Humanity" (1993) *International Journal on Group Rights* 27.

Greenberg Michael D. "Creating an International Criminal Court" (1992) 10 *Boston University International Law Journal* 119.

Greenwood, Christopher. "Is there a Right of Humanitarian Intervention?" (1993) 49: 2 *The World Today* 40.

Guillot, Philippe. "France, Peacekeeping and Humanitarian Intervention" (1994) 1: 1 *International Peacekeeping* 30.

Haas, Peter M. "Introduction: Epistemic Communities and International Policy Coordination" (1992) 46 *International Organization* 1.

Halberstam, Malvina. "The Copenhagen Document: Intervention in Support of Democracy" (1993) 34 *Harvard International Law Journal* 163.

Han, Sonia. "Building A Peace that Lasts: The United Nations and Post-Civil War Peace-Building" (1994) 26 *New York University Journal of International Law and Politics* 837.

Harff, Barbara. "Rescuing Endangered Peoples: Missed Opportunities" (1995) 62: 1 *Social Research* 23.

Hassan, Farooq. "Realpolitik in International Law: After Tanzanian-Ugandan Conflict 'Humanitarian Intervention' Reexamined" (1980-1981) 17 *Willamette Law Review* 859.

Hehir, Bryan. "Expanding Military Intervention: Promise or Peril" (1995) 61: 1 *Social Research* 41.

Henrikson, Alan. "How Can the Vision of a 'New World Order' be Realized" (1992) 16 *Fletcher Forum of World Affairs* 63.

Higgins, Rosalyn. "The New United Nations and Former Yugoslavia" (1993) 69 *International Affairs* at 469.

Hindell, Keith. "An Interventionist Manifesto" (1996) XIII *International Relations* 23.

Hoffmann, Stanley. "The Politics and Ethics of Military Intervention" (1995-96) 37: 4 *Survival* 29.

Hohfeld, Wesley N. "Some Fundamental Legal Conceptions as Applied in Judicial Reasoning" (1913) 23 *Yale Law Journal* 16.

Hutchinson, Mark R. "Restoring Hope: UN Security Council Resolutions and an Expanded Doctrine of Humanitarian Intervention" (1993) 34 *Harvard International Law Journal* 624.

Ignatieff, Michael. "The Seductiveness of Moral Disgust" (1995) 62: 1 *Social Research* 77.

Ikenberry, John. "A World Economy Restored: Expert Consensus and the Anglo-American Postwar Settlement" (1992) 46 *International Organization* 289.

Jackson, Robert. "Quasi-States, Dual Regimes, and Neoclassical Theory: International Jurisdiction and the Third World" (1987) 41 *International Organization* 519.

Jackson, Robert. "Armed Humanitarianism" (1993) XLVIII *International Journal* 579.

Jhabvala, Farrokh. "Unilateral Humanitarian Intervention and International Law" (1981) 21 *Indian Journal of International Law* 208.

Jones, Mary G. "National Minorities: A Case Study in International Protection" (1949) 14 *Law & Contemporary Problems* 599.

Jones, Bruce. "Intervention Without Borders: Humanitarian Intervention in Rwanda, 1990-1994" (1995) 24: 2 *Millennium: Journal of International Studies* 225.

Kaufmann, Chaim. "Possible and Impossible Solutions to Ethnic Civil Wars" (1996) 20: 4 *International Security* 136.

Keating, Thomas & Gammer, Nicholas. "The 'New Look' in Canada's Foreign Policy" (1993) XLVIII *International Journal* 720.

Kegley Jr., Charles W. "The New Global Order: The Power of Principle in a Pluralistic World" (1992) 6 *Ethics and International Affairs* 21.

Khushalani, Yougindra. "Human Rights in Asia and Africa" (1983) 4 *Human Rights Law Journal* 403.

Kloepfer, Stephen. "The Syrian Crisis, 1860-61: A Case Study in Classic Humanitarian Intervention" (1985) 23 *Canadian Yearbook of International Law* 246.

Knight, Andy & Gebremariam, Kassu. "United Nations Intervention and State-Building in Somalia: Constraints and Possibilities" Paper presented at 8th Annual Meeting of the Academic Council on the United Nations System, 19-21 June 1995, New York City.

Krasner, Stephen. "Compromising Westphalia" (1995/96) 20: 3 *International Security* 115.

Krylov, Nikolai. "Humanitarian Intervention: Pros and Cons" (1995) 17 *Loyola of Los Angeles International and Comparative Law* 365.

Kufuor, Kofi O. "The Legality of the Intervention in the Liberian Civil War by the Economic Community of West African States" (1993) *African Journal of International and Comparative Law* 523.

Kufuor, Kofi O. "Starvation as a Means of Warfare in the Liberian Conflict" (1994) XLI *Netherlands International Law Review* 313.

Kutner, Luis. "World Habeas Corpus and Humanitarian Intervention" (1985) 19 *Valpraiso University Law Review* 593.

Levitin, Michael J. "The Law of Force and the Force of Law: Grenada, The Falklands and Humanitarian Intervention" (1986) 27 *Harvard International Law Journal* 621.

Lewy, Guenter. "The Case for Humanitarian Intervention" (1993) Fall *Orbis* 621.

Lillich, Richard. "Intervention to Protect Human Rights" (1969) 15 *McGill Law Journal* 205.

Lillich, Richard. "Forcible Self-Help by States to Protect Human Rights" (1967) 53 *Iowa Law Review* 325.

Lillich, Richard. "The Role of the UN Security Council in Protecting Human Rights in Crisis Situations: UN Humanitarian Intervention in the Post-Cold War World" (1994) 3 *Tulane Journal of International and Comparative Law* 1.

MacFarlene, Neil & Weiss, Thomas G. "Regional Organizations and Regional Security" (1992) 2: 1 *Security Studies* 6.

Makinda, Samuel. "Sovereignty and International Security: Challenges for the United Nations" (1996) 2: 2 *Global Governance: A Review of Multilateralism and International Organizations* 149.

Martin, Guy. "International Solidarity and Cooperation in Assistance to African Refugees: Burden-Sharing or Burden-Shifting" (Paper presented at the Eighth Annual Meeting, Academic Council on the United Nations System, New York, 19-21 June 1995).

Martin, Laurence. "Peacekeeping as a Growth Industry" (1993) 32 *The National Interest* 3.

Mayall, James. "Non-intervention, Self-Determination and the 'New World Order'" (1991) 67: 3 *International Affairs* 426.

McCormack, Timothy L. & Simpson, Gerry J. "The International Law Commission's Draft Code of Crimes against the Peace and Security of Mankind: An Appraisal of the Substantive Provisions" (1994) 5: 1 *Criminal Law Forum: An International Journal* 1.

McDougal, Myres & Reisman, Michael W. "Response by Professors McDougal and Reisman" (1969) 3 *International Lawyer* 438.

McDougal, Myres & Bebr, Gerhard. "Human Rights in the United Nations" (1964) 58 *American Journal of International Law* 603.

Mills, Kurt. "Eclipsing Sovereignty: The Legitimacy of Humanitarian Intervention" (Paper Presented at the Academic Council on the United Nations System/American Society of International Law Summer Workshop, Providence, Rhode Island, July 28-August 9, 1996).

Moore, John N. "The Control of Foreign Intervention in International Conflict" (1969) 9 *Virginia Journal of International Law* 205.

Morgenthau, Hans. "To Intervene or not to Intervene" (1967) 45 *Foreign Affairs* 425.

Mutharika, Peter. "The Role of the United Nations Security Council in African Peace Management: Some Proposals" (1996)17: 2 *Michigan Journal of International Law* 537.

Nafziger, James. "Humanitarian Intervention in a Community of Power Part II" (1994) 22 *Denver Journal of International Law and Policy* 219.

Nanda, Ved P. "Tragedies in Northern Iraq, Liberia, Yugoslavia, and Haiti – Revisiting the Validity of Humanitarian Intervention Under International Law – Part I" (1992) 20 *Denver Journal of International Law and Policy* 305.

Nanda, Ved P. "The United States' Action in the 1965 Dominican Crisis: Impact on World Order-Part I " (1966) 43 *Denver Law Journal* 439; Part II (1967) 44 *Denver Law Journal* 225.

Nanda, Ved P. "A Critique of the United Nations Inaction in the Bangladesh Crisis" (1972) 49 *Denver Law Journal* 53.

Nariman, Fali S. "The Universality of Human Rights" (1993) 50 *The Review – International Commission of Jurists* 8.

Natsios, Andrew. "Food Through Force: Humanitarian Intervention and U.S. Policy" (1993) 17: 1 *The Washington Quarterly* 129.

Note, "Entebbe: Use of Force for the Protection of Nationals Abroad" (1977) 9 *Case Western Journal of International Law* 117.

O'Manique, John. "Universal and Inalienable Rights: A Search for Foundations" (1990) 12 *Human Rights Quarterly* 465.

Ofodile, Anthony C. "The Legality of the ECOWAS Intervention in Liberia" (1994-95) 32 *Columbia Journal of Transnational Law* 381.

Oglesby, Ross. "A Search for Legal Norms in Contemporary Situations of Civil Strife" (1970) 3: 1 *Case Western Reserve Journal of International Law* 30.

Orentlicher, Diane F. "Settling Accounts: The Duty to Prosecute Human Rights Violations of a Prior Regime" (1991) 100 *Yale Law Journal* 2537.

Paasivirta, Esa. "Internationalization and Stabilization of Contracts Versus State Sovereignty" (1990) *British Yearbook of International Law* 315.

Parekh, Bikhu. "Rethinking Humanitarian Intervention" (1997) 18: 1 *International Political Science Review* 49.

Pastor, Robert. "Forward to the Beginning: Widening the Scope for Global Collective Action" (1993) XLVIII *International Journal* at 642.

Pease Kelly & Forsythe, David. "Human Rights, Humanitarian Intervention, and World Politics" (1993) 15 *Human Rights Quarterly* 290.

Perera, Rohan. "Towards the Establishment of an International Criminal Court" (1994) 20 *Commonwealth Law Bulletin* 298.

Philpott, Daniel. "Sovereignty: An Introduction and Brief History" (1995) 48 *Journal of International Affairs* 353.

Pogany, Istvan. "Humanitarian Intervention in International Law: The French Intervention in Syria Re-examined" (1986) 35 *International and Comparative Law Quarterly* 182.

Posen, Barry R. "Military Responses to Refugee Disasters" (1996) 21: 1 *International Security* 72.

Prunier, Gerard. "Somalia: Civil War, Intervention and Withdrawal (1990-1995)" (1996) 15: 1 *Refugee Survey Quarterly* 35.

Regensburg, Kenneth. "Refugee Law Reconsidered: Reconciling Humanitarian Objectives with the Protectionist Agendas of Western Europe and the United States" (1996) 29 : 1 *Cornell International Law Journal* 225.

Reisman, Michael W. "Criteria for the Lawful Use of Force in International Law (1985) 10 *Yale Journal of International Law* 279.

Reisman, Michael W. "Sovereignty and Human Rights in Contemporary International Law" (1990) 84 *American Journal of International Law* 866.

Reno, William. "The Business of War in Liberia" (May 1996) *Current History: A Journal of Contemporary World Affairs* at 212.

Roberts, Adam. "Humanitarian War: Military Intervention and Human Rights" (1993) 69: 3 *International Affairs* 429.

Roberts, Adam. "The Road to Hell': A Critique of Humanitarian Intervention" (1993) 16: 1 *Harvard International Review* 11.

Rodley, Nigel. "Human Rights and Humanitarian Intervention: The Case of the World Court" (1989) 38 *International and Comparative Law Quarterly* 321.

Rubenstein, Richard. "Silent Partners in Ethnic Cleansing: The UN, The EC, and NATO" (1993)3: 2 *In Depth – A Journal for Values and Public Policy* 35.

Ruddick, Elizabeth. Note, "The Continuing Constraint of Sovereignty: International Law, International Protection, and the Internally Displaced" (1997) 77 *Boston University Law Review* 429.

Russet Bruce, O'Neill Barry, & Sutterlin, James. "Breaking the Security Council Logjam" (1996) 2: 1 *Global Governance: A Review of Multilateralism and International Organizations* 65.

Ryan, Christopher M. "Sovereignty, Intervention, amd the Law: A Tenuous Relationship of Competing Principles" (1997) 26: 1 *Millennium: Journal of International Studies* 77.

Sajoo, Amyn B. "Islam and Human Rights: Congruence or Dichotomy?" (1990) 4: 1 *Temple International and Comparative Law Journal* 3.

Sandoz, Yves. "'Droit' or 'Devoir d'Ingerence' and the Right to Assistance: The Issues Involved" (1992) 49 *The Review: International Commission of Jurists* 12.

Schachter, Oscar. "The Right of States to Use Force" (1984) 82 *Michigan Law Review* 1620.

Scharf, Michael. "The Jury is Still Out on the Need for an International Criminal Court" (1991) 135 *Duke Journal of International and Comparative Law* 135.

Scharf, Michael. "A Critique of the Yugoslavia War Crimes Tribunal" (1997) 25: 2 *Denver Journal of International Law and Policy* 313.

Scheffer, David. "Toward A Modern Doctrine of Humanitarian Intervention" (1992) 23 *University of Toledo Law Review* 253.

Schwartzberg, Joseph E. "A New Perspective on Peacekeeping: Lessons from Bosnia and Elsewhere" (1997) 3: 1 *Global Governance: A Review of Multilateralism and International Organizations* 1.

Schwelb Egon. "International Measures of Implementation of the International Covenant on Civil and Political Rights and the Optional Protocol" (1977) 12 *Texas International Law Journal* 141.

Sikkink, Kathryn. "Human Rights, Principled Issue Networks, and Sovereignty in Latin America" (1993) 47 *International Organization* 411.

Simon, Steve. "The Contemporary Legality of Unilateral Humanitarian Intervention" (1993) 24 *California Western International Law Journal* 117.

Slater, Jerome & Nardin, Terry. "Nonintervention and Human Rights" (1986) 48 *Journal of Politics* 86.

Slim, Hugo. "Military Humanitarianism and the New Peacekeeping: An Agenda for Peace?" (1995) *Journal of Humanitarian Assistance* 1. [http: //www-jha.sps.cam.ac.uk].

Sloan, James. "The Dayton Peace Agreement: Human Rights Guarantees and their Implementation" (1996) 7: 2 *European Journal of International Law* 207.

Smith, Tony. "In Defense of Intervention" (1994)73: 6 *Foreign Affairs* 34.

Smith, Gaddis. "Haiti: from Intervention to Intervasion" (1995) 94: 589 *Current History: A Journal of Contemporary World Affairs* 54.

Sohn, Louis B. "The Shaping of International Law" (1978) *Georgia Journal of International and Comparative Law* 16.

Solana, Javier. "NATO's Role in Bosnia" (1996) April 15, *Review of International Affairs* 1.

Sornarajah, M. "Internal Colonialism and Humanitarian Intervention" (1981) 11 *Georgia Journal of International and Comparative Law* 45.

Stedman, Stephen J. "The New Interventionists" (1993) 72: 1 *Foreign Affairs* 1.

Tesón, Fernando R. "Collective Humanitarian Intervention" (1996) 17: 2 *Michigan Journal of International Law* 323.

Torrelli, Maurice. "From Humanitarian Assistance to 'Intervention on Humanitarian Grounds'?" (1992) *International Review of the Red Cross* 228.

Tyagi, Yogesh. "The Concept of Humanitarian Intervention Revisited" (1995) 16 *Michigan Journal of International Law* 883.

Umozurike, U.D. "Tanzania's Intervention in Uganda" (1982) 20 *Archiv Des Volkerrechts* 301.

Urquhart, Brian. "For a UN Volunteer Military Force" (1993) 40 *New York Review of Books*, June 10, 3.

Van Dijk, P & Bloed, A. "Conference on Security and Cooperation in Europe, Human Rights and Non-intervention" (1983) 8 *Liverpool Law Review* 117.

Verhoeven, Joe. "Sovereign States: A Collectivity or Community" (1994) *Hitotsubashi Journal of Law and Politics* 149.

Verwey, W.D. "Humanitarian Intervention Under International Law" (1985) 32 *Netherlands International Law Review* 357 at 399.

Walzer, Michael. "The Politics of Rescue" (1995) 62: 1 *Social Research* 53.

Weber, Cynthia. "Dissimulating Intervention: A Reading of the US-Led Intervention in Haiti" (1995) 20 *Alternatives* 265.

Wedgwood, Ruth. "War Crimes in the Former Yugoslavia: Comments on the International War Crimes Tribunal" (1994) 34 *Virginia Journal of International Law* 267.

Weisberg, Howard L. "The Congo Crisis 1964: A Case Study in Humanitarian Intervention" (1972) 12 *Virginia Journal of International Law* 261.

Weiss, Thomas G. "UN Responses in the Former Yugoslavia: Moral and Operational Choices" (1994) 8 *Ethics and International Affairs* 1.

Weiss, Thomas G. "Whither the United Nations" (1993) 17: 1 *The Washington Quarterly* 109.

Weiss, Thomas G. "On the Brink of a New Era? Humanitarian Interventions, 1991-1993" (1994) *The Brown Journal of World Affairs* 235.

Weiss, Thomas G. "Triage: Humanitarian Interventions in a New Era" (1994) *World Policy Journal* 11.

Weiss, Thomas G. "The United Nations at Fifty: Recent Lessons" (1995) 94 *Current History* 225.

Weiss, Thomas G. "Military – Civilian Humanitarianism: The 'Age of Innocence' is Over" (1995) 2: 2 *International Peacekeeping* 158.

Weiss, Thomas G. "Overcoming the Somalia Syndrome – 'Operation Rekindle Hope'?" (1995) 1 *Global Governance: A Review of Multilateralism and International Organizations* 171.

Weiss, Thomas G & Campbell, Kurt M. "Military Humanitarianism" (1991) 33: 5 *Survival* 451.

Weiss, Thomas G. "The United Nations and Civil Wars" (1994) 17: 4 *The Washington Quarterly* 139.

Weller, Marc. "The International Response to the Dissolution of the Socialist Federal Republic of Yugoslavia" (1992) 86 *American Journal of International Law* 569.

West Africa Magazine, June 14-20, 1993.

West Africa Magazine, January 8-14, 1990.

West Africa Magazine, July 22-28, 1996.

Weston Burns, Lukes Robin, & Hnatt, Kelly. "Regional Human Rights Regimes: A Comparison and Appraisal" (1987) 20 *Vanderbilt Journal of Transnational Law* 585.

Wheeler, Nicholas. "Pluralist or Solidarist Conceptions of International Society: Bull and Vincent on Humanitarian Intervention" (1992) *Millennium: Journal of International Studies* 463.

Wheeler, Nicholas. "Agency, Humanitarianism and Intervention" (1997) 18: 1 *International Political Science Review* 9.

Whitman, Jim. "A Cautionary Note on Humanitarian Intervention" (1995) *Journal of Humanitarian Assistance* 1.[http: //www-jha.sps. cam.ac.uk].

Winfield, P.H. "The History of Intervention in International Law" (1922-1923) 3 *British Yearbook of International Law* 130.

Wolf, Daniel. "Humanitarian Intervention" (1988) *Michigan Yearbook on International Legal Studies Annual* 333.

Wright, George. "A Contemporary Theory of Humanitarian Intervention" (1989) 4 *Florida International Law Journal* 435.

BOOKS

African Rights, *Rwanda: Death, Despair and Defiance* (London: African Rights Publications, 1994).

Agarwal, Hari O. *Implementation of Human Rights Covenants: With Special Reference to India* (Allahabad: Kitab Mahal, 1983).

Akehurst, Michael B. *Modern Introduction to International Law* (London: George Allen & Unwin, 1985).

Amos, Sheldon. *Political and Legal Remedies for War* (New York: Harper, 1880).

Asrat, Belatchew. *Prohibition of Force Under the UN Charter: A Study of Art. 2 (4)* (Uppsala: Juridiska Foreningen i, 1991).

Bassiouni, Cherif M. *International Crimes: Digest/Index of International Instruments 1815-1985*, Vols. I & II (1986).

Bay, Christian. *Toward a Postliberal World Order of Human Rights* (Dept. of Pol.Sci. University of Toronto: Working Paper A7, 1983).

Beigbeder, Yves. *The Role and Status of International Humanitarian Volunteers and Organizations: The Right and Duty to Humanitarian Assistance* (Dordrecht: Martinus Nijhoff Publishers, 1991).

Bennet et al. *Meeting Needs: NGO Coordination in Practice* (London: Earthscan Publications, 1995).

Bernhadt, Rudolf. ed. 3 *Encyclopedia of Public International Law* (Amsterdam: North-Holland Publishing Co., 1981).

Biersteker, Thomas & Weber, Cynthia. eds. *State Sovereignty as Social Construct* (Cambridge: Cambridge University Press, 1996).

Bodin, Jean. *Six Bookes of a Commonweale* (London, 1606) trans. Knolles, MacRae ed., (Cambridge, Mass: Harvard University Press, 1962) bk.1.

Borchard, Edwin. *The Diplomatic Protection of Citizens Abroad* (New York: The Banks Law Publishing Co., 1922).

Boutros-Ghali, Boutros. *An Agenda for Peace: Preventive Diplomacy, Peacemaking and Peace-keeping*, Report of the Secretary-General pursuant to the statement adopted by the Summit Meeting of the Security Council on 31 January 1992 (New York: United Nations, 1992).

Boutros-Ghali, Boutros. *Supplement to An Agenda for Peace: Position Paper of the Secretary-General on the Occasion of the Fifthtieth Anniversary of the United Nations* (UN Doc.A/50/60-5/1995/1, January 1995).

Brown, Michael E. ed., *The International Dimensions of Internal Conflict* (Cambridge, Mass: MIT Press, 1996).

Brownlie, Ian. *The Principles of Public International Law* 4th ed. (Oxford: Clarendon Press, 1990).

Brownlie, Ian. *International Law and the Use of Force by States* (Oxford: Clarendon Press, 1963).

Buergenthal, Thomas. *International Human Rights* (St.Paul, Minn: West Publishing Co., 1988).

Bull, Hedley & Watson, Adam. eds., *The Expansion of International Society* (New York: Clarendon Press, 1894).

Bull, Hedley. ed., *Intervention in World Politics* (Oxford: Clarendon Press, 1984).

Canadian Department of Foreign Affairs and International Trade, *Towards a Rapid Reaction Capability for the United Nations* (1995).

Carey J. ed. *The Dominican Republic Crisis* (Dobbs Ferry: Oceana Publications Inc., 1967).

Carlyle, Robert W. *History of Mediaeval Political Theory in the West* (London: Blackwood & Sons, 1950).

Carty, Anthony. *The Decay of International Law? A Reappraisal of the Limits of Legal Imagination in International Affairs* (Manchester, 1986).

Cassese, Antonio. ed. *UN Law/Fundamental Rights – Two Topics in International Law* (Sijthoff & Noordhoff, 1979).

Cassese, Antonio. ed. *The Current Regulation of the Use of Force* (Dordrecht: Martinus Nijhoff Publishers, 1986).

Charlton, Mark & Riddle-Dixon, Elizabeth. eds. *International Relations in the Post-Cold War Era* (Scarborough: Nelson Canada, 1993).

Chen, Bin & Brown, eds. *Contemporary Problems of International Law: Essays in Honour of Georg Schwarzenberger* (London: Stevens & Sons Ltd., 1988).

Childers, Erskine & Urquhart, Brian. *Renewing the United Nations System* (Uppsala: Dag Hammerskjold Foundation, 1994).

Claude, Richard P & Weston, Burns H. *Human Rights in the World Community – Issues and Action* (Philadelphia: Univ. of Pennsylvania Press, 1989).

Conference Report, *The Challenge to Intervene: A New Role for the United Nations?* (Uppsala: Life & Peace Institute, 1992).

Corbett, Percy E. *Law and Society in the Relations of States* (New York: Harcout, Brace & Co.1951).

Cotler, Irwin & Eliadis, Pearl. eds. *International Human Rights: Theory and Practice* (Montreal: Canadian Human Rights Foundation, 1992).

Cranston, Maurice W. *What are Human Rights?* (London: Bodley Head, 1973).

Crawford, James. *The Creation of States in International Law* (Oxford: Clarendon Press, 1979).

Crocker Chester, Hampson Fen O, & Aall, Pamela. eds. *Managing Global Chaos: Sources of and Responses to International Conflict* (Washington, DC: United States Institute of Peace Press, 1996).

D'Amato, Anthony. *International Law: Process and Prospect* (New York: 1987).

Damrosch, Lori Fisler & Scheffer David. eds. *Law and Force in the New International Order* (Boulder: Westview Press, 1991).

Damrosch, Lori Fisler. ed. *Enforcing Restraint: Collective Intervention in Internal Conflicts* (New York: Council on Foreign Relations Press, 1993).

Daniel, Donald & Hayes, Bradd. eds. *Beyond Traditional Peacekeeping* (London: Macmillan Press Ltd., 1995).

De Lima, F.X. *Intervention in International Law – With A Reference to the Organisation of American States* (Den Haag: Uitgeverij Pax Nederland, 1971).

Deng, Francis *Protecting the Dispossessed: A Challenge for the International Community* (Washington, DC: The Brookings Institution, 1993).

Digest of United States Practice in International Law (U.S. Government Printer's Office: Washington, 1975).

Dominguez, Jorge. et al. eds. *Enhancing Global Human Rights* (New York: McGraw Hill, 1979).

Donini, Antonio. *The Policies of Mercy: UN Coordination in Afghanistan, Mozambique, and Rwanda* (Providence: Watson Institute for International Studies, 1996) Occasional Paper no. 22.

Esman, Milton & Telhami, Shibley. eds. *International Organizations and Ethnic Conflict* (Ithaca: Cornell University Press, 1995).

Farer, Tom. *Collectively Defending Democracy in a World of Sovereign States: The Western Hemisphere Prospect* (International Centre for Human Rights and Democratic Development, 1993).

Fawn, Rick & Larkins, Jeremy. eds. *International Society after the Cold War: Anarchy and Order Reconsidered* (London: Macmillan Press Ltd., 1996).

Ferris, Elizabeth. ed. *The Challenge to Intervene: A New Role for the United Nations?* (Uppsala: Life and Peace Institute, 1992) 113 at 114.

Forbes, Ian & Hoffman, Mark. eds. *Political Theory, International Relations and the Ethics of Intervention* (London: Macmillan Press, 1993).

Forsythe, David. *The Internationalization of Human Rights* (Lexington, Mass.: Lexington Books, 1991).

Ganji, Manouchehr. *International Protection of Human Rights* (Geneve: Librairie E. Droz, 1962).

Gilpin, Robert. *War and Change in World Politics* (Cambridge: Cambridge University Press, 1981).

Goldstein, Judith & Keohane, Robert. eds. *Ideas and Foreign Policy: Beliefs, Institutions and Political Change* (Ithaca, NY: Cornell University Press, 1993).

Goodrich, Leland M., Hambro, Edvard., and Simons, Anne P. *Charter of the United Nations: Commentary and Documents*, 3rd ed. (New York: Columbia University Press, 1969).

Gotlieb, Allan. *Human Rights, Federalism and Minorities* (Toronto: Canadian Institute of International Affairs, 1970).

Green, Leslie C. *Law and Society* (Leyden: A.W. Sijthoff, 1975).

Grotius, Hugo. *De Jure Belli ac Pacis Libri Tre* (1625), Kelsey trans. (New York: Bobbs-Merrill Co., 1925).

Haka, Tamijula. *Human Rights in Islam vis-a-vis Universal Declaration of Human Rights of the United Nations* (Washington, DC: World Peace through Law Center, 1981).

Hall, Willliam E. *A Treatise on International Law* 2nd ed. (1884).

Harbeson, John & Rothchild, Donald. eds. *Africa in World Politics: Post-Cold War Challenges* (Boulder: Westview Press, 1995).

Harff, Barbara. *Genocide and Human Rights: International Legal and Political Issues* (Denver: Graduate School of International Studies University of Denver, 1984).

Harriss, John. ed. *The Politics of Humanitarian Intervention* (London: Pinter Publishers, 1995).

Held, David. ed., *Political Theory Today* (Stanford University Press, 1991).

Henkin Louis, Hoffmann Stanley, & Kirkpatrick, Jeane. et al. eds. *Right v. Might: International Law and the Use of Force* (New York: Council on Foreign Relations Press, 1991).

Higgins, Rosalyn. *The Development of International Law Through the Political Organs of the United Nations* (London: Oxford University Press, 1963).

Higgins, Rosalyn. *Problems and Process: International Law and How We Use it* (Oxford: Clarendon Press, 1994).

Hinsley, Francis H. *Sovereignty* (London: Watts & Co. Ltd., 1966).

Hoffmann, Stanley. et al. *The Politics and Ethics of Humanitarian Intervention* (Notre Dame: University of Notre Dame Press, 1996).

Humphrey, John. *No Distant Millennium: The International Law of Human Rights* (Paris: UNESCO, 1989).

Independent Commission on International Humanitarian Issues, *Modern Wars: The Humanitarian Challenge* (London: Zed Books, 1988).

International Federation of Red Cross & Red Crescent Societies, *World Disasters Report 1996* (Oxford: Oxford University Press, 1996).

International Commission of Jurists, *The Events in East Pakistan, 1971* (Geneva, 1972).

Israel, Fred L. *Major Peace Treaties of Modern History: 1648-1967* Vol.1 (New York: Chelsea House, 1967).

Jean, Francois. ed. *Life, Death and Aid: The Médecins Sans Frontières Report on World Crisis Intervention* (London: Routledge, 1993).

Jessup, Philip. *A Modern Law of Nations* ((New York: MacMillan, 1948).

Jones, Dorothy. *Code of Peace: Ethics and Security in the World of the Warlord States* (Chicago: The University of Chicago Press, 1991).

Keohane, Robert. *International Institutions and State Power: Essays in International Relations Theory* (Boulder: Westview Press, 1989).

Larson Arthur, Jenks, Wilfred. et al. *Sovereignty Within the Law* (New York: Dobbs Ferry, 1965).

Laski, Harold J. *A Grammar of Politics* 4th ed. (London: Allen & Unwin, 1938).

Lauterpacht, Hersch. *International Law and Human Rights* (London: Stevens, 1950).

Lawrence, Thomas J. *The Principles of International Law* 4th ed. (London: Macmillan & Co., 1910).

Legault Albert, Murphy Craig, & Ofuatey-Kodjoe, Wentworth B. *The State of the United Nations: 1992* (Academic Council on the United Nations System Reports and Papers No.3, 1992).

Leurdijk Henk J. *Intervention in International Politics* (Leeuwarden: Eisma B.V. Publishers, 1986).

Lillich, Richard B. ed. *Humanitarian Intervention and the United Nations* (Charlottesville: University of Virginia Press, 1973).

Lowe, Vaughan & Warbrick, Colin. eds. *The United Nations and the Principles of International Law – Essays in Memory of Michael Akehurst* (London: Routledge, 1994).

Lyons, Gene & Mastanduno, Michael. eds. *Beyond Westphalia? State Sovereignty and International Intervention* (Baltimore: Johns Hopkins University Press, 1995).

Macdonald, Ronald St. John. ed. *Essays in Honour of Wang Tieya* (Dordrecht: Martinus Nijhoff Publishers, 1994).

Mahoney, Kathleen & Mahoney, Paul. eds. *Human Rights in the Twenty-First Century: A Global Challenge* (Dordrecht: Martinus Nijhoff Publishers, 1993).

Makinda, Samuel. *Seeking Peace from Chaos: Humanitarian Intervention in Somalia* (Boulder: Lynne Rienner Publishers, 1993).

Mayall, James. ed. *The New Interventionism 1991-1994: United Nations Experience in Cambodia, Former Yugoslavia and Somalia* (Cambridge: Cambridge University Press, 1996).

McDougal Myres, Lasswell Harold & Chen, Lung-chu. *Human Rights and World Public Order: The Basic Policies of an International Law of Human Dignity* (New Haven: Yale University Press, 1980).

Meron, Theodore. *Human Rights Law-Making in the United Nations* (Oxford: Clarendon Press, 1986).

Meron, Theodore. ed. *Human Rights in International Law*, Vol.1 (Oxford: Clarendon Press, 1984).

Merriam, Charles E. *History of the Theory of Sovereignty since Rousseau* (New York: Ams Press, 1968).

Mills, Kurt. *Human Rights in the Emerging Global Order: A New Sovereignty?* (London: Macmillan Press, 1998).

Minear, Larry & Weiss, Thomas G. *Humanitarian Action in Times of War: A Handbook for Practitioners* (Boulder: Lynne Rienner Publishers, 1993).

Minear Larry, Clark Jeffrey, Cohen Roberta. et al. *Humanitarian Action in the Former Yugoslavia: The UN's Role 1991-1993*, Occasional Paper no. 18 (Providence: Watson Institute for International Studies, 1994).

Minear, Larry. *Humanitarians and Intervention* (Oslo: Norwegian Institute for International Affairs, 1994).

Minear Larry, Weiss Thomas G & Campbell, Kurt. *Humanitarianism and War: Learning Lessons from Recent Armed Conflicts, Occasional Paper no.8* (Providence: Watson Institute for International Studies, 1991).

Moore, John N. ed. *Law and Civil War in the Modern World* (Baltimore: Johns Hopkins University Press, 1974).

Moskowitz, Moses. *Human Rights and World Order* (New York: Oceana Publications, 1958).

Mullerson, Rein. *Human Rights Diplomacy* (London: Routledge, 1997).

Murphy, Sean. *Humanitarian Intervention: The United Nations in an Evolving World Order* (Philadelphia: University of Pennsylvania Press, 1996).

Na'im, Abdullahi A. & Deng, Francis. eds. *Human Rights in Africa* (Washington, DC: The Brookings Institution, 1990).

Newman, Frank & Weissbrodt, David. *Selected International Human Rights Instruments* (Cincinnati: Anderson Publishing Co., 1990).

O'Connell, Daniel P. *International Law* (London: Stevens, 1970).

O'Halloran, Patrick. *Humanitarian Intervention and the Genocide in Rwanda* (London: Institute for the Study of Conflict & Terrorism, 1995).

Onuf, Nicholas ed. *Law-Making in the Global Community* (Durham, NC: Carolina Academic Press, 1982).

Oppenheim, Lassa. *International Law* (London: Longmans & Co., 1905).

Our Global Neighbourhood: The Report of the Commission on Global Governance (Oxford: Oxford University Press, 1995).

Oye, Kenneth. et al. eds. *Eagle Entangled: US Foreign Policy in a Complex World* (New York: Longman, 1979).

Parry, Clive. ed. *The Consolidated Treaty Series (1655-1658)* Vol.4 (Dobbs Ferry: Oceana Publications, 1969).

Perez De Cuellar, Javier. *Report of the Secretary-General on the Work of the Organization: 1991* (1991).

Phillipson, Coleman. *The International Law and Custom of Ancient Greece and Rome*, Vol. 1 (London: MacMillan & Co. Ltd, 1911).

Pollis, Adamantia & Schwab, Peter. eds. *Human Rights: Cultural and Ideological Perspective* (New York: Praeger, 1979).

Puchala, Donald. *The Ethics of Globalism* (Providence: Academic Council on the United Nations System Reports and Papers No.3, 1995).

Ramcharan, B.G. ed. *Human Rights: Thirty Years After the Declaration* (Dordrecht: Martinus Nijhoff, 1979).

Ramcharan, B.G. *The Concept and Present Status of the International Protection of Human Rights – Forty Years after the Universal Declaration* (Dordrecht: Martinus Nijhoff Publishers, 1988).

Ramsbotham, Oliver & Woodhouse, Tom. *Humanitarian Intervention in Contemporary Conflict: A Reconceptualization* (Cambridge: Polity Press, 1996).

Reed, Laura & Kaysen, Carl. eds. *Emerging Norms of Justified Intervention* (Cambridge, Mass: American Academy of Arts and Sciences, 1993).

Report of the Independent Working Group on the Future of the United Nations, *The United Nations in its Second Half-Century* (New York: Ford Foundation, 1995).

Righter, Rosemary. *Utopia Lost: The United Nations and World Order* (New York: The Twentieth Century Fund Press, 1995).

Roberts, Adam & Kingsbury, Benedict. eds. *United Nations, Divided World: The UN's Roles in International Relations* (Oxford: Clarendon Press, 1988).

Robinson, Jacob. *Were the Minorities Treaties a Failure?* (New York: Institute of Jewish Affairs, 1943).

Rodley, Nigel ed. *To Loose the Bands of Wickedness-International Intervention in Defence of Human Rights* (London: Brassey's 1992).

Ronzitti, Natalino. *Rescuing Nationals Abroad Through Military Coercion and Intervention on Grounds of Humanity* (Dordrecht: Martinus Nijhoff Publishers, 1985).

Sarooshi, Danesh. *Humanitarian Intervention and International Humanitarian Assistance: Law and Practice* (London: HMSO, 1993).

Scheffer David, Gardner Richard & Helman, Gerald. *Post-Gulf War Challenges to the UN Collective Security System: Three Views on the Issue of Humanitarian Intervention* (Washington, DC: United States Institute of Peace, 1992).

Schwarzenberger, Georg. *Power Politics – A Study of World Society* (London: Stevens & Sons, 1964).

Schwarzenberger, Georg & Brown, Edward D. *A Manual of International Law* (Milton: Professional Books, 1976).

Scott, James B. *The Spanish Origins of International Law, Francisco de Vitoria and His Law of Nations* (Carnegie Endowment for International Peace, 1934).

Scott, Colin. *Humanitarian Action and Security in Liberia 1989-1994* (Providence: Watson Institute for International Studies, 1995 Occasional Paper no. 20).

Shaw, Malcolm. *International Law* 3rd.ed. (Cambridge: Grotius Publications Ltd., 1991).

Sieghart, Paul. *The International Law of Human Rights* (Oxford: Clarendon Press, 1988).

Skinner, Quentin. *The Foundations of Modern Political Thought*, 2 Vols. (Cambridge: Cambridge University Press, 1978).

Slater, Jerome. *Intervention and Negotiation: The United States and the Dominican Crisis* (New York, 1970).

Sohn, Louis & Buergenthal, Thomas. *International Protection of Human Rights* (New York: Bobb-Merrill Co., 1973).

Stanger, Roland J. ed. *Essays on Intervention* (Cleveland: Ohio State University Press, 1964).

Stone, Julius. *Aggression and World Order* (London: 1958, reprinted 1976).

Stowell, Ellery C. *Intervention in International Law* (Washington DC: John Byrne & Co., 1921).

Tesón, Fernando R. *Humanitarian Intervention: An Inquiry into Law and Morality* (Ardsley-on-Hudson, New York: Transnational Publishers, 1988).

Thomas, Caroline. *New States, Sovereignty and Intervention* (Aldershot: Gower Publishing Co.Ltd., 1985).

Thomas, Ann V. & Thomas, A.J. *Non Intervention- The Law and its Import in the Americas* (Dallas: Southern Methodist University Press, 1956).

Thompson, Kenneth W. ed. *The Moral Imperatives of Human Rights: A World Survey* (Washington, DC: University Press of America, 1980).

Tilly, Charles. *Coercion, Capital, and European States, AD 990-1990* (Oxford: Basil Blakwell, 1990).

UNESCO ed., *International Dimension of Humanitarian Law* (Paris: Martinus Nijhoff Publishers, 1988).

Vassal-Adams, G. *Rwanda: An Agenda for International Action* (London: Oxfam Publishers, 1994).

Vincent, R.J. *Human Rights and International Relations* (Cambridge: Cambridge University Press, 1986).

Vincent, R.J. *Nonintervention and International Order* (Princeton: Princeton University Press, 1974).

Von Glahn, Gerhard. *Law Among Nations: An Introduction to Public International Law* (New York: MacMillan Publishing Co., 1992).

Walker R.B.J. & Mendlovitz, Saul. eds. *Contending Sovereignties: Redefining Political Community* (Boulder: Rienner, 1990).

Walzer, Michael. *Just and Unjust Wars: A Moral Argument with Historical Illustrations* (New York: Basic Books Publishers, 1977).

Weiss, Thomas G. ed. *Collective Security in a Changing World* (Boulder: Lynne Rienner Publishers, 1993).

Weiss, Thomas G. ed. *Beyond UN Subcontracting: Task-Sharing with Regional Security Arrangements and Service-Providing NGOs* (London: Macmillan Press, 1998).

Weiss, Thomas G. & Minear, Larry. eds. *Humanitarianism Across Borders: Sustaining Civilians in Times of War* (Boulder: Lynne Rienner Publishers, 1993).

Weiss Thomas G, Forsythe David & Coate, Roger. *The United Nations and Changing World Politics* (Boulder: Westview Press, 1994).

Weiss, Thomas G. & Gordenker, Leon. eds. *NGOs, the UN and Global Governance* (Boulder: Lynne Rienner Publishers, 1996).

Westlake, John. *International Law* Part I, Peace (Cambridge: Cambridge University Press, 1904).

Yearbook of the United Nations, 1964 (New York: United Nations, 1966).

DOCUMENTS

United Nations General Assembly Resolutions.

United Nations Security Council Resolutions.

United Nations Chronicle.

Various United Nations documents.

INDEX